Gordon knows all the excuses students give about why they don't read. With a finger on the pulse of teen lives, she has developed a coherent plan for reintroducing them to the joy of reading. Using the techniques outlined in this book, students can't help but become engaged, especially as they discover contemporary issues in time-honored classics. The most important message in the book? When students are secure in the company of a caring and accomplished teacher, great things happen.

—**Nancy Frey**
Author of *Visible Learning for Literacy*
San Diego State University, San Diego, California

There is so much to love about this book! Grounded in the authority of classroom practice, it makes independent reading work in new ways by actively teaching and sharing *how* to read, and by leveraging the social power and pleasure of reading. The approach is based on an elegant principle of cognitive apprenticeship: meet students at their current state of being with their current interests and use this as the platform to help them outgrow themselves. The approach allows for authentic and democratic differentiation—through various materials, levels of support, groupings—while all students are working in complementary ways on a common project. This approach mirrors what expert adult readers do: they put texts into conversation with each other to make global meanings.

—**Jeffrey D. Wilhelm**
Professor of English Education, Boise State University
Boise, Idaho

After attending an eye-opening workshop with Berit Gordon, I followed her lead and tried something new with my freshman college prep students. I'd been teaching *Great Expectations* to this age group for years, and it was always a challenge for them and for me. The assigned nightly reading went unread, and if the students did read, they did not understand it. Every day felt exhausting as I would reteach the previous night's assignment. This year, using Gordon's ideas as a guide, I opted to use the novel as an in-class text, analyzing passages to teach close reading skills while the students chose books to read on their own. Students delved into these high-interest contemporary books and made consistent meaningful connections between *Great Expectations* and their independent novels. They wrote literary essays about their choice books and took a test on *Great Expectations*, for which they received extremely high marks, demonstrating their mastery of a sophisticated—and previously dreaded!—text.

The experiment was a huge success! Working through a complex text together with focused instruction enabled students to engage with a difficult book, and appreciate it in a way they never had before. Interestingly, they enjoyed Dickens so much that I taught more of the book than I had originally planned!

—**Ellin Glassband**
High School Teacher, West Windsor-Plainsboro High School South
Princeton Junction, New Jersey

While I had spent over twenty years implementing book clubs and independent reading in my language arts classroom, I had never quite approached it in the same way Berit Gordon outlines in *No More Fake Reading*. Now, my students are reading at least double the previously required amount, and they are thrilled with the large amount of choice. I found it effortless to create a curriculum where I match in-class texts with independent reading. The students find the more challenging texts enjoyable when sampling them rather than haranguing through the truly difficult ones or just reading SparkNotes!

—**Rose Leonard**
English Teacher, West Windsor-Plainsboro High School South
Princeton Junction, New Jersey

How can we inspire reading and critical thinking in a time of widespread student distraction and disengagement? Berit Gordon helps bridge the gap between theory and action with classroom-friendly strategies that work. Test them out, and like me, you may find your students begging for more time to read.

—**Jessica Miller**
English Teacher and Literacy Coach, Keenan High School
Columbia, South Carolina

Berit Gordon is the best word whisperer, lighting a love for words in even the most reluctant of readers and writers. Her techniques create an atmosphere of electricity in a classroom that has lost its spark for communication. Many books that I've read only speak to the strategy and provide anchor charts. Gordon goes further and explains the what, why, how, and when of the strategy in use. This is key. Gordon is key. For many of us, we know what we want our students to do. We just need a little direction to get there. Gordon provides the map, serves as GPS, and leads us to a place where our classrooms are now abuzz with engaged readers and inspired writers.

—**Wendy Platt**
Eau Claire High School
Columbia, South Carolina

*To the official and unofficial teachers in
my family, which is all of you.*

# NO MORE FAKE READING

## MERGING THE CLASSICS WITH INDEPENDENT READING
### TO CREATE JOYFUL, LIFELONG READERS

**BERIT GORDON**

resources.corwin.com/nofakereading

CORWIN LITERACY

FOR INFORMATION:

Corwin

A SAGE Company

2455 Teller Road

Thousand Oaks, California 91320

(800) 233-9936

www.corwin.com

SAGE Publications Ltd.

1 Oliver's Yard

55 City Road

London EC1Y 1SP

United Kingdom

SAGE Publications India Pvt. Ltd.

B 1/I 1 Mohan Cooperative Industrial Area

Mathura Road, New Delhi 110 044

India

SAGE Publications Asia-Pacific Pte. Ltd.

3 Church Street

#10-04 Samsung Hub

Singapore 049483

Publisher and Senior Program Director:  Lisa Luedeke

Editorial Development Manager:  Julie Nemer

Editorial Assistant:  Nicole Shade

Production Editor:  Amy Schroller

Copy Editor:  Melinda Masson

Typesetter:  C&M Digitals (P) Ltd.

Proofreader:  Dennis W. Webb

Indexer:  Sheila Bodell

Cover and Graphic Designer:  Rose Storey

Marketing Manager:  Rebecca Eaton

Printed in the United States of America

ISBN 978-1-5063-6551-0

This book is printed on acid-free paper.

SUSTAINABLE FORESTRY INITIATIVE

Certified Chain of Custody
Promoting Sustainable Forestry
www.sfiprogram.org
SFI-01268

SFI label applies to text stock

19 20 21 10 9 8 7 6 5 4 3

# Contents

CHAPTER THREE

## Building a Blended Curriculum for Fiction-Based Units ........... 71

CHAPTER FOUR

## Building a Blended Curriculum for Nonfiction-Based Units ........... 95

## CHAPTER EIGHT

## Building Teacher–Student Relationships Through the Blended Model

## Final Words

## Resources

For downloadable versions of tools and
resources, please visit the companion website at
resources.corwin.com/nofakereading.

# Acknowledgments

It's a mind-altering thing to write a book after spending so much of my life reading books by others. My long-held image of authors holed up in a room by themselves and then magically getting that work into my hands is forever changed. This book *is* the result of countless solo hours at the computer, but it's equally a product of others' voices and generous contributions. Never again will I look at one person's name on a book jacket without imagining all the unwritten names that belong there, too.

First and foremost, I'd like to thank the teachers who open up their classrooms and minds to me. A day in the life of a teacher is not easy. My work with teachers adds one more layer of suggestions, goal setting, dialogues, and ideas to the flurry of mental juggling they balance so beautifully. It was their hard work that turned ideas from this book into teens who identify as readers. These teachers kept up the dialogue between my visits with emails, student work, and smart questions. I'm grateful to all of them for their work ethic, their commitment to students, and their tireless ability to keep getting even better. In particular, I'd like to thank teachers who let me take pictures in their classrooms, sent me student work, took surveys with their classes, and went the extra mile (or two) when they didn't have to: Vanessa Astore, Daniel Bailey-Yavonditte, Melissa Calamari, Ed Chambers, Katie Daly, Ellin Glassband, Sebastian Hill, Kelly Kosch, Sheena Lall, Rose Leonard, Jessica Miller, Beth Pandolpho, Wendy Platt, Laura Prosdocimo, Jill Ramacciotti, Dara Sheller, Robby Suarez, Ashley Tarasiewicz, Becky Territo, Jacki Tur, Christina Van Horn, and Kristin Whitmore.

Without support from administrators with vision and a belief that teachers make it all happen, I wouldn't see these ideas put into practice. Thank you to Tempie Bowers, Ronnie Dougherty, Kathy Foster, Jabar Hankins, Nancy Hoch, Amanda Matticks, Cathy Reilly, Tamika Shuler, Kim Tew, Cheryl Watson, and Adam Zygmunt. And thank you to the women who first connected me with great work in schools: Pam Allyn and Leah Danziger.

These ideas wouldn't be in print if it weren't for amazing colleagues who encouraged me to write them down. I'm thankful for the invitation from Kirsten Widmer and Jennifer Serravallo to join the learning group, and to bring "whatever you're working on." That casual request was wildly intimidating and then wildly invigorating. To be told that yes, I have something to say, and to name my fledgling idea was a game changer. Everyone's voice and smart thinking in this group is such a boost. Jen, your bottomless generosity in supporting others is an inspiration, and you make a mean frittata to boot. I'm grateful to be a recipient of both on multiple occasions.

Helping students to love reading was always a way to feel closer to my teen idol and high school English teacher, Judy Vaill. She inspired this book in many ways as she not only merged class novels with choice reading, but she tucked books in my hand, telling me she chose them "just for me." Seeing this same connection happen with teachers and teens in the schools where I work reminds me she lives on. In graduate school, I had the joy of being in classes with Ruth Vinz, the least assuming and yet smartest person in the room, always. She helped me trust myself as an educator and to respect that there are many ways to teach well. She continues this theme of women who take great pleasure in supporting others to succeed, which carries over to my staff developer and friend, Andrea Lowenkopf. Andrea's honest advice stays with me in my work twenty-some years later. I'm grateful I got to work with Stephanie Smith, Laura Rigolosi, and Jill Myers, whose work ethics and "students first" styles I still try to emulate. I'm also thankful for the friend voices that have shaped me since grad school: Jenn McDermott, Clare Hagan, Glenn Powers, and Kiry Widmer; and new friends and writers Alix Clyburn and Judith Wolochow.

I'm deeply appreciative to my editor at Corwin, Lisa Luedeke, who provided unwavering support for a new author as well as spot-on advice throughout. Nicole Shade impressed me to no end with her quick answers to any question. I'm also grateful to Lisa and her team at Corwin for their hard work, and for inviting me to a lovely dinner at the National Council of Teachers of English where I got to sit next to authors I adore. Any English teacher understands that is celebrity spotting at its finest. And a huge thank-you to Melinda Masson, copy editor extraordinaire. I'd like to shake her former English teachers' hands.

My parents and sister have operated on one mode with this project: constant cheerleader. I could have told them I was working on a book about test prep, and they would have oohed and aahed. But they encouraged me with extra gusto because they are readers, they know just how much books enrich our lives, and they care about empowering kids. They listened in car rides, sent articles and follow-up emails, read chapters, and listened some more. Julia, thank you for reading every word and mailing me supportive and smart penciled-in comments. You helped my drafts immensely and taught me as a writer, too. Mom, you taught me to be a reader, to connect over books, and to be kind to myself and others. I hope those philosophies underlie these chapters and more.

Finally, I'd like to thank the people who graciously bore the brunt of a working and writing family member: Andrew, Naomi, Violet, and Sam. You are all my favorite mix of smart and kind. I love that you let me write and then pull me back into life with you.

## Publisher's Acknowledgments

Corwin gratefully acknowledges the contributions of the following reviewers:

Lynn Angus Ramos
Language Arts Curriculum and
Instruction Coordinator
Decatur, GA

Lydia Bowden
Assistant Principal
Peachtree Corners, GA

Cindy Gagliardi
English Teacher
Chatham, NJ

Andy Schoenborn
English Teacher
Midland, MI

Sayuri Stabrowski
Dean of Instruction
New York, NY

Marsha Voigt
Educational Consultant
Barrington, IL

# Introduction: "What Book Should I Read Next?"

## Vignette of a High School Reader

Carlos walks into his sixth-period sophomore English class where other students are already seated and lost in books. Pages are turning, students have eyes on print, and it's library silent. No one is rapt in Dickens or poring over *The Odyssey*, but students are immersed in Sherman Alexie's *The Absolutely True Diary of a Part-Time Indian*, the latest by John Green, and *Enrique's Journey*, a nonfiction narrative about a boy crossing illegally into the United States. After years of fake reading, these students are racking up page counts ten times those from the previous year when they were assigned (but didn't read) one novel a marking period.

As a literacy consultant, I've been working with Carlos's teacher toward our common goal of sparking joy in high school readers. Today I'm observing the lesson we planned together.

Meanwhile, Carlos, a self-professed nonreader, takes *Grasshopper Jungle* by Andrew Smith out of his backpack. He picks up from where he left off last night. I'm watching this all from my own seat, having arranged to coach into today's lesson if necessary. So far, I'm not needed—why disturb a room of students lost in books?

Then Mr. Valentine hustles into the room. He uses the quiet to put his copy of *Of Mice and Men* on the document camera, collect the pile of double-entry notes from the corner of his desk, and post plot and character charts on the board as a refresher.

He catches his breath, then asks the kids to come to a stopping point and dives into the lesson.

"Wow, wow, wow. I have read and reread this book so many times. And do you know last night I noticed something else that Steinbeck manages to do? Well, I had characters in mind since that's what we've been talking about this week, so I was paying close attention to our friends Lennie and George. But last night, I slowed down on a part where we meet Curley's wife. Before I show you, let me get you up to speed." I'm nodding along with Mr. Valentine. I'm with him, and so is the class.

In a few sentences, Mr. Valentine summarizes the fifteen pages between yesterday's excerpt of the book and the one they'll look at today. This summary consists of a must-know plot turn and character development. I see students nodding, getting the gist. He provides this summary not because students were supposed to read *Of Mice and Men* and didn't, which used to be the case, but because it simply wasn't assigned.

After the recap, Mr. Valentine looks in depth at a short section of text by projecting the book from the document camera. He reads aloud from pages 76–77, stopping every paragraph or so to tell students what he's thinking. He's getting more comfortable sharing out *how* he reads, instead of just reading. I smile from the back that he's thinking aloud with them, letting them into his reading mind.

Students don't notice any inner awkwardness on their teacher's part, even though this is new to him. They look attentive, following along as Mr. Valentine shares the questions he had about Curley's wife, what he started out thinking about her motivations, and how he came around to wondering what happened beforehand to make her so bitter. He poses questions aloud and writes them on a blank piece of paper on the document camera:

- What does this character want?

- What's in her way of getting it?

- How is she affecting the people around her?

- What is she not saying?

He also jots down his thoughts in double-entry format: on the one side, lines from the text so there's evidence to back up his thoughts, which he lists on the other side.

"I feel like Curley's wife supports the theme we were talking about yesterday: how weak characters want to take someone else down who is even weaker. So, I'm using this tiny pop-up of a character to keep looking at theme. Make sense?" Mr. Valentine says. A few kids nod. He and I have talked about taking what he does as a strong reader and making it something all students can try with their books. I smile at him—it's happening. Even if some students are still unsure how this will work, they see a universal reading strategy and not just something limited to Steinbeck's work.

Mr. Valentine tells them, "Think about your book right now, and one of the characters who doesn't get a lot of airtime. Try answering one of these questions for the character, and then jot down your thinking."

He walks around, checking their notes. After looking at a few, he shares how one reader used Rachel, a minor character in *Speak*, to look at the theme of nonconformity and how it leads to isolation. Then he recaps another student's reading of *The Absolutely True Diary of a Part-Time Indian*. This student noted that someone tells Junior he's a nomad, even though Junior goes to the same home every night. That got the student thinking about the theme of home. Maybe, he writes, it's a place where you belong, not just the place you sleep in at night.

After walking around, Mr. Valentine comes over to chat with me. He noticed that some students didn't manage to connect theme and minor characters, but everyone viewed minor characters with heightened attention, and that's something. Then, hearing examples from other readers helped push their thinking. Not knowing those readers' books didn't stop them from getting the idea. Once they saw instances in *Of Mice and Men*, all the readers, at different stages, started to ask and answer questions about minor characters. They were willing to try the strategy with their own books, sensing it wasn't hard to do.

Mr. Valentine reminds his students they've got lots of ways to pay attention to characters as they read, and then he stops. The kids are used to this—they know he doesn't talk for long. No more marathon listening sessions or passive chunks of time when their attention wanders, behavior takes a nosedive, and phones start to drift out. Now, after a short burst of instruction, the kids are back to their books, books they chose. Somewhat disappointingly for Mr. Valentine, they've never asked him to keep talking. Books are more enticing.

Now that he's off the stage, Mr. Valentine can spend his time circulating among readers. He sees Carlos frowning and goes over to him. And indeed, Carlos is ticked off that the author of *Grasshopper Jungle* lets the world collapse. "Why couldn't Austin and Robby stop the apocalypse?" he asks. Mr. Valentine nods, listening. Carlos wonders whether Robby isn't just as important in the book even though he's a secondary character, and he and Mr. Valentine discuss this for a bit.

Mr. Valentine moves on, and Carlos adds some thoughts to his double-entry journal for the day.

| Text | My thoughts, questions |
|------|------------------------|
| p. 133, paragraph 3: "I tried all day . . ."* | This makes me think that Austin isn't as honest as he started out. He used to say he'd never lie to Shann, but now he's trying to think up a story for her. He loves her, but he's confused. I totally get that. |
| | It also reminds me that characters have lots of traits, and sometimes those traits are almost opposites. Like, Austin can be honest with his friends, but sometimes he covers things up so they don't get mad. He's got these big ideas about who he wants to be, but he's not always living up to them. I think Shann is smart enough to see through him. |
| p. 137: "*Transient* is a nice way of saying homeless . . ." | Austin is always trying to poke holes in other people's hypocrisies. I hate it, too, when people are fake or try to gloss over stuff that's real. But I think it's going to catch up to Austin, kind of like when Curley's wife judges everyone else, but she's the one who's horrible. |

*Carlos and others aren't required to copy the whole quote. It takes them out of their reading for too long, and often serves as a tempting misuse of time instead of keeping eyes on print, their minds on task with questioning and responding to the text.

After a half-hour of reading and teacher–student conversations, it's almost the end of the period. The teacher doesn't have to beg kids to stay seated until the bell, because everyone is still reading.

Mr. Valentine asks them to come to a stop. He recaps the character work they did that day and has a couple students show their notes on the SMART Board. He reviews the homework: they should continue reading and thinking about major and minor characters in double-entry note form. He reminds them that they can look at his models from *Of Mice and Men* on Google Docs if they need help.

As students walk out, Daniela stops to show Mr. Valentine the new book she's reading, and Julia and Jayden compare notes on *Insurgent* and whether the movie is as good as the book. And Carlos mentions to Mr. Valentine that he should be finished with *Grasshopper Jungle* by tomorrow. He's got a long bus ride to a soccer game, and he's planning on reading that whole time. He wants to know, what book should he read next?

This blend of choice reading and classic literature is a marriage of what we know works (independent reading) and what we long to keep (the classics). It's a blend of the research-based practice of letting students choose what they want to and can read and the traditional approach of exposing students to quality literature already rooted in many of our current curriculums.

We should be able to build on the classics, and still hear our students ask, "What book should I read next?" Here's why and how we can make that happen.

## CHAPTER ONE

# WHY ARE MY STUDENTS SNAPCHATTING THEIR WAY THROUGH *THE ODYSSEY*—AND WHAT CAN I OFFER INSTEAD?

Perhaps you have tried to get your kids to fall in love with a big white whale or a little girl named Scout. I have. And I fell flat on my face, or rather right into a group of resistant readers.

The problem Mr. Valentine set out to overcome in the Introduction is one many of us battle every day: how to get our middle and high school students to love to read. But the challenge doesn't end there. Even if we give up on getting our students to love literature and settle for simply getting them to read the assigned classic, we face defeat. Forget appreciating the richness of those books—most students aren't even cracking them open.

Consider what happened in an honors English class I recently visited. The students were on their sixth week of *The Odyssey*, and not into it. This—despite the teacher trying to connect it to their lives, incorporate creative assignments, and break it down in discussion. All that hard work, yet most of the class was checked out, one girl blatantly so.

Perhaps you remember the trick of cutting an inner square out of the pages of a book to hide a pack of cigarettes or contraband candy. This girl taught me a new reason: hiding a phone. She had taken an X-ACTO knife to her copy of *The Odyssey* and was now swiping her way through Snapchat and Instagram during the forty-minute discussion of the text, all while giving the appearance of intently reading. When I asked her why, she said the book was boring. She didn't like listening to her teacher explain it, and it didn't make sense anyway. This A-level student felt that listening in on the discussion was enough to get by, even though she was "listening" while swiping through her phone.

## Why We Have to Minimize the Role of, but Not Abandon, the Classics

Imagine if her six-plus weeks not reading *The Odyssey* had been spent immersed in novels of her choice. My work in middle and high school classrooms tells me that many students carry figurative cell phones in their class copies of the text, appearing to be on task but meanwhile absorbing little of what the teacher so desperately wants them to know.

You wouldn't be reading this book if you weren't also discouraged by students who balk at what you hold closest to your teaching heart—a love of books. So many of us struggle with students' lack of engagement and motivation to read. As a lifelong reader, I wonder how some can deny themselves the habit of reading. But it's no mystery to me, as a reader who chooses what she wants to read and is good at reading, why others resist difficult texts that are disconnected from their lives and interests.

I just picked up *The Scarlet Letter* and opened a page at random. Even as an avid reader, I had to reread this passage a few times to "get it," let alone to analyze craft:

> *It may appear singular, and, indeed, not a little ludicrous, that an affair of this kind, which in later days would have been referred to no higher jurisdiction than that of the select men of the town, should then have been*

*a question publicly discussed, and on which statesmen of eminence took sides. At that epoch of pristine simplicity, however, matters of even slighter public interest, and of far less intrinsic weight than the welfare of Hester and her child, were strangely mixed up with the deliberations of legislators and acts of state.* (Hawthorne, 1850/2003, p. 89)

Whew. How many of us skimmed that?

"Selling" this kind of text to already resistant readers is a huge hurdle. But we don't want to abandon master authors such as Hawthorne, either. We want to use complex classic texts without resorting to reading them aloud in class, chapter by chapter, or making the film version at the end of the unit the only carrot to get students through.

Most middle and high school English teachers I work with worry about denying their students the texts that, as "literature" lovers, we long to teach. David Denby, author of *Lit Up* (2016), makes an impassioned plea to keep critically praised literature in the canon in today's middle and high school curricula, and many teachers I work with share this sentiment.

We don't have the option of dismissing those books anyway. Now we have the added pressure to get our students reading complex literature in order to meet the Common Core State Standards or the state-designed equivalent. The suggested level of texts outlined in Appendix B of the standards is almost shockingly difficult. Most teachers I know would be amazed if their students read and understood works by Cervantes, Chaucer, Chekhov, Dostoyevsky, Molière, Thoreau, Emerson, and Poe. Yet there they are, serving as models for the level of texts that we are to use with our middle and high schoolers.

The expectations laid out in the standards are meant to minimize the gap between what high school students are asked to do now and what they will be asked to do as college freshmen. This makes sense: when we only use texts at a level that is accessible and palatable to our students, we set them up for a shock on standardized tests and at college.

But if students are SparkNoting and Snapchatting their way through the complex texts we teach, what's the point? We can't keep relying on this outdated model of one class novel every six (ahem, sometimes twelve) weeks. Most of our students are not only not reading the classics; they're simply not reading.

One educator I work with told me how she recently asked a high school senior if he was reading.

"No," he answered honestly.

When she asked, "Why not?" he shrugged.

Then she asked, "How does that work?"

"Do you really want to know?" he said.

After she nodded, he quickly jotted down a list in his notebook and showed her. It looked something like this:

- Look up and nod every minute or two

- Write song lists or scribbles in the margins of the book so it looks like you're taking notes

- When the teacher asks a question, flip through pages of the book, then stop at one and look like you're trying to find something as evidence

- Repeat as needed until someone else answers the question or until class is over

This student managed to pass each year without actually reading any of the assigned texts. He artfully avoided reading in part because the text was hard or impossible to understand, and in the meantime developed a clear series of coping mechanisms.

When I heard this story, I pictured so many of my former students nodding eagerly, then avoiding eye contact. Maybe this wasn't such a secret list. If only these students were all able, instead, to just as quickly jot down a list of steps they used to navigate, comprehend, and analyze texts, not fake read them.

We do not want our students to be among the numbers of college freshmen (1.7 million every year) who must take remedial classes in literacy, for which they pay and get no credit (National Center for Education Statistics, 2010). Nor do we want them to be among the nearly 50 percent of students who will drop out of college before graduating. In addition to the high risk of not graduating, our students will run an average debt of almost $30,000 (Bidwell, 2014). The deck is stacked against our students, and deficient literacy skills impair their slim odds of success.

No pressure, right?

As if it's not enough to get our students to read right now, and maybe even enjoy it a little, we face the crushing need to get them reading enough so they can survive the workload in college. It's no wonder some teachers start checking out the health benefits offered at Starbucks or downloading Peace Corps applications when it all starts to feel like too much. But there must be a way to tackle these challenges without drowning under the pressure: how can we turn our students into capable robust readers who also know and appreciate the classics?

And so we're agreed: if schools are to be a place for empowering all students, we need to keep complex texts, including some of the classics we cherish, although we can't limit our curriculum to those potentially alienating books, either. Alfred Tatum (2005) confirms the need to provide a rich variety of texts to get to culturally responsive teaching. When teaching students already disempowered in our society, he says, such as Black adolescent males, we must use texts that reflect students' culture and knowledge, as well as texts that do not. His research shows that the best literacy instruction provides a purposeful blend of texts, those that rely on what is already culturally familiar to our students, along with those that expand their knowledge and value sets into the unknown.

This is smart teaching for any and all students, not only those already facing distinct challenges. If we want all our students to be engaged readers, we cannot remain in the model of only the classics, and if we want them to be empowered in our society, we cannot ignore those complex works, either. But we need to get our students to *be* readers. It's a fine balance.

As English teachers, we're used to working in a pressure cooker. I've never met an English teacher who is scared of hard work—would we take on grading papers if we were? We want to help our students thrive in our classes and beyond. We want to be that changing force that many of our former English teachers were for us, and we're not afraid of working hard to get there. But, we want to feel like those efforts pay off in the form of engaged robust readers, not cell-phone-carrying resisters.

Thankfully, there are ways to be that inspiration, to support our students and boost their reading lives, to keep the dust off our copies of *Walden*, and to remove that cell phone from the pages of their books. And luckily, it doesn't mean working even harder to get there.

## Why We Need to Incorporate Choice Reading

Just as Mr. Valentine overcame reluctant resistant readers, so can we. The turn-around in Carlos isn't a blip, a miracle, or a pipe dream. He has become a reader because of the way Mr. Valentine has structured this and every day.

What works is that literacy is no longer limited to the one book in the curriculum that the whole class is supposed to be reading. That book still exists—it's the template to show students powerful ways to read and to acquaint them with the classics. But afterward there are choices for what students want to read, and that element of choice entices them to crack open a book and develop the habit of reading.

Choice reading has been and continues to be the single most powerful move in supporting all students in becoming authentic readers with robust reading skills. After numerous studies, Stephen Krashen (2004a) documented how choice reading led not only to students' greater enjoyment of reading, but to a marked improvement in their grammar, vocabulary, spelling, and writing skills. Gay Ivey and Peter H. Johnston's (2015) research shows how self-selected reading benefits students' sense of agency as well as their overall intellectual, moral, and personal lives. Penny Kittle (2013), Kelly Gallagher (2009), Stephen Krashen (2004a), Richard Allington (2002), Kylene Beers (2003), Nancie Atwell (2007), Lucy Calkins (2000), and Donalyn Miller (2014) are renowned educators and writers who champion putting choice books into readers' hands. They have been leading countless teachers on this path for decades, and the results are clear. Choice reading, when done right, grows authentic readers. In *The Power of Reading*, Krashen (2004a) reminds us that the single greatest factor in reading ability is how much we read. But how can we expect students to become readers with books they can't, and/or don't, want to read?

We owe it to all of our students, especially those already reading below grade level, to provide the opportunity for prolific reading experiences in books they can read well and want to read. By limiting our instruction to texts that are well above students' reading level, which is the case so often in the schools I work in, we deny students this ability to read well—and to enjoy reading. And, as Allington (2002) reminds us, texts above our students' abilities keep them from growing: "Simply put, students need enormous quantities of successful reading to become independent, proficient readers" (p. 743). One novel every marking period provides anything but.

Mr. Valentine knew a book every couple months wasn't cutting it. He wanted to move his students to do more with their reading, but he also knew they had to be reading in the first place. That's where choice came in, but it wasn't either–or; he could turn them into readers without abandoning the class text. In fact, Mr. Valentine could use the class text as a powerful tool for close reading—excerpting passages of highly complex literature that students are willing to grapple with and appreciate for a few paragraphs, if not necessarily the entire tome.

First he had to feel comfortable embracing young adult (YA) and nonclassic texts as part of his curriculum, knowing most students wouldn't elect to read *To Kill a Mockingbird*, but they'd fly through the pages of *Mockingjay*. Indeed, reading popular literature is a proven way to become a strong reader. It was good enough for David Foster Wallace's college students at Illinois State University in 1994. In his English 102 syllabus, Wallace provided a book list that included Stephen King, Larry McMurtry, and Jackie Collins. As he explained to his students, "Don't let any potential lightweightish-looking qualities of the text delude you into thinking that this will be a blow-off-type class. These 'popular' texts will end up being harder than more conventionally 'literary' works to unpack and read critically. English 102 aims to show you some ways to read fiction more deeply, to come up with more interesting insights on how pieces of fiction work, to have informed, intelligent reasons for liking or disliking a piece of fiction" (Harry Ransom Center, 2010). Wallace used so-called commercial fiction to get his students thinking critically about literature.

So choice reading helps reluctant readers actually read, and as Wallace showed in his course, it's not the death of in-depth literary analysis. Text complexity is not so much about the text, then, but about what you do with the text and the interaction(s) between text and reader.

Thanks to work by Kittle (2013), Gallagher (2009), Miller (2014), Atwell (2007), Calkins (2000), Ivey and Johnston (2015), Krashen (2004a), Allington (2002), and many others, we know the impact of letting students choose books they want to read. We can take these researchers' well-documented successes of turning students into readers to our own classrooms. When we allow our students to pick their books, resistance to reading fades. Not only will students read regularly for the first time in years—or ever—but they may even enjoy it! So the habit gets reinforced, again and again.

## What the Blended Model Offers

If having our kids read regularly, even if it's not the classics from cover to cover; if having a class that's manageable, even enjoyable, to teach; if getting to know our students through their books has some pull, then this book will show you the way. Here's what can happen for you and your students in this blended model.

## STUDENTS READ MORE,
## AND READING MORE MATTERS

Penny Kittle, renowned high school English teacher and author of *Book Love* (2013), filmed her students openly admitting to reading only the SparkNotes, if anything, for their English classes. A startling image shows her students displaying a total of all of the books they read in three years of high school. Most show between zero and five. Then, students display the number of books read *in one semester* after being able to choose what they want to read. Every student's number jumps considerably, most to double digits.

A great thing about reading more is that it builds on itself, naturally strengthening stamina and fluency, which in turn leads readers to read more. We all enjoy doing things we're good at. The only thing I do as an adult that I'm not good at is karaoke, and that is once a decade. Teens are no different—they're drawn to what they feel competent doing, and they avoid what bruises their already vulnerable egos.

> I read much more because I am able to pick books I understand and connect to. Being able to choose has made me look forward to reading whereas before I dreaded it.
>
> —Jolie Sheerin, high school student

Students choose what they read, and that autonomy creates buy-in to read at high volume. No more assigned marriage of tenth grader to *The Scarlet Letter*. Students still read excerpts of that novel, they're familiar with Hawthorne's language and craft, and they know the plot. But they're not expected to read it from cover to cover, which they weren't doing anyway. They are, however, expected to read a lot and to learn strategies of how to read any book. And they do so in books they choose.

> When I do enjoy the book, I can finish it in a matter of days. And sometimes I'll read it over and over again, just to be able to relive my favorite moments in the book.
>
> —Adideb Nag, high school student

By simply introducing choice reading, I've seen classrooms transformed. Teachers who felt it was impossible to get their kids to read can't wait for me to visit their rooms and see all (yes, all) of their students quietly immersed in books. This didn't mean teachers had to completely overhaul their practice. They got students to read by putting engaging books in the classroom, letting them pick out what they want, and giving them time to read. Lessons still incorporate the novels teachers know and love and provide strategies within those beloved texts.

One teacher recently told me how a mom stopped her at the local ShopRite. "I have to tell you the most amazing thing," she told this ninth-grade teacher.

Teens still like getting a sticker for books completed.

This section of tenth-grade English collectively read over one hundred thousand pages by early November.

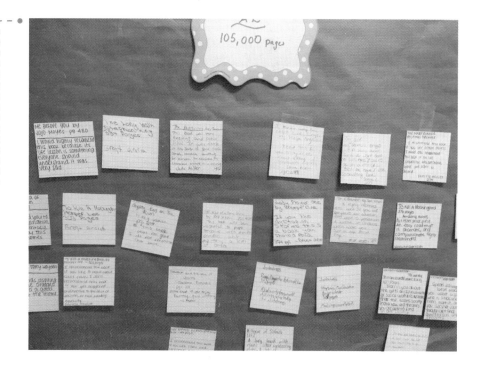

Another way to celebrate students' success as readers: posting lines they love from their independent books.

"My son is reading for the first time since sixth grade. His little brother will play the Wii, and he opts to read." Other parents expressed delight during conferences that their children included books on birthday and holiday gift lists.

When we offer the choice of books that help students feel confident as readers, versus books that are a struggle to comprehend, we offer a path to a feel-good habit that students want to replicate on their own. Once this confidence is established, using excerpts of challenging texts isn't painful. Students have the craft and tools to navigate their own reading, which often grows to include increasingly harder and harder texts. Complex excerpts move our readers to think critically as they read any text and to be aware of sophisticated craft.

While we'll talk about meeting the standards and developing high-level reading skills, reading for volume is a worthwhile goal in and of itself. The more students read, and it doesn't matter what they read, the better they get at reading (Krashen, 2004b). And it's not hard to do—we just give students books they can and want to read (Allington, 2013)! Malcolm Gladwell's (2012) famous statistic tells us that to get good at anything, we need to do it for at least ten thousand hours. Time spent on books that students aren't reading is a massive loss of opportunity, but we can turn that around.

## WE SUPPORT STUDENTS GETTING TO THE HIGHEST LEARNING GOAL: TRANSFER

This book will show two things we can start doing in our classrooms that have significant impact on students:

1. **Provide a focused lesson at the beginning of class, often a close read within a challenging text.** This brief lesson consists of the teacher using an excerpt from the class novel to model his or her thinking as a strong reader with a singular focus (e.g., paying attention to how setting is introduced).

2. **Turn the lesson over to students to try that process with their own books.**

The first instructional method is a think-aloud and is well documented in its ability to empower readers (Wilhelm, 2001). It also provides an opportunity for students to do a close reading of a challenging text with the teacher's support. The second method supports what Douglas Fisher, Nancy Frey, and John Hattie

(2016) refer to as the highest level of learning: transfer. Both are essential to high-level literacy instruction.

The think-aloud is how we make our thinking visible to students, revealing the "secret" moves we employ, so students know how to think as readers. Jeffrey Wilhelm (2001) explains, "Think-alouds ensure that the hallmarks of engaged reading don't remain a big secret to any child in our classrooms" (p. 66). The moves we make as skilled readers are made visible, and students then try these moves on their own while the teacher circulates, scaffolding and guiding as needed. This transition to guided practice and then independent practice is the hallmark of the gradual release of responsibility (Fisher, 2008). It's what deepens comprehension, helps students to make meaning, and empowers them to approach texts with confidence. Basically, it's the essential step before asking readers to go try good reading on their own.

This focused lesson also gets to *close reading*, a current buzzword for good reason. Close reading refers to the process of doing in-depth analysis of a text, using a specific lens for examining key details, patterns, and more. Close reading is essential in helping students arrive at deep understandings of author's craft, underlying meaning, text structures, and all of our literacy standards. Asking students to join us in an intense examination of a passage in a classic text, then apply it anew to a choice text, allows us to incorporate choice reading in a way that is anything but "lite."

Close reading isn't meant to be done for an entire novel or nonfiction book—that wouldn't be realistic or particularly useful. It's meant to be done within paragraphs, passages, or select pages of text in order to lift our understanding and thinking about how we read. Pulling excerpts of our class texts to do this heavy lifting provides access to challenging literature as well as practice with the habit of close reading. Then, readers try that same careful attention within books of their own.

Transfer is what happens when readers take what we show them and use it in a new way, or in this instance with their own book. Fisher et al.'s (2016) scale of learning sets transfer as the most valuable goal we can aim for when teaching, and yet their research shows it is rare in most instruction.

By asking students to take what we show them in the class novel and apply that reading strategy to their own books, we are teaching them to transfer essential reading understandings. This is what reading workshops, à la Kittle, Miller, Atwell, Calkins, and more, have showcased for decades. We ask students to apply a strategy to their own work, and see the results. Transfer is where we need to go in our teaching, but it requires that students aren't using skills in the same book that we're teaching: they must try that skill in a new text.

For example, let's look at an excerpt from *The Scarlet Letter* to show students how to pay attention to repeated images. The teacher chose this passage to help students consider author's craft, knowing that images described in detail may stand for a bigger idea in the book.

The teacher read this passage aloud from the beginning of *The Scarlet Letter*:

> *The rust on the ponderous iron-work of its oaken door looked more antique than anything else in the New World. Like all that pertains to crime, it seemed never to have known a youthful era. Before this ugly edifice, and between it and the wheeltrack of the street, was a grass plot, much overgrown with burdock, pigweed, and apple peru, and such unsightly vegetation, which evidently found something congenital in the soil that had so early borne the black flower of civilized society, a prison. But on one side of the portal, and rooted almost at the threshold, was a wild rosebush, covered, in this month of June, with its delicate gems, which might be imagined to offer their fragrance and fragile beauty to the prisoner as he went in, and to the condemned criminal as he came forth to his doom, in token that the deep heart of Nature could pity and be kind to him.* (pp. 42–43)

After he read, the teacher spoke about why the rosebush seemed to stand for something bigger than just a glimpse of something pretty at the prison door. He talked informally about how the prison seems to stand for Puritan judgment, and how the rosebush's natural beauty counteracts that harshness of the Puritans. As he spoke, he'd go back and point to specifics in the text that drew his attention. He connected his theories to a lesson from the day before in which students learned about Puritanism and the themes of punishment and forgiveness. This all took about eight minutes.

Then, the teacher asked his students to pay attention to images in their books that are repeated or described in detail. Students were asked to question why the author included those descriptions, and to assume the objects are mentioned for a reason. He sent students off to read, and at the end of class, he had them write for a little less than ten minutes about the images they saw in their books and how those images might connect to the way Hawthorne used the rosebush in *The Scarlet Letter*.

After watching the teacher analyze the symbol of the rosebush in *The Scarlet Letter*, this reader considers possible symbols in *Grasshopper Jungle*.

Repeated Images and Symbolism in Grasshopper Jungle

Nathaniel Hawthorne focuses on the rose near the prison to show something about Puritanism without just saying it. Andrew Smith does this a lot in Grasshopper Jungle, too. Smith repeats images to show things about his characters. Austin keeps mentioning the Xanax that his and Robby's moms take and calls the Xanax kayaks. It seems like he might call them kayaks because their moms are kind of floating on the surface and not really getting involved. They are basically clueless about what their kids do outside the house.

This reader of *Inside Out and Back Again* considers how the main character's choice of a doll to bring to America from Vietnam is more than just a random detail, but stands for something bigger in the story.

Symbolism in Inside Out and Back Again

Just like the rosebush represents something bigger in The Scarlet Letter, Ha's doll means more than just that she brought a doll with her when she leaves Vietnam. She describes the doll as her "one choice". Ha chooses something nonessential but important to her, because she doesn't want to completely leave Saigon. Just like the specific description of the rosebush tells us something important in The Scarlet Letter, the description of the doll is important, too. Lai writes that the doll was left outside by a neighbor and has marks from where a mouse bit it. I think this shows that the doll is like Ha, and that it might be left outside or harmed, too. It might not always be safe or kept intact, so we know that her trip to America is probably not going to be all easy. That's why Ha says she loves the doll even more because it has scars. Ha has scars, too, and this makes me think that the author

When students transfer reading skills into a book of their choice, there is also the chance they'll be better able to transfer those skills to their history or science class's readings, not to mention the state tests. If we want our students to be skilled readers in all content areas, on high-stakes tests, in college, and in life, then having them apply and transfer reading skills in our classes means we are getting them ready.

## AUTHENTIC ASSESSMENT AND DIFFERENTIATION HAPPEN NATURALLY

These routines of modeling reading strategies and asking students to transfer them to their own books also allow for authentic assessment. We will see our readers master the strategies. Time spent reading isn't fluff, it's immediate and useful data for us, and it produces results for our students.

Now the guessing work is gone. If students can take a reading strategy we've modeled in *The Scarlet Letter* and use it with a book of their choice, we can be confident they truly "got" that concept. And we don't have to worry that they used SparkNotes to get there.

Carlos didn't, and frankly couldn't, fake meeting standard RL.9–10.3: *Analyze how complex characters (e.g., those with multiple or conflicting motivations) develop over the course of a text, interact with other characters, and advance the plot or develop the theme.* He did this work when reading *Grasshopper Jungle*, and he showed it in his double-entry notes. There's immediate proof. Trying to see if a student mastered a strategy by listening to a comment she makes in class discussion around a common text is much harder. And it makes it more difficult to assess whether or not the student did the reading at all.

Fake reading turns into authentic reading when students do it in class, every day. As teachers, we already work hard to create thoughtful lessons with impact—this is a way to make that expertise and hard work pay off. And, it pays off with all students: nonreaders, fake readers, and even already capable readers.

> By writing sticky notes and answering questions, I enjoy reading more. I think more about characters and I look deeper into the story, so I have a better understanding.
>
> -Miranda Maley, high school student

Every reader is working at his or her own pace and ability. We don't need to differentiate for the range of learners we all teach; differentiation is naturally embedded for interest and level when students apply reading skills to books they want to and can read.

As Carol Ann Tomlinson (2014) reminds us, there is no such thing as a class of homogeneous learners. Differentiating for individual needs and interests is essential to good teaching. By offering up choice reading as a way to demonstrate student learning, we meet our students' needs.

## BLENDING THE CLASS NOVEL WITH STUDENTS' NOVELS ISN'T FOR MARTYRS

This blend of excerpts from the class novel to show high-level reading skills mixed with students going off to try it in their own choice books is a game-changing structure. And yet sometimes, as hardworking and devoted professionals, we might hesitate. It's understandable. After years of being "on" during the whole class period, we might feel guilty that we lead the class for a short time, and then students take on the hard work of critical reading while we coach them. It feels too easy! Are we really earning our keep if we aren't doing all the heavy lifting?

But this change in ownership of learning is the idea. First of all, there's still plenty to do in preparing a tight lesson and helping readers, but second, we put the onus on those who most need these strategies: the students! No more hiding behind a cell-phoned copy of *The Odyssey*; students are on task with the important work of critical thinking and reading. And they're actually doing it.

Typically, any hesitation disappears as we see the profound change in students' reading habits, engagement, and motivation. We witness students' joy and confidence surge, without giving up the classics to get there, either. Being less exhausted at the end of the day is just icing on the cake. The biggest reward is seeing the transformation in our students: not just in a few high flyers, but in everyone.

> I discovered that I'm actually an avid reader. I just need to have a novel that I like to read.
>
> -Suchita Kanala, high school student

> I read more now that I choose an independent book. Now I am more interested in the story. Before I would never be excited to pick up the class book because I wasn't intrigued.
>
> -Miranda Maley, high school student

Now all students get in the habit of reading, building up stamina, choosing books they want to read, and passing around hot titles as soon as they finish, all while being exposed to the classics. Students read in the hallways and on bus rides to games, and sometimes put away cell phones in favor of books. They enjoy reading.

Teachers I work with know this because they're also implementing a research-proven instructional move that fosters achievement: reflecting on what and how they're teaching. Fisher et al.'s (2016) studies show that

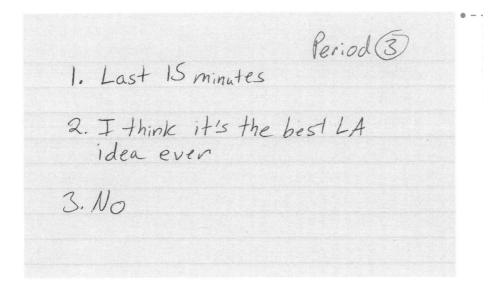

No. 1 is an answer to the question, "When would you like to read your choice book in class?" and No. 2 answers, "What do you think of adding choice reading to the curriculum?" No. 3 answers whether there is anything else the student's teacher should know.

stopping to consider what is working and what isn't is transformative. This blended model came about with teachers who tried it, fed off of students' immediate enthusiasm, and modified it according to the informal and formal data they collected.

## A HIGH VOLUME OF READING GETS OUR STUDENTS COLLEGE-READY

The ability to read well is essential in helping students prepare for college. Yet many middle and high schoolers are ill prepared. Most of us as teachers have been forced to let go of the assumption that by middle or high school our students will be solid readers, prepared to tackle literary analysis in the classics. It's clear we lost this battle awhile ago. Analyzing symbolism in *The Great Gatsby* isn't what lures these students back. So, instead of pushing them into the class novel and further away from reading, we must teach the habits of intense sustained reading through choice texts.

Developing stamina as readers is essential if students are going to manage the hundreds of pages a week of college reading. We can help them develop stamina with higher degrees of independence so they will be ready for flying solo in college. We can't expect to nag and threaten and babysit middle and high schoolers into skimming the class novel, and later being able to direct themselves as readers on their own. The time to get students reading a lot on their own is now.

Students will see the reading skills outlined in the standards as you model them with the class novel, and they'll do that same work with their own books. Plus, our love of classic novels and texts will be contagious. Some students might even pick up those classics—by choice.

I've seen students pick up *Go Set a Watchman*, *Invisible Man*, *The Catcher in the Rye*, and *Animal Farm*, all because their teachers used excerpts from these texts in their lessons and inadvertently plugged them as captivating reads. Regardless of what they choose, students are getting fit as readers, ready for the marathon of reading they'll do in college.

We'll also see how the blended model moves beyond a class discussion around one novel, in which typically just a few students take part, toward a seminar-like conversation in which all students use their own books as textual evidence for complex concepts and theories. Reading and talking about choice books in class won't feel elementary because students will be engaging in the meaningful complex analysis they'll be asked to do in college.

Through the blended model, we help all students be capable robust readers. Not only the very few who go on to be English majors, but all of our students, will be able to think critically, identify and discuss literary techniques in a range of works, and feel confident in themselves and their reading skills. In a world in which a college degree is nonnegotiable for professional careers, we must steep our students in the habits they'll need once they get there.

## KEEPING THE CLASSICS GIVES OUR STUDENTS CULTURAL CAPITAL

While much good can be done with volume in choice reading, our students get the best of both worlds when we keep the classics, too. By exposing students to summaries and close reading within well-regarded texts that have stood the test of time, we give students much more than the plotline of *Macbeth* or an appreciation for Harper Lee. We also give them the touchstone texts for so many other works, the reference points on which so many contemporary narratives are built. Our students gain the sense that story lines in modern film, TV, and literature were not created in a vacuum.

A familiarity with the classics is cultural capital: it enables our students to navigate and succeed within our world. Students are more likely to understand references to someone's Jekyll and Hyde personality, a Scrooge type, or a Pollyannaish optimism, and to pick up on allusions to literary texts within contemporary works. When they hear Selena Gomez sing, "The heart wants what it wants," they might do so with the awareness that Woody Allen said it before her, and Emily Dickinson before that.

Readers can gain a broader view of the world and appreciate how attitudes have changed over time when experiencing Austen, Shakespearean sonnets, *Uncle Tom's Cabin*, and *Fahrenheit 451*, alongside contemporary lit. Exposure to classics also helps students navigate and understand language in unfamiliar styles and contexts. And again, students might be tempted to pick up those classics because they are becoming more confident as readers.

Reading literary fiction not only helps us understand our world and historical contexts, but it improves our social skills, such as empathy and understanding (Kidd & Castano, 2013)—not to mention it feeds our brains. Reading texts like Jane Austen's actually activates parts of our brain that popular literature cannot. When students are exposed to complex texts that require high levels of inference, brain activity expands (Goldman, 2012). Complex classics are worth keeping around, even if we're not holding onto a pipe dream that students will read them from cover to cover.

While keeping the classics is vital, the term *classic* can and should be broadly defined beyond what we may have read as students in English class. If classics worth teaching are deemed to have "outstanding or enduring" qualities (Wheeler, 2017), then our book lists don't have to be limited to texts written by White men from previous centuries. Having just finished Colson Whitehead's *Underground Railroad*, I'm itching to use this profound book to showcase characterization, symbolism, text structure, and more. Many high schools use *Speak* by Laurie Halse Anderson as a class novel, and for good reason. It's beautifully written, and it was written for young adults, with teen characters, issues, and conflicts. Just because it's not hard to understand or relate to, or because as teachers we didn't read this book in school, doesn't mean this YA classic shouldn't be an option for teaching students how to read well.

For every *Romeo and Juliet* that we keep, we can model reading strategies with a fresher text that's equally complex, rich in technique, and relevant to our teen students. I urge teachers to model reading strategies with complex well-written books that include teen characters, issues, and conflicts whenever possible. *To Kill a Mockingbird, Code Name Verity, Wonder*, and *Chew On This* over *Animal Farm* in middle school. *The Book Thief, The Catcher in the Rye, The Absolutely True Diary of a Part-Time Indian, Pride and Prejudice*, and *I Am Malala* over *Ulysses* and *Great*

*Expectations* in high school. As middle and high school English teachers, we usually have some choice in what we teach: let's use that choice to pull readers into the classics (broadly defined), not push them out.

No matter what complex, "outstanding" classic literature we choose to teach, we also need to keep the classics in our classrooms because our students deserve access to those texts. Challenging classic literature should not exist solely in rarified environments for highly literate students. We live in a society of polarized classes, where a few have access to privilege and many do not. If we leave the classics out, we risk sending a message that our students can't handle those texts, don't deserve them, or won't need them in the futures where they are headed.

Keeping the classics, while using them in the summarized form, means our students get the message that they deserve access to all texts, at all levels. We subtly reinforce the message that they can be anything they want to be and do anything they want to do because we are not dumbing down our classes or withholding challenging texts. We use complex literature because we know that all of our students, not just the privileged or AP classes, deserve to be taught that way.

## WE PREPARE OUR STUDENTS FOR CAREERS

This blended model turns students into engaged readers who can succeed in middle school, high school, and college, and it gets students ready for the literacy demands of their future work lives, too.

According to the National Center for Education Statistics (2002) and a survey from company executives, the most important job skill hiring managers look for is the ability to communicate and manage information. Findings from the International Adult Literacy Survey found that only half of the U.S. population between sixteen and sixty-five years of age were proficient in the minimum standards for success in today's labor market (National Center for Education Statistics, 2002). We know students will need to read a high volume of information and emails, complex instructions, loan applications, and legal documents; conduct fluent correspondence; and, ideally, still have pleasure reading as a part of their lives. And we know that when they're carrying that cell phone in the pages of *The Odyssey*, it's impossible to get them there. All of us want our students to enter the working world able to showcase their minds and abilities, and by turning them into fluent readers, we're readying them to do so.

Many teachers face the challenge of making this all meaningful to high school juniors and seniors with no interest in or plans to attend college. We need to

These students aren't reading *Lord of the Flies* and *The Bluest Eye* because they were assigned. They picked them up by choice. Not assigning the classics doesn't mean readers won't ever read them. It means they'll get there when they are ready.

remind them that career options, even in what we once thought of as blue-collar jobs or those that require only a high school diploma, will be limited without strong reading skills. Research shows that the need for reading comprehension in factory work and other positions is increasing at a rapid rate. A recent production plant opening in North Carolina was able to accept only 15 percent of job applicants due to the proficiency on a test measuring reading, writing, and math. The head of Siemens Energy declared that there are no longer any jobs on the plant floor for high school graduates, and a director at the John Deere farming machinery company also explained that comprehension skills are a necessity. Our students simply don't have the option of being nonreaders and having strong careers (Selingo, 2017).

Whether we teach students rich in privilege or lacking in resources and opportunity, we want all of our students to head off into their futures equipped with every literacy skill, every advantage, and every ounce of confidence we can supply them with. And we only have forty-five minutes to do that. But this is a doable structure, a method that can work for any combination of ability and need. It will supply our students with what's needed to take on a world steeped in text and information.

We know literate lives aren't a privilege. They are a right and a cornerstone of an informed society, and by getting students to independently manage the work of adept readers, we're also graduating students who can take part in an educated civic body and workplace.

## WE DEVELOP RELATIONSHIPS WITH OUR STUDENTS—EVERY ONE

Apart from the blended model's benefits that empower our students later on, we also reap rewards in the here and now. A big part of what makes Mr. Valentine's class inviting to kids, and enjoyable for him to teach, is that he's gotten to know his students through books they love. For the majority of class, kids are reading. And during that time, the teacher can rotate through the class, talking to each kid about his or her book, or lead discussions in which students exchange ideas around their personal reading. At a time in their lives when kids most need and seldom have one-on-one time with adults, teachers can get to know their teen students. These conversations also help students solidify their sense of self as a reader.

In the old model of the class novel, there's no time for one-on-one. We're too busy running a class discussion and keeping students on task. Reading in class, essential and valuable work, opens up room for other important opportunities, too. We've now created space to talk to students about their ideas, questions, and struggles as they relate to their reading. This is a results-producing powerful time of an adult listening intently to each student. "Bad" students tend to lose their negative labels; quiet students emerge from their shells; superstars slow down and find an authentic way to connect. The time invested is a win-win: the relationships that are fostered by talking about books are enriching for all.

## STUDENTS DEVELOP COMPASSION, EMPATHY, AND UNDERSTANDING

The students in classes like Mr. Valentine's are readers, but they're also members of a reading community. That community can see rich growth not just in skills, but in kindness and understanding. This might sound like a fantasy, but compassion flourishes within this new structure.

Peter Johnston and Gay Ivey, educators and authors, discovered in their research that by simply introducing students to a range of YA fiction and telling students to read what they liked, each student read on average forty-two books in the first year (Johnston, 2012). In addition to amassing this tremendous volume, there were a myriad of social benefits: a reduction in behavior problems, an increase in students talking about books, improved maturity, compassion and empathy toward one another, a strengthening of peer and student–teacher relationships, and, quite simply, an increase in happiness. And to prove this was not just a feel-good exercise but one that administrators could invest in without hesitation, Johnston and Ivey also noted that test scores shot up.

As further testimony to the power of reading fiction, former president Barack Obama recently attributed his most essential growth and learning to novels. "When I think about how I understand my role as citizen, setting aside being president, and the most important set of understandings that I bring to that position of citizen, the most important stuff I've learned I think I've learned from novels," he said. "It has to do with empathy. . . . And the notion that it's possible to connect with some[one] else even though they're very different from you" (quoted in Schaub, 2015). In our increasingly global world, what better skill to foster among our students than empathy?

As kids read about characters both like and unlike themselves, as they fall in love with them and follow their journeys, they strengthen core qualities of kindness and understanding. These readers bring that compassion and empathy to their friendships in school and beyond to their families and communities. Reading isn't just academic literacy—it expands our hearts and deepens our consideration of the world.

In case we ever lose faith in the strengths, abilities, and compassion of the coming generations, we can read this student's writing about choice reading and how it pushed her thinking and understanding of the world:

> *She hated novels. She hated reading. She hated books with small text and thick binds. She hated the smell of it; she hated the look of it. She hated the countless hours spent on reading assignments. She hated the sound of the clock ticking as she read the same words over and over again, turning to the same page over and over again, only to realize that she didn't know what she had just read.*
>
> *"Pick out two books and read them by January 20," her teacher had said. She groaned. "Time to read another book that will bore me to death," she thought. She walked over to the pile of books laid upon books and more books. Her hands grazed over each and every cover. "Too big," "Too small of a text," or "Looks lame," she thought. But her hands stopped at one and only one book:* The Color of Water. *She skimmed through the pages, and "Perfect," she thought. "Just one semester, and this is finally over," she sighed.*
>
> *She sat back down in her seat and read the first few pages. Few pages turned to few chapters, minutes turned to hours, and hours turned to days. She was captivated. She was captivated by the story of Ruth, who was chained to her Jewish traditions all throughout childhood. She was captivated by how Ruth, as a single mother, was able to take care of all her twelve children. Her favorite quote was the one that showed Ruth's lack of support. "My mother knew I was pregnant and in trouble. Looking back, she knew. All she did was sit by the door of the store and fix up the vegetables" (p. 129). She was captivated by James's struggle to find individuality and to finally find a balance with his mixed race. The story of the mother and*

*the son motivated her to turn the pages and to read. The idea of losing family helped her realize how important they really are. She no longer paid attention to the clock ticking. She was content with the text of the book and the width of the bind. She liked the reading. She loved the book.*

*—Surabhi Sahay*

## What's Next: Sparking Joy in Our Classes

These wonderful things can happen in our classrooms, too. They don't require a 180-degree turn from what currently exists. What can look different, however, are the new levels of student engagement with texts. And this book is here to help make this process doable for any teacher.

We'll start by outlining in depth the building blocks for exposing kids to the classics and other complex literature, while also sweetening the pot with choice reading.

First I'll explain how to get ready for independent reading. I'll go through ways to get lots of books, how to set them up in our classrooms, and how to help students find books they won't want to put down. Then, we'll see frameworks for how to make a consistent time for students to dive into their books *and* a time to teach the class novel or nonfiction text.

Next, we'll see the process for figuring out what to teach, using the novels we love and grade-level standards as a foundation. I'll break down this process, providing models, tips, and templates for each step so we see the "how to" clearly. The planning out of a unit will feel doable, not daunting.

We're all aware, sometimes overwhelmingly, that nonfiction needs to be an equal player in our curriculums. In Chapter 4, I'll show how to create units based on nonfiction texts and standards, too. Just as in the previous chapter on fiction texts, the planning process will be illustrated with a sample nonfiction text, model lessons, and more to make the methods easily accessible. I'll also show how to choose excerpts and give summaries of the class text, and anticipate possible challenges and what to do about them. There will be resources so we can take on this process without hesitation.

Once we're comfortable building lessons and units using this structure, I'll explain how to bring those lessons to life in our classrooms. Chapter 5 will help us get a sense of timing for a single class period or block, and a sample script will help us envision what it all looks like. We'll see how to do read-alouds, what kinds of writing students can do to show their understanding of their reading, and samples of what that all looks like. This chapter will demystify the day-to-day and lay out the teaching moves that can transform a room of reluctant readers to engaged ones.

Once we've covered these building blocks, I'll explain how to foster reading discussion among groups of students and as a class in Chapter 6. Most of us love leading class discussion, and we don't want that talk to disappear! We'll look at ways to encourage discussion around the class text so talking about a shared text still exists. Then we'll also see how students use their expertise in their own books to make pair, group, and whole-class discussion rich and engaging.

And, of course, middle and high school is a high-stakes world of assessment, so we must consider how to come up with a grade when using this structure. Chapter 7 will look at the huge benefits of grading within choice reading and excerpting the class text. Then we'll go over how to create formative and summative assessments. With these strategies, grading tends to be more authentic, useful for both teacher and student, and easier to manage.

Finally, Chapter 8 will show results where they count: in *our* classrooms. As educators, we will see how this process builds relationships among readers in powerful ways. Through talk about books, through modeling ourselves as readers, through getting to know students as readers, meaningful bonds develop. As Fisher et al.'s (2016) research shows, the impact of student–teacher relationships is considerable and worth prioritizing. By nurturing that tie, teachers stand to get about a year and a half of learning for one year of teaching. Not to mention, a healthy relationship and mutual fondness increase the likelihood that teacher and students enjoy time together in school. Win-win.

The lifelong impact of fostering strong readers is clear, but the here and now in the classroom is also a rich pleasurable experience. We will find that individual reading identities emerge, and that crucial communities of readers impact one another in positive and far-reaching ways.

Now, let's get started!

## CHAPTER TWO

# GETTING READY FOR THE BLENDED MODEL

Mr. Miller sees me in the hallway and flags me down. He's the head football coach for the winning team of this high school, and his presence commands attention. As I get closer, I see him bouncing on the balls of his feet, egging me on.

"You have to come see this." He's grinning and looks almost boyish. "Look—they're *all* reading!"

Indeed, they are. Every one of his sophomores has a book propped on his or her desk. The book jackets show everything from historical nonfiction about communicable diseases to a bio of LeBron James to manga. In some ways, it's about as unglamorous as it gets. It's not exactly a scene from *Dead Poets Society* with a captivating teacher pontificating to a group of enthralled students. It's just a room of teens silently reading. What's the big deal? But Mr. Miller and I know. This is a very big deal.

It's like getting every single thing on a teaching wish list: a group of sixteen-year-olds, all with eyes on print. I don't see a phone, a distracted gaze, a person off task. And I see an utterly invigorated teacher standing next to me, beaming with pride. Rightly so. This room of rapt readers is a championship trophy.

# How to Set Up Your Classes
## So Students Really Read

Let's look at ways to turn your classroom into one like Mr. Miller's, to get your energized smile to emerge, and to spark reading joy and habits in your students.

Of course, it may be you have already immersed yourself in the works of Nancie Atwell (2007), Donalyn Miller (2014), and Penny Kittle (2013), all experts in independent reading and reading workshops, and you have libraries and choice reading up and running. If so, well done. You might still skim this chapter, however, to see how other middle and high school teachers have taken that expert instruction and modified it through trial and error, creating personalized adaptations that can work for your middle or high school classroom. And if you haven't taken those steps yet, you will find this important. These steps provide a condensed and adapted blend of what premier educators have been teaching for years—how to get our kids to read.

This chapter will show you how to lay the groundwork for "real" reading, providing big and small steps to establish classroom libraries, organize those libraries, and help students access books they'll want to read. You will see engaged readers, not SparkNote skimmers. Subsequent chapters will show you the way to blend students' choice reading with the classics, but for now we'll start with laying this foundation on which everything else will be built.

The chapter is structured so that you'll take on one step at a time, setting yourself up for success and not frustration. You might jump ahead at times, or save certain things for when you can get to them. While you're troubleshooting one step, you might move ahead to another or go back and strengthen a previous one. That's okay—just remember to allow for the habit of independent reading to go in fits and starts and to acknowledge the successes and shining moments when they happen. And trust me, they'll happen.

Keep your eyes tuned to celebrate the growth of readers along the way. Then flag a colleague or two down and show them your room of readers, saying, "Look— they're doing it!"

## STEP 1: GET BOOKS INTO YOUR CLASSROOM THAT STUDENTS WILL WANT TO READ

Perhaps you are lucky enough to already have a classroom library inherited from a previous teacher or funded by a principal who ordered up a rich stock of books for every classroom. This is like finding a unicorn, however. If you have generous administrators or library-donating colleagues, find a way to thank them. They are a rare species!

Most teachers create classroom libraries over time, pulling from a range of resources. When I say time, I mean years, not weeks or months. I will show you how to access those resources to save you time and energy, and still, creating a candy store of books will be an ongoing effort. Just remember it's an effort well worth the reward—a class filled with literacy-rich authentic readers.

Gather your energies by picturing your future classroom like Mr. Miller's. Instead of running discussion, struggling to pull out smart comments, or finding ways to tell if anyone really read *The Scarlet Letter*, picture a room of students quietly reading. In order for that to happen, they'll need books right there, books that beckon them to open the cover and start to read.

## Have enticing books close at hand

For students accustomed to years of being told what to read and often resisting that reading, finding books isn't an easy task. You and I, as experienced readers, find going to Barnes & Noble or scanning the new releases at the library as delicious as students find an iTunes gift card or going to GameStop. It's important not to assume they'll be given the choice to read in class and immediately salivate at the chance. We want to eliminate all the obstacles that keep them from wanting to read, and one of the most important things we can do is put those tantalizing, perfect-match, must-read books right within arm's reach.

## Generate a wish list of books with students, and use other go-to lists as resources

There are lots of book lists that will likely apply to almost any high school student. Here are a few to start with:

- **Nancie Atwell's fabulous lists** "Pleasure Reading for High School Guys" and "Pleasure Reading for High School Girls" (Center for Teaching and Learning, 2017)

- The myriad of **lists on Goodreads** (2017) such as "Popular Teen Books" (Just browse them with a discerning eye tuned into your population.)

- **Penny Kittle's *Custom Booklist*** (2014), devised with her high school students

This middle school classroom library showcases organized shelves and an inviting spot to read.

Another middle school classroom library keeps books facing out—covers are enticing!

This high school teacher took advantage of any shelves she could find, and then organized books so students can easily find a captivating read.

Organizing books could be as simple as using masking tape to mark genres such as graphic novels (always a hit).

- The **Nerdy Book Club "Top Ten Lists"** (2017)—for instance, "Top Ten Books for Harry Potter Fans," "Top Ten New Classics," or "Top Ten Sci Fi/Fantasy Villains" (Use these lists, and eventually consider contributing to them—and having your students do so, too!)

- The ***Nerdy Book Club* awarded books** (2015), vetted by experienced teachers and school librarians who choose the best books every year in a ton of excellent categories, such as graphic novels, young adult books, and reading for the middle grades (This is my go-to place to find books that I know I will love and can recommend to students. In addition to the yearly awards, check out the posts by teachers and students.)

Readers tend to gravitate to what they know, to characters like them, and to familiar settings and conflicts, and they especially enjoy texts that make them feel good about reading. Realistic fiction is a go-to genre, but so are fantasy, narrative nonfiction, graphic novels, anime, and more. Students will gravitate toward texts in which they can share an emotional world with characters, and that appeal exists across a wide variety of genres. Look for books that will be easy to read, not those that feel like a challenging chore. I like going to Amazon and using its "look inside" feature; when you click on the cover image, you can see what a text looks like as if you're actually picking up a real book in a bookstore. Keep a certain reader in your head as you scan the first pages of books—maybe one of your strugglers who actively resists reading. Then view lists of books with an at-grade-level reader in mind, and again with a high flyer. Remember them, not just your own personal reading tastes, as you create a wish list of titles or put books in your cart.

Goodreads is a wonderful website for students to use on their own, and for you to find books for them. Readers can personalize lists for themselves, and you can also access lists such as "Best Young Adult Books," "Best Young Adult Dystopian Novels," "Best YA Romance," "Best Series," and "Best Kick-Ass Female Characters From YA and Children's Fantasy and Science Fiction." Again, use the site to find books for your library, and remember it as a place to direct students as users and contributors. Such sites are amazingly helpful because of readers like you and your students.

## The Best Books of 6th Grade!

Divergent series *******
Legend series
Warrior Cats series
H2O series ***
A Tale Dork and Grimm series **
A Night Divided *
The Best Bad Luck I Ever Had *
Because of Mr. Terupt ******
Out of My Mind *
Auggie and me **
Amulet series *****
Harry Potter series **********
Rump **
Is it Night or Day?
The Crossover **********
Victor Cruz: Out of the Blue
Gym Candy **
The Magisterium series *
Nightmares series *
Goodbye Stranger
Girl Online series
Sisters *****
The Hunger Games series ***
Drums, Girls, & Dangerous Pie
House Arrest *
Between Shades of Gray **
Buddy
The Honest Truth

The Terrible Two
A Work in Progress **
A Mango-Shaped Space *
Flipped *
When My Name Was Keoko
Anna and the Swallow Man
The Secret series **
Smile *******
El Deafo *
Percy Jackson series ***
Pretty Little Liars series
Wonder *********
Trials of Apollo *
Land of Stories series *****
Love, Lucas ***
Shug
One for the Murphys ***
Fish in a Tree *
Sunny Side Up
Roller Girl
The Heroes of Olympus **
Maze Runner series *
Bone series
~~Kingdom~~ Kingdom Keepers
The Swap
Booked ****
The Westing Game
The Finisher *

This list of popular favorites is generated completely by student readers and is added to throughout the year. Why keep an amazing title to yourself?

## Rely on the advice of good readers right in your building

Ask librarians, often an underappreciated resource. If you're lucky enough to have a school librarian, ask him or her to generate a list of books that get checked out frequently, as well as books he or she recommends. Establish a relationship with your local librarians, too—especially those specializing in young adult books. They'll be a treasure trove of information, and they may likely even jump-start your library collection with books they need to phase out.

Ask your students, your very best resource. It may be they haven't read in years and struggle to generate a list, in which case ask them to list their favorite movies, sports figures, heroes, and interests. Use those as search starters. And, don't assume they haven't heard of books they'd want to read or that there aren't closet readers in your ranks. When told they are going to help create a classroom library, they often have great ideas and opinions.

One way students can both share and create a useful resource is to craft a list of books they want to read before the school year is over, ideally outlining categories such as a range of genres and challenging titles to push readers out of their comfort zones at times.

This student's reading plan was generated after a month or so of talking about books in class and looking at Goodreads and BookYap. The genres were up to the students, but everyone had to have some nonfiction and a "challenge" list.

## My Reading Plan

**Fiction**
- To Catch a Watchman by Harper Lee
- The Bluest Eye by Toni Morrison
- Thirteen Reasons Why by Jay Asher
- The Alchemist by Paulo Coelho
- Will Grayson, Will Grayson by John Green
- The Poisonwood Bible by Barbara Kingsolver
- Kindred by Octavia Butler
- Room by Emma Donoghue

**Graphic Novels**
- Persepolis by Marjane Satrapi
- Maus I: A Survivor's Tale by Art Spiegleman

**Poetry**
- Honeybee by Naomi Shihab Nye
- On the Bus with Rosa Parks by Rita Dove

**Nonfiction**
- Freakonomics by Steven Levitt
- Fast Food Nation by Eric Schlosser
- Bird by Bird by Anne Lamott

**Challenges**
- The Autobiography of Malcom X by Malcom X
- The Jungle by Upton Sinclair
- The Omnivore's Dilemma by Michael Pollen
- A Passage to India by E.M. Forster
- The Underground Railroad by Colson Whitehead

What I'll read by June 23rd
                    by Andrew

Fiction
The Curious Incident of the Dog in Night-time by Mark Haddon
Life of Pi by Yann Martel
The Absolutely True Diary of a Part-Time Indian by Sherman Alexie
The Bourne Identity by Robert Ludlum
Aristotle and Dante Discover the Secrets of the Universe by Benjamin Alire Saenz
The Martian by Andy Weir
Grasshopper Jungle by Andrew Smith

Humor
Me Talk Pretty One Day by David Sedaris
A Walk in the Woods by Bill Bryson

Memoir
A Long Way Gone by Ishmael Beah
The Glass Castle by Jeanette Walls

Other Nonfiction
Enrique's Journey by Sonia Nazario
Drowned City: Hurricane Katrina and New Orleans by Don Brown
Into Thin Air by Jon Krakauer
The Boys on the Boat by Daniel James Brown

Challenges *
No Country for Old Men — Cormac McCarthy
The Brief Wondrous Life of Oscar Wao — Junot Diaz
A Man Without a Country — Kurt Vonnegut
Unbroken — Laura Hillenbrand

This student included such genres as humor and memoir. His class also talked about when they might fit in their "challenge" books, such as right after midterms when life wasn't as stressful, after a varsity sports season, or during school breaks.

## STEP 2: GET THOSE BOOKS OFF THE WISH LIST AND INTO YOUR CLASSROOM

We all know teachers spend a greater percentage of their salary on their jobs than professionals in any other field. The average is $500 a year, so try not to add to that number by funding the library yourself. Most teachers I know can't resist buying a few (okay, armloads of) books at a library sale, then another few (heavy bags) at the book fair. High school teachers in Chattanooga, Tennessee, directed me to their favorite used bookstore, McKay's, as a gem of a place to

# 2016-2017 READING LIST

Every time you select a new book to read, enter the title, author, and the date started. When you have completed it, enter the date completed, number of pages read, and your 5-star rating. If you abandoned it, place an *A* in the date completed column. Your goal is to read a minimum of **100 pages per week** and at least 4 **books per marking period**.

| Title | Author | Date Started | Date Completed | # of Pages Read | 5-Star Rating |
|---|---|---|---|---|---|
| MP1 | | | | | |
| Upside down in the middle of nowhere | Julie T. Lamana | 9/19/16 | 9/28/16 | 313 | 5! |
| Goose Bumps Ghost Beach | RL Stine | 9/29/16 | 9/6/16 | 119 | 3 |
| Goosebumps Go eat worms! | RL Stine | 9/29/16 | 10/8/16 | 118 | 4 |
| Goosebumps A Night more on Terror Claus | RL Stine | 10/9/16 | 10/9/16 | 148 | 4 |
| The Swap | Megan Shull | 10/19/16 | 10/27/16 | 383 | 5! |
| Ghosts | Raina Telgemeir | 10/28/16 | 11/1/16 | 240 | 4 |
| MP2 | | | | | |
| One for the Murphys | Lynda Mullaly Hunt | 12/3/16 | 12-14/16 | 274 | 5! |
| Auggie's Me | RJ Palacio | 12-14-16 | 12-20- | 303 | 5! |
| Jessica Darling | Megan M. | 12-20-16 | 1-10-17 | 213 | 4! |
| Not Enough to eat | Kawra La Belia | 1-11-17 | 1-14-17 | 55 | 3! |
| Fishin A tree | Lynda Mullaly Hunt | 1-12-17 | 1-23-17 | 264 | 5! |
| MP3 The Thing about Jellyfish | Ali Benjamin | 1-24-17 | 2/5/17 | 333 | 5! |
| Half a chance | Cynthia Lord | 2-6-17 | | 278 | |

find excellent books at a low price. Like those teachers, I left with a trunk full of phenomenal books without breaking the bank. Maybe there's a similar place in your town, but use it sparingly, and start with places that will cost you only time, not money.

The most likely starting point is your school's administration. Often schools have budgets specifically for books. If that exists and it's not already depleted, you may be lucky enough to hand over a list of ISBNs and await beautiful boxes of books. Whether you have that jackpot or not, however, you'll want to go to other avenues, too. There's simply no such thing as having too many fantastic books in your classroom, and the more choices you offer, the better.

Some websites to register on right away include

- AdoptAClassroom.org

- DonorsChoose.org

- FundMyClassroom.com

- ClassWish.org

- Penny Kittle's BookLoveFoundation.org

The first two sites allow teachers to request resources for their classroom and receive funding from organizations or single donors who want to support educators. The last site awards starter classroom libraries to passionate teachers such as yourself.

The easiest, and most likely to show quick results, is AdoptAClassroom.org. It takes only a few minutes to register your classroom and quickly write about your need for books. I can't tell you how many teachers I work with registered and received generous funds to buy books. Big-name companies like JCPenney, Office Depot, and Quaker donate heavily, as do individuals. One teacher I work with asked for a long list of books that students requested. The next day, author Neil Gaiman funded her entire wish list. If you haven't added some of his books to your list, do so now—students love them! And if you already know him as an author, it makes you love him even more. Over 90 percent of all projects receive funding, so odds are in your favor.

Social media is your friend. Post on Facebook and Twitter that you're look-ing for books for your classroom. I like to specify that friends only pass on books that they or their kids love, along with making specific requests for genres, levels, and so on. That helps weed out junk books that could fill your shelves but never turn on a reader. Outdated, uninteresting, too-hard, boring books stand the chance of reminding your students why they don't like to read. After posting, await bags of books on your doorstep, as many friends and families love a reason to clean out their bookshelves and help a teacher.

Boxes of book still arrive on my doorstep from families who know I'll pass them on to student readers.

You might be even more direct in your requests. I work

with a teacher who loves hosting at family holidays. She texts all her guests the week before to remind them, "No book, no eat!" Bringing a good book to donate is evidently a small price to pay for her cooking.

Consider a school book drive. This demands a little more outreach, but it works wonders to generate donations as well as to establish the culture of the school as a community of readers. Some schools I work with give a different spin each month to the book donations—Halloween is "mystery/horror," Thanksgiving is "thankful for books," December is "gift a book," and so on. I've seen bins placed in the front office, in guidance, in the auditorium—anywhere parents and students might be reminded to pass on a book. Written reminders go out in weekly newsletters, eblasts, and any communication home. Teachers also give rewards or set up class competitions for most books donated. A few teachers I work with had the lovely problem of too many books to sort through after offering up a pizza party reward.

So, how many books should you go for? There are plenty of professional opinions about what makes an adequate classroom library. I'll spare you some of the numbers, as "adequate" will likely feel "impossible." Go for as many great books as you can get. It's better to have two hundred books of hot titles getting passed around than five hundred dusty books no one wants to touch. For instance, I was sure Laura Ingalls Wilder and the Nancy Drew series would be checked out quickly because I loved those books, but they sat there, untouched. Revamping my library so students found books they wanted to read meant listening to their tastes, not mine. When I asked students what they'd like, I heard of genres that surprised me: manga, anime, books on gaming, Misty Copeland bios, the *Clique* series, and more.

When I stopped expecting them to want to read Dickens or my old favorites and remembered that I wanted their eyes on the pages of books, things improved. My library needed to reflect my students' tastes and provide options for when they were ready to challenge themselves, too. Classroom libraries need the same combination of eye candy, complex books, and various genres that our own bookshelves have at home.

Keep in mind that your libraries should house fiction and nonfiction. Remember, however, that there is a tiny footnote in the Common Core State Standards showing high schoolers should be reading 70 percent nonfiction by twelfth grade. The footnote states that the percentage is reflected over the course of students' *entire school day*. As students will read only nonfiction in science, history, and other classes, it is okay that your English class is still a hotbed for fiction! Narrative nonfiction is also a great way to ease students into informational texts if they aren't already fans. While I lean toward contemporary fiction, I'm constantly reminded of how many students, often boys, gravitate to fact-heavy nonfiction. "If it didn't happen, what's the point?" is a question I've heard more than one student ask when choosing a sports biography or memoir over a novel. So, while my experience still shows fiction pulling in the greatest percentage of readers, don't make too many assumptions. All it takes is one charismatic student to talk up a book within a genre to shift the tastes of large swaths of readers.

In general, avoid putting books in your library that are above students' reading abilities. There is an outdated rule still used in some elementary schools called the five-finger rule: if you don't know five words on the first page, it's too hard; if you don't know two to three, it's just right; and if you don't know zero to one, it's too easy. I've never picked up a book and not known three words on the first page and thought, "Perfect." In fact, I put that book right back on the shelf. I'm a lifelong reader, and I still choose books in which I know every word. It feels good! Strive to provide the same feel-good choices for your readers.

## STEP 3: YOU'VE GOT BOOKS. NOW, WHERE TO PUT THEM?

Something many teachers find a challenge is where to put the books. Classrooms are often cramped, and shelving may be taken up with other resources. We might share the room with other teachers. Finding both space and shelving is a legitimate challenge, and one that isn't necessarily as fun to take on as finding books.

Again, start with administration and even scouting out other classrooms. Sometimes there are unused shelves in the art room, behind a stage, or collecting dust in a storage closet. Or, your principal might have funding to order new shelves.

Teachers often use the same avenues, such as AdoptAClassroom.org and social media, to drum up bins and shelves. I've seen everything from IKEA bookcases donated from family members to boards on cinder blocks. One teacher I know received beautiful bookcases by

going on Craigslist and asking sellers to consider donating them to a good cause if they didn't receive an offer. One seller not only donated the shelves but also brought them to the school and bolted them to the walls.

Whatever system you can find, go for putting books at eye level, and remember you're working with big people. Elementary classroom libraries are sweet with their bins on the floor, but you'll want to go for more of a bookstore setup—tall shelves and tables with books you can see without squatting down. Think, too, of book displays that catch your interest; many teachers I know organize books covers out, and books are sorted by genre or even catchier groupings such as

- Award-Winning Books

- Books That Make You Laugh

- Books That Get Your Heart Racing

- Brutally Honest Memoirs

- Books About Wanderlust

- Graphic Novels: Pictures Aren't Just for Kids

- Books About Life as a Refugee

- Offbeat Memoirs

- Books to Get You Inspired

- Books About Real Places, Real People, or Real Events

Creating a display is a surefire way to attract readers. Consider some of the following displays:

- Monthly Picks (curated by you to start and by students thereafter)

- Books [insert name here] Loves (created by individual or small groups of students who "own" their choices and are publicists for their books)

- Books That Will Change You

- Staff Picks (Ask teachers in various departments to bring in a recent favorite, along with a description on an index card of why they liked it. Expect conversations about reading in gym, science, math, and more to happen. Don't forget to invite guidance counselors, custodial and secretarial staff, and administrators to contribute.)

- Hot New Titles (As you gather new titles from book sales, donations, or orders, draw attention to these fresh picks.)

- Sleeper Titles (You may notice certain books being passed over that deserve a second look. Putting them on display with covers out may get them into students' hands.)

- Books on Film (If students liked the movie, they'll love the book!)

- Banned Books (These always seem to draw a crowd.)

- Books About Skateboarding, Fashion, Soccer, Food, Romance, Scary Stuff, or Other Topics (Find out what your students are interested in and curate a collection—or, better yet, ask them to do so.)

Speaking of organization, you'll want to devise a system so readers know where to find certain books. At a minimum, separate fiction from nonfiction.

Then, a tedious but necessary task is labeling all of your books. To ensure they will get returned to you,

- As you put them on shelves, write your name on the outer pages or inside cover. Including the genre so readers know where to reshelve books is very helpful. You don't want to be the one reorganizing your library every week.

- Have every reader tape a sticky note on the front of his or her choice book with the classroom number on it. That way, if the student leaves it on the bus, on the soccer field, or in the cafeteria, anyone can bring it back to where it belongs.

No matter what, you can expect to lose some books every year, but labels are one of the best ways to guard against big losses.

## STEP 4: CREATE A CHECKOUT SYSTEM

In order for you and your students to keep track of what books go home and come back, you'll need a checkout system. You can go high-tech and use an iPad app that scans in the bar codes and shows each reader's book record. Here are a few user-friendly apps:

- **Book Retriever** allows you to print out bar code labels to facilitate checkout and features a "hotlist" of ten books that changes monthly.

- **Booksource Classroom Organizer** lets you easily import titles, import your student roster, and receive a report on library activity.

You can use an app to help students electronically check out books.

- **IntelliScanner** catalogs books, creates printed resource lists for your students such as all the books in a genre with a thumbnail of the covers, and offers a great checkout system, too.

Or, go low-tech and put a sign-out system on a clipboard or on index cards. One teacher uses a duplicate "message" notebook in which students sign out their books. This way, the student gets a copy, and there's always another copy in the classroom. Just make it something that you can show students once and then they can independently manage. Simple is best!

## OPTIONAL STEP: CAPITALIZE ON OLDER STUDENTS' ABILITY TO GET BOOKS ON THEIR OWN

A big bonus of teaching older students who already manage a great deal of their lives independently is that you can tell them, "If you don't see what you want in our classroom, here's where else you can look":

- Amazon
- Wattpad
- The school library
- The town library
- Your friends' bookshelves, or maybe even your own

To make this more likely to happen, get students jump-started with a field trip to the local library. I know teachers who've organized such outings, and the librarians preselected stacks of books for each student, who received a friendly tour and left with a library card. Who knew there were personal reading shoppers?

If your library offers electronic checkout, students with e-readers can now virtually check out books without even leaving the classroom. To help make these

| Name | Title of Book | Date Out | Date In | Kosch ONLY |
|---|---|---|---|---|
| Alexis Kim | The Wild Robot | 9/9/16 | ✓ | Ⓚ |
| Madison Wright | Divergent | 9/9/16 | 10/13 | Ⓚ |
| Emma Hart | Amulet | 9/9/16 | 9/14 | Ⓚ |
| Daniel Novak | Year in Sports | 9/10/16 | | |
| Jacob Johansen | Middle School Worst Year | 9/13/16 | 9/26 | Ⓚ |
| Emily Mirza | Bones | 9/13/16 | 9/19 | Ⓚ |
| Ryan Clarke | Prisoner B-3087 | 9/13 | 9/14 | Ⓚ |
| Ethan Hu | Hilo The boy Who Crashed to earth | 9/13 | ✓ | Ⓚ |
| Michael Chakma | amulet | 9/13 | 9/19 | Ⓚ |
| Sam Das | Pr Die 9/11 | 9/13 | ✓ | Ⓚ |
| Jose Diaz | Amulet #3 | 9/14 | 9/21 | Ⓚ |
| Logan Green | The Fourth Horseman | 9/14 | 9/16 | Ⓚ |
| Olivia Wilson | Booked | 9/14 | 9/26 | Ⓚ |
| Hannah Ruiz | Counting by Sevens | 9/15 | | Ⓚ |
| Abigail Wood | Dream jumper | 9/14 | 9/16 | Ⓚ |
| Will Lin | The Wild Robot | 9/9/16 | 9/16/16 | Ⓚ |
| Anthony Acosta | The Serpents Shadow | 9/16 | 9/16 | Ⓚ |

Ms. Kosch has her students simply sign out her books on a sheet of paper, then she initials it when she sees the book go back.

kinds of resources available, another teacher provided extra credit for any student who showed her a library card in the student's name.

Another district I work in has students' school ID cards automatically linked to the local library. Students frequently access electronic books through the local library's database with just a few clicks. Teachers in this district rarely suffer from hearing kids say, "I don't have anything to read," and the students now have the tools for reading in the digital era. As a side note, none of the teens I work with consider reading on a phone a hindrance or a visually cramped experience. They see it as *the* way to read for pleasure. I've also spied them quickly cross-referencing a detail, looking up words, or simply checking out a photo of the author as they read. So while a phone in hand can feel like the opposite of what we're going for, we may need to check our biases against digital reading.

Some teachers also remind parents at holidays and breaks to consider gifting their teens books, along with distributing lists of popular titles. Not just affluent communities respond to this, but economically struggling districts do as well. These teachers operate on the assumption that every parent wants his or her child to succeed and cares deeply about his or her education. Providing a good book is a relatively easy way to put that emotional investment to use.

## STEP 5: BOOKS ARE THERE. THEY'RE ORGANIZED. HOW DO YOU GET STUDENTS TO READ THEM?

Some of your students will surprise you. When given the option of reading a book of their choice, they'll act like they're getting away with something to sit with a book for thirty minutes. Others, however, will struggle. It may have been years since they read anything that wasn't assigned, and many didn't even read those assigned texts. Some of them have never completed a book at all. Finding a book they want to read uses a muscle so atrophied that it needs serious boot camp training.

Spend time helping your students find books they'll want to read to build that habit up. One great place to start is a reading interest survey. Jennifer Serravallo's *The Literacy Teacher's Playbook, Grades 3–6* (2013) and Donalyn Miller's *Reading in the Wild* (2014) offer great examples. Or, just ask your students to write you a letter about their reading likes and dislikes. Use those as a starting place to gauge entry points for readers, to make suggestions, and to help your students reflect on their reading histories and how prior positive experiences can guide them to good fits.

Many classrooms also benefit from a modified survey that asks for information about the students' interests, period. This survey doesn't assume students have a lot to say about their reading tastes, because many students may identify strongly as nonreaders. Starting off the year by forcing these teens to admit that they don't read or don't like reading, or to lie about their reading habits, isn't the tone to set.

Instead, ask them what they are interested in: TV shows? Video games? Movies? Sports? What classes most interest them? What book do they remember enjoying, even if it was in elementary school?

Use the information about your students' likes to help them find books attached to those interests. One student I worked with was an adamant nonreader and could not provide me with a single reading experience he ever enjoyed. He was quick, however, to tell me about the clothing brands he loves, where he shops, how he customizes outfits, and his fashion icons. We started out with copies of *GQ Magazine* from the media center and then crafted a reading list that included *Twisted: My Dreadlock Chronicles* and a book by fashion designer Tom Ford. For a professed nonreader, this student began to immerse himself in a lot of books. They were simply books on topics he cared about.

> Now that I choose my own books, I find that reading is something I truly enjoy to do.
>
> —Susan George, high school student
>
> I read a lot more now because I'm allowed to read what I like. I'm more interested.
>
> —Olivia Sloan, high school student
>
> I read way more than before. It's because I have the power to choose exactly what I want to read. Choosing my own books has helped me understand what my interests are and what really entices me.
>
> —Michelle Enkhbayar, high school student

After asking students to reflect on what turns them on to and off from reading, I know the best way to get them to find the right book is to conduct a book talk. Penny Kittle's *Book Love* (2013) and Donalyn Miller's *Reading in the Wild* (2014) both offer examples and guidelines. Also referred to as a book buzz or commercial, this is an opportunity to quickly "sell" a book to students by holding it up, saying what you love about it, and reading a snippet so students get a sense of the language and writing style. Wendy, a teacher I work with in South Carolina, recently did a sound bite version of a book buzz for *Touching Spirit Bear* (Mikaelsen, 2001): "Boy beats up boy. Gets sent to an island. Has to eat throw-up to survive." Then she left the book on the chalk tray. Five boys raced up to grab it.

You'll want to start by modeling these yourself. Dive in with book buzzes at the beginning of every class, holding up a book from your library and giving it a quick sell. Say briefly what it's about, read a short passage, and share what kind of reader might enjoy it. Then watch it fly into the hands of readers. Also check out great examples on ReadingRants.org. This middle school librarian's site is a goldmine of book recommendations, many sorted by headings such as "Fanging Around," "Inquiring Minds Want to Know," and "Nail Biters." As you keep doing book buzzes, invite student readers to do the same. As much as your students love and respect your opinions about books, there is no greater sales pitch than one by a peer.

Here is an example of one classroom's scheduled book buzzes, done the minute students walk in to set the tone: "We are a room of readers."

Book Buzz Dates

| | 10/17 | 10/18 | 10/19 | 10/20 | 10/23 |
|---|---|---|---|---|---|
| 6R | | 1. Massiel 2. Frogelina 3. Diego | 1. Melina 2. Ellyn 3. MJ | 1. Justin 2. Hailee 3. Kayla | 1. Caitlyn 2. Gio 3. AJ |
| 6W | 1. Jack 2. Jonathan | 1. Gabby 2. Elena | 1. Carsten 2. Ava | 1. Will 2. Madison | 1. Alandra 2. Harli |
| 6S | 1. Maia 2. Aurelia 3. Katie | 1. Rachel 2. Anthony | 1. Jackie 2. Rafael 3. Hannah | 1. Mark 2. Sam 3. Kailey | 10/24 1. Jordan 2. Uyanna |

Getting readers to review their books not only helps show you whether they read; it also shares the wealth by helping other potential readers make the right choice. Writing a review is an opportunity for teen readers to do authentic writing about reading. Why not start here and then assign entries on the websites for Goodreads, *Nerdy Book Club*, *Cuddlebuggery Book Blog*, and more?

Name: Salma Marma          Date: _____

Period:   1   2   ④   5   8

### Independent Reading Book Review

Title of Book: Courage for Beginners

Author of Book: Karen Harrington

Genre: Realistic Fiction

Star Rating (Please circle how many Stars you give this book): ★ ★ ★ ★ ★

Review: *(Possible responses: Why did you give this book the rating that you did? What specifically did you like about this book? What specifically did you not like? Did this book change your perspective or world view?)* Please attach additional paper if needed.

The book "Courage for Beginners" by Karen Harrington I would rate it 4 stars, I rated it 4 stars because at the end it seemed unfinished. I thought this was unfinished because they didn't go more in depth with the dad's sickness. If they went with more detail the story would have felt complete because Mysti the main character would have become a better person. But what I did like about the book was how Mysti handled her problems, she took matters into her own hands. In the beginning she wasn't doing what she wanted instead she followed everything Anibal would say.

If you've got a SMART Board or another way to project videos, show your students book trailers online. These are sexy commercials just as enticing as trailers for the hottest new blockbuster movie, but for new-release book titles. You can also show them student book talks, "shelfies," and student videos about books to make reading feel less like an outdated chore and more like an alluring pursuit.

Technology is also a great way to showcase teachers' reading picks and promote a culture of reading school-wide. The following Twitter display from by a high school English department is one example. Other schools have begun book clubs for staff members, including everyone from administrators to secretaries and custodial staff, with the prerequisite that adults must choose books that they think will appeal to their students.

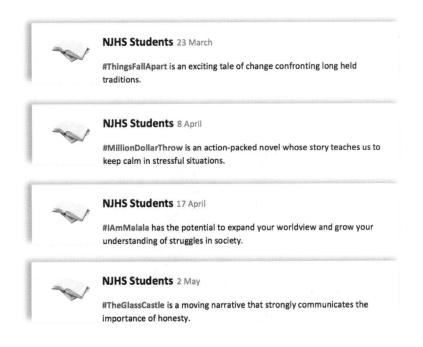

**NJHS Students** 23 March

#ThingsFallApart is an exciting tale of change confronting long held traditions.

**NJHS Students** 8 April

#MillionDollarThrow is an action-packed novel whose story teaches us to keep calm in stressful situations.

**NJHS Students** 17 April

#IAmMalala has the potential to expand your worldview and grow your understanding of struggles in society.

**NJHS Students** 2 May

#TheGlassCastle is a moving narrative that strongly communicates the importance of honesty.

Some high schools use Twitter book buzzes as a way to quickly disseminate students' favorite choice reads, and capitalize on technology. As a bonus, it becomes a way both to showcase your school as a hotbed of reading and to share the wealth of your students' top picks.

Dexter talking about his book so others might check it out.

Naomi recorded her book talk on her phone. This helps students with anxiety about presenting to the class because they can redo it as many times as they want.

Naomi book talk video

By having students record their book talks, Violet's teacher can pull up video files whenever she wants to share a book title with the class, as opposed to asking for a volunteer to do so on the spot.

Violet book talk video

This group of middle school students "buzzed" about favorite books and created a book spine with the title to post around the room. The line of book spines is starting to stretch around the perimeter of the room, thereby providing a "What to Read Next" source of ideas at just a glance.

Another teacher had students follow up their book buzz by drawing a spine with a QR code attached, linking interested peers to their recorded discussion of the book. The assignment for the book reviews and QR codes is included in **Resource 1**.

The QR codes on book spines are grouped by genre to further assist readers in finding the book that's best for them.

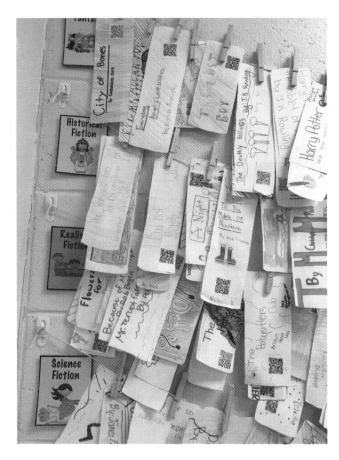

Even mock technology has a place in this middle school classroom with faux Instagram shots of students reading.

Such infusions of catchy tech-minded visuals probably work best in middle school. By high school, just do the real thing!

Rating a book with an emoji is another easy way to tap into students' social media fluency.

In fact, this school also created a useful list of ways to integrate technology and independent reading into a middle or high school classroom. That list of ideas can be found in **Resource 2**. Teachers there are committing to boosting the culture of reading throughout the entire school, and it's working!

When your school welcomes everyone into identifying as a reader, you can start using a new greeting with students you see outside of class: "What are you reading?" Imagine the power of every school member asking one another what they're reading as the new "How are you?" I shared this idea with some teachers in South Carolina, and it caught on surprisingly fast. Hopefully this becomes a larger trend and a question for which all of our students have a ready answer.

Remember, teens are fluent in devices, and books can still feel flat and dead compared to Instagram, Snapchat, and Vine. Whether they confess to it or not in their surveys, many of your students haven't read with pleasure since elementary school. Start small, keep talking it up, and don't despair. When you see even the smallest moves toward reading habits—someone at the cafeteria with a book chosen from a book talk, or a student completely immersed in reading—celebrate it loudly!

## STEP TO TAKE THROUGHOUT: MAKE THE CASE FOR WHAT YOUR STUDENTS ARE DOING: READING

The best approach to implementing this method is total transparency, and practicing this from the start of the year. When parents, administrators, and students know these new routines of your classroom and why they benefit readers, they are likely to be your biggest cheerleaders.

| TOP PICKS | |
|---|---|
| **Realistic Fiction** | **Science Fiction/Dystopian Literature** |
| *To Kill a Mockingbird* by Harper Lee | *Maze Runner* series by James Dashner |
| *Mosquitoland* by David Arnold | *Hybrid Chronicles* series by Kat Zhang |
| *Looking for Alaska* by John Green | *Divergent* series by Veronica Roth |
| *Paper Towns* by John Green | *Ender's Game* by Orson Scott Card |
| *The Fault in Our Stars* by John Green | *Elsewhere* by Gabrielle Zevin |
| *All the Bright Places* by Jennifer Niven | *Life as We Knew It* by Susan Beth Pfeffer |
| *Tears of a Tiger* by Sharon M. Draper | *Ready Player One* by Ernest Cline |
| *The Absolutely True Diary of a Part-Time Indian* by Sherman Alexie | *Maximum Ride* series by James Patterson |
| *Of Mice and Men* by John Steinbeck | *Among the Hidden* by Margaret Peterson Haddix |
| *13 Reasons Why* by Jay Asher | *Hunger Games* series by Suzanne Collins |
| *A Little Something Different* by Sandy Hall | *1984* by George Orwell |
| *Lord of the Flies* by William Golding | *Uglies* by Scott Westfield |
| *Freak the Mighty* by Rodman Philbrick | *Matched* by Ally Condie |
| *The Secret Life of Bees* by Sue Monk Kidd | *The Program* by Suzanne Young |
| *A Tree Grows in Brooklyn* by Betty Smith | *Michael Vey* series by Richard Paul Evans |
| *Son of the Mob* by Gordon Korman | *Delirium* by Lauren Oliver |
| *Bang!* by Sharon Flake | |
| *The Perks of Being a Wallflower* by Stephen Chbosky | |
| *Monster* by Walter Dean Myers | |
| **Historical Fiction** | **Fantasy** |
| *To Kill a Mockingbird* by Harper Lee | *Before I Fall* by Lauren Oliver |
| *A Tree Grows in Brooklyn* by Betty Smith | *The Summoning* series by Kelley Armstrong |
| *The Secret Life of Bees* by Sue Monk Kidd | *A Song of Ice and Fire* by George R. R. Martin |
| | *Harry Potter* series by J. K. Rowling |
| | *Cinder* by Marissa Meyer |
| | *Alex Rider* series by Anthony Horowitz |

High school students' favorite books within multiple genres listed on their class website.

Share quick stats around volume data and how important it is that students read not just high-level texts but simply a lot of text. There are plenty of stats in Chapter 1 (and online) showing that having eyes on print is one of the single best ways to set up students for success in high school, for the huge reading volume in college, for the literacy demands of the working world, and on tests right now.

Sadly, the literacy demands in the work world are skyrocketing at the same time that skills are plummeting. "Between 1996 and 2006, the average level of literacy required for all occupations rose by 14 percent. Both dropouts and high school graduates demonstrate significantly worse reading skills than they did ten years ago" (Alliance for Excellent Education, 2006, cited in Gallagher, 2009, p. 115). Remind your school community that we're all on the same page: we want to graduate lifelong readers who are ready to handle the literacy challenges of high school, college, and beyond.

Consider articulating what your students are doing with reading and how it benefits them on your website, in letters home, in postings around your room, and at back-to-school night. Testimonials from any newly inspired readers will work wonders in showing the power of this new approach. Remind everyone involved, both directly and indirectly, that you are still giving students the cultural capital of exposure to the classics, but that you aren't limiting them to only those chosen texts. Students not only read at much higher volumes, but they grapple with productive struggle in challenging texts on a regular basis. Your students benefit from rich knowledge about classic texts as well as the immense boost of regular authentic reading.

## Possible Follow-Up Steps

If you have put together a classroom library and students are in the habit of choosing books and sitting down with them on a regular basis, take a moment to pat yourself on the back. You've given a gift to every potential reader who walks through your doorway: to enjoy class, school, and a life with books. Then, consider these steps to bring your class to the next level as literacy experts.

### MODEL AND SET READING GOALS WITH STUDENTS

Getting regular reading up and going is the foundation, but now it's time to build all the necessary reading skills to make your students empowered and highly literate readers. A great way for middle and high school students to self-assess and for you to guide them is to establish specific goals. Five areas to look at include

- **How much they read and for how long** (Volume and stamina are always worth monitoring and building.)
- **Reading habits** (Will they jot down their thinking about characters as they go? Share favorites in a book talk? Reread when it gets confusing?)

- **Genre** (How will they stretch themselves to become familiar with new and unfamiliar styles of writing? If they always choose sports bios, will they try historical fiction? Books in a series? Dystopian literature?)
- **Reading strategies**
- **Titles that are next on their list** (including books that present a bit of a challenge in terms of unfamiliar content or style, or increased complexity)

You'll show your class your own goals in these areas. Make them real—teens are so good at sniffing out fakers! Then, revisit those goals periodically, revising the ones you've met so you can add new ones and adjusting goals you didn't meet so they are more realistic or apt. See the student example in **Resource 3**. Your students will do the same, and in doing so, they will take ownership of their reading lives in a new way that was never accessible to them when they were assigned pages of a book they rarely read.

## SUPPORT STUDENTS IN THE HABIT OF BRINGING BOOKS HOME AND BACK TO CLASS

Whether students actually read is one of the big worries of teachers, and for good reason. You go to this tremendous effort to get them books and give them time to read, but what if they still don't do it? Remember, most of them weren't reading beforehand. Any improvement—and trust me, there will be a great deal—will feel significant.

Part of building the habits of good readers is having a book on you at all times. Therefore, you must let readers bring books home. I understand the reluctance— you've spent so much time and energy to get them in your classroom, and we all know how forgetful teens can be. It's important, however, that students create reading lives inside and outside of the classroom.

If we want books to be respected and remembered, we can make it happen. I worked at a charter school in the South Bronx serving some of the poorest children in the country, and many students went home to different shelters on a nightly basis. The teachers worked hard to establish the expectation that whatever book went out of the building must come back the next day. It became as much of a habit as remembering to wear clothing—nonnegotiable. Establishing the routine of books coming back each day might not be instantaneous, but you can get there, too.

One teacher makes bringing books back to class every day her only homework for the first two weeks of school. Students love the easy A. And, don't underestimate the power of a gallon-sized Ziploc bag. Many teachers have adapted this lower-grade "book baggie" for students to store the book, along with sticky notes, a pen, and a notebook for writing about their reading. Teachers might add a piece of gum to the bags of those who bring their books back the next day. You can do the same; just don't call it a baggie unless you want to see eyes roll. Call it an organizer, book tote, hold-all, or even book bag.

One ninth-grade teacher asked me, "What magic goes into those Ziploc bags?" Her students went from constantly forgetting books to actually bringing them home and back again regularly. I've seen them decorated with faux Gucci stickers, *washi* tape, and Redbubble icons. The bags are a cheap, painless tool to help your students craft adult reading lives. They're a simple crutch until readers are shoving a paperback in their glove compartments and coat pockets like we do, fearful we might find ourselves with nothing to do and no book.

## CREATE A SYSTEM TO TRACK VOLUME OF READING

It's important that students track how much they're reading, and that they do it honestly. For good reason, many teachers fear faked reading logs or overly optimistic recollections of how much students are actually reading. Here is one of the best ways for students to log their reading that I've seen. It's tried and true across many classrooms!

A teacher at Paramus Middle School in New Jersey devised a great system. It is easy to do, requires no signatures, and lets you, anyone around the student, and the student him- or herself quickly spot-check his or her reading volume and stamina. See the blank template for your use in **Resource 4**.

When students begin a new book, they divide the total amount of pages their book has into ten days. They take the suggested amount of pages they should read per day and find a good place to stop, give or take. If they are reading more than forty pages a night, they decide whether they should give themselves three weeks to read the book.

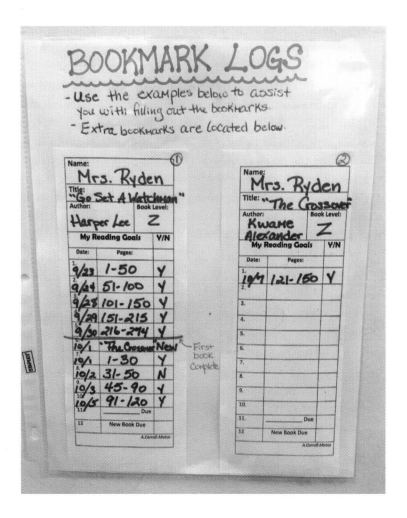

The benefit is that they have ten reading days within a fourteen-day span, so if they know they have a game plus lots of homework on Thursday, they might move that reading night to the weekend. Another benefit is that it gives readers a way to keep the volume of reading up. Also, you can quickly eyeball what page the reader has his or her book open to during reading time and cross-check it with the bookmark. If students are way off, you know it's probably time to talk about what's getting in the way of their reading. Parents, if they're into patrolling homework, can also spot-check.

Readers hand in their completed bookmarks when they finish their books. It's an easy way to catalog their reading, their pace, and more. This kind of data is invaluable to help them build up the stamina they'll need to be robust readers in college and beyond.

Another teacher simply outlines how long students will be spending on the class novel, typically no more than four weeks, with approximate demarcations such as "By Thanksgiving break, we'll be halfway through *Great Expectations*." Students are expected to read their choice books accordingly so that if they are looking at how setting is introduced at the beginning of Dickens, students are able to do the same thinking at the beginning of their books. This teacher adds reminders within homework assignments, such as "You should be close to finishing your book by now so we can all work on evaluating the predominant themes across our novels as well as in *Great Expectations*." This helps differentiate across reading levels, as robust readers can handle getting through half of *1984* (yes, a few may *choose* that book) while less proficient readers feel successful by reading half of something more like *Eleanor & Park*.

Choice Book, Reading Response #17: Analyzing the Tempo

Today in class we considered how authors such as Dickens speed up and slow down the action in a plot, often tightening the pace toward the end of the story. What do you notice about the tempo of events and how the author structured timing and tempo **toward the end of your novel**? What effect does the quickening or slowing of events have on us as a reader? Why did the author make those choices?

Choice Book, Reading Response #18: Taking a Second Look at Titles

Today in class we took a second look at the title of *Great Expectations* and why it may have been chosen, now that we have read almost all of the book. **You also should be almost finished with your book**. How has your understanding of the author's choice of title changed or deepened? What new information has shed light on the author's title and what it means in relation to the work?

*These assignments reflect how students are expected to keep pace in their own books with the correlating sections (beginning, middle, and end) of the class novel excerpts. That way, students can do similar work from that day's lesson using their choice books. Students are allowed to read further, even finishing books when they are still halfway through the class novel, but they aren't allowed to fall behind. If readers go ahead, and many do, they can always go back to the appropriate parts of their choice book as a reread, or try it using their current book.*

You can also find many templates online for reading logs. The more information students need to record, such as genre, rating, pages, and minutes, the more tedious it may feel, but the more data students have to measure progress and set goals. You'll know best what is realistic to ask of them. Just don't require parent signatures—that seems to teach faking signatures more than any other skill. In fact, the more you praise honestly on these accountability measures, the better. If someone admits to not reading and documents that, celebrate it! No one grows through fake reading.

There are also apps to help students monitor and organize their reading lives. You-Log Reading, Reading Log, and Readmore are all examples of apps to track reading. Most teachers I know haven't needed these, as the bookmarks worked for them, but tech options might be more appealing to you and your students.

Regardless, keep emphasizing a higher volume of reading.

## BE KIND TO YOURSELF

You'll notice there are a lot of to-dos here. You're checking out library sales, filling up car trunks with boxes of books, soliciting donations, organizing, and

This middle school teacher starts by assigning one hundred pages a week and adds to the total across the year. Imagine how well these students will be prepared for two hundred pages a week or more in high school, and double that in college.

labeling. You're thinking, "I also have my other job to do that involves grading, planning, running student council, cooking dinner . . . This library thing feels like another full-time job!"

Don't set out to run a marathon, but begin with a light jog around the block. It helps to set goals that are manageable, like devoting one prep period a week to organizing your class library or adding fifty books each marking period. You can also ask students to help label and organize. And still, it *will* be a lot of work.

When you look at those boxes and bags of books stacking up in your garage or in the corner of your classroom, remember this 2014 tweet from James Patterson: "There's no such thing as a kid who hates reading. There are kids who love reading, and kids who are reading the wrong books." Indeed, the most important thing you can do to help turn all students into readers is to put books they'll want to read within arm's reach. That just doesn't mean it's a cinch to do so.

What will feel easy, though, is looking around your room like Mr. Miller did and seeing a group of teens with noses in books. That will come, and witnessing that joy of reading will feed you.

## CHAPTER THREE

# BUILDING A BLENDED CURRICULUM FOR FICTION-BASED UNITS

In this chapter, we look at *The Scarlet Letter* and see how to create a unit that uses this novel to help students transfer skills to their own novels. Just as your daily lessons will model smart reading of the class novel so students can apply it to their novels, we'll think through one book together so you'll feel confident duplicating this process with the books in your curriculum.

You might wonder where to start with this kind of planning. I recently worked with a group of high school teachers who decided to start with their least accessible class novel unit, based on *Great Expectations*. Revamping the entire curriculum at a go is a lot to ask of yourself. Think about what class novel results in the most fake reading, and begin there.

## Why Start With Fiction?

Quick! Think of a favorite book from your teen years. My hunch is it's a fiction title. Fiction is a great place to try out this planning work for several reasons. Most reluctant readers are more easily hooked with stories than with dense fact-packed nonfiction. Narrative plots have a power to grip us; fictional characters stir up our empathy, affection, and disdain; and the evolution of those plots and characters provide powerful ways to teach us about ourselves and the world. Fiction doesn't just help us read; it helps us be better human beings. Why not take advantage of that potential?

Also, despite the valid push for nonfiction in the standards, it's still our job as English teachers, and our job alone, to teach literature. As stated in Chapter 2, a footnote in the introduction to the Common Core State Standards explains that although students' reading should weigh heavily in favor of informational texts, that includes all the texts students see across the scope of their day. Since students get only nonfiction in history, science, health, and every other class besides English, we are still doing our job by emphasizing literature.

Another reason to start with story is that we tend to feel confident teaching fiction. If you're an outlier and your heart is with nonfiction, skip to the next chapter. It will include a similar breakdown of planning steps and walking through the process using a nonfiction book. By starting with our strengths, we'll make our enthusiasm contagious to our readers.

## What's Important to Know About This Planning Process Before Diving In?

Whether you're a novice or you've taught for years, adopting a new approach will demand a learning curve. Most of us were never taught this way, so we can't rely on what we know best: our own lives as students. We will rely on our expertise with class novels, but a shift in how we use that expertise is needed. Just like we swear we'll never be like our parents and then find ourselves saying the exact same things they did, we tend to regress to what we know best. After a stellar training in education, I found myself re-creating my student life in Mrs. Dayton's ninth-grade English class, teaching *A Tale of Two Cities* for an entire marking period. The routines we know best from our own student histories not only won't help us; they won't even fit.

This careful planning work will help us avoid that comfy old sweatshirt of the class novel anytime we feel frustrated or challenged by resistant students.

## YOU'RE PLANNING A UNIT THAT TEACHES HOW TO READ WELL

We'll plan using what we do as readers of fiction, and that can be hard to articulate at first. Often we can't look back on how we were taught reading skills—most of us just *are* good readers. We got good at it by doing a lot of reading, not necessarily by having someone show us what to do.

Conversely, when we plan lessons to show students how to *write* well, we dive in. We recall everything we were taught about organizing ideas or composing a strong thesis. But when we think about how we learned to come up with a book's theme, our minds draw a blank.

There's no tangible example like a rough draft to show what we do as readers. It's tucked away in a series of subconscious moves. So, we'll need to look at how to make those moves visible and therefore make them tangible for students, too. We'll listen in on ourselves as readers, and it will remind us, as well as our students, that good reading results not from some secret genius ability, but rather from specific strategies that we can all employ.

In just a minute, we'll get started on demystifying what it means to be a good fiction reader. First, however, it's helpful to problem-solve for potential issues.

## YOUR OWN IDENTITY AS A READER PLAYS A PART

Many of us harbor insecurities about our own résumé of reading expertise. We don't have a wealth of markers or milestone achievements for "good reading." Maybe we remember being put in the high-level reading group in elementary school or making the cut to AP English. Those moments, however, exposed not what we did as "readers," just that we passed a certain test.

Usually, we feel like good readers because we read a lot, enjoy it, or feel confident tackling tough texts. However, teaching students to be readers can feel like a bigger roadblock when we don't feel like reading superstars.

From my experience working with English teachers in middle and high schools, having a lack of confidence as a reader, or in knowing how to show what good readers do, is normal. With busy lives, many of us no longer feel like robust readers.

Teaching, as you well know, is not a lightweight profession. It's physically and emotionally demanding; it requires us to work well beyond the last-period bell, and our energy is sapped by spending hours with exhilarating, diverse, funny, challenging teens. For many of us, going home to a good book simply isn't in the cards. Maybe we were passionate "literature people" at one point, but our lives became swamped with family or chores or just keeping up with the never-ending pile of papers to grade.

The same temptations that pull our students away from reading can keep us from good reading habits; think Netflix, Facebook, and a desire for more sleep. Books can become something to cram into summer vacations, not an intellectual daily activity. If any of those are true for you, then sharing your reading self with students can feel less like a lesson in what to do and more like an exercise in what not to do.

## YOUR READING IDENTITY IS STILL VALUABLE

Whether you're a devoted reader who feels twitchy when you don't have a great book in hand, or whether you'd like to expand your reading skills, it's okay. What we need to be able to do is tune into ourselves as readers and share what we notice, question, and do as we read. Who we are as English teachers and readers will be as diverse as the students in our classes. Some of us will be passionate voracious readers; others will be analytical readers who tune in easily to this metacognitive process; and others might be described as "when we can" readers. Any of those personalities can be represented as we show what readers do. And, if we can model our own paths from "when it fits in my schedule" readers to regular, thoughtful readers, it will serve as an excellent example for our students.

## Getting Started

If this is your first time trying out this planning work, take forty-five minutes to an hour to do the following activity. This exercise helps us to transition into teaching the reader instead of the book, even though we don't need to do it every time we plan a unit. And while you can do this activity on your own, the results will be better (if slightly more time-consuming) if you do it with a colleague. In fact, you'll notice I refer to pairs or groups of teachers throughout, as I do this work collectively to draw on everyone's expertise.

## STEP 1: SPY ON YOURSELF AS A READER

We're going to spy on ourselves as we read the first chapter in *The Scarlet Letter*. In doing this, we'll generate a list:

1. What we pay attention to

2. What we question

3. What we think about as we read

It's important that we try this as readers at least once, rather than just generate a list straight away of what we want our students to be able to do. Otherwise, it's easy to slip back into our old habits of teaching the novel or adopting the language of what we feel pressured to teach. Without looking at what we do as readers, we tend to list terms like *synthesize* and *make inferences*. While we hope to get to those very skills, the terms can lead us right back to the issue that what good readers do, such as synthesize, often feels elusive.

Try this process at least once, but remember you can rely heavily on your existing units, too. If you've taught the class novel for years, much of your new focus lessons might lie right in those old lesson plans! You likely outlined all of what you notice and think about as a good reader already—don't let that expertise go to waste.

If I tell students to synthesize, they'll nod and go do *something*, because they like me or they don't want to get a bad grade. Or, they might check out and get out their phone because *synthesize* makes no sense to them. But if I show what synthesizing actually *looks* like—if I put it into the language of what I'm paying attention to, what I'm rereading, what I'm putting together—that becomes something students can try. So, that's what we're going to do: remind ourselves what we do and notice as we read.

Let's get started with the first chapter!

Although here I'll walk you through the process with *The Scarlet Letter*, you'll start your planning by reading the first chapter of your chosen novel. You can use a short story, too, even though you're preparing to teach a novel. Remember, it isn't the text that is critical; it's what we do with any work of fiction. What we notice and think about in our chosen classic needs to transfer to our students' novels, and we can do that same work noticing and thinking in a short story. The advantage of trying it with a short story is that you will feel comfortable listing out what you think about across an entire text, from beginning to end. It's the process I care about for this exercise, not the text, so choose what works best for you.

It can also be helpful *not* to use your class novel to remind yourself you're teaching what good readers do in any work of fiction. With that in mind, here is a list of short stories I've used with teachers before planning a fiction unit:

Bambara, Toni Cade: "Raymond's Run"

Cisneros, Sandra: "Eleven"

Dahl, Roald: "The Landlady"

Howe, James (Ed.): Any story from *13: Thirteen Stories That Capture the Agony and Ecstasy of Being Thirteen*

Olsen, Tillie: "I Stand Here Ironing"

Poe, Edgar Allan: "The Black Cat"

Salinas, Marta: "The Scholarship Jacket"

Soto, Gary: "Mother and Daughter"

Tan, Amy: "Rules of the Game"

Tolstoy, Leo: "The Two Brothers"

Go to this Oklahoma school's website to find PDFs of many popular short (and long) works of literature: www.woodland.k12.ok.us/217497_3.

Everyone needs a stack of stickies or a blank piece of paper for notes, along with a copy of the text. Pens are in hand. Take time to silently read and mark up everything you notice. Again, don't feel like your job is to "make inferences"; instead it is to write honestly about what you're thinking about, noticing, and questioning. You might jot things like "Huh, that surprised me" or "I had to reread that part three times!" Of course, go for the more "literary" things, too, like noticing repetition, themes, and more. Just make your jots genuine.

We'll use sentence starters with students, too. As you read, try using these sentence starters to help you track your thinking:

I'm thinking . . .

I'm noticing . . .

I'm surprised . . .

I wonder . . .

## STEP 2: SHARE OUT WHAT YOU NOTICED

Okay, now that we've marked up the text, it's time to share out what we noticed. Here's what a list looked like after tenth-grade teachers read the introduction to *The Scarlet Letter*:

*I found myself wondering who the narrator really is.*

*I wondered why he's so critical of the custom house.*

*Tons of detailed description of the custom house and Salem.*

*I was tempted to skim this part but made myself slow down.*

*There's already a conflict set up between the narrator and his Puritan ancestors.*

*I'm thinking about the purpose of the introduction, and why the story doesn't start right away with the story, so to speak.*

*How much of the narrator is Hawthorne? And can we even assume that they overlap?*

*It's already clear your reading of this book will be limited if you don't know about Puritans and their history.*

*The language is jarring at first. Hawthorne uses very high-level vocabulary that might scare off a lot of my students. Also, the sentences and paragraphs here are extremely dense and long. I know how to break down these sentences so they make sense, but my students might not.*

*The romance genre is stated in the introduction, but we know it's not necessarily the kind of romance that our students are familiar with.*

*The story is twice removed. We are learning about Hester Prynne's story through Jonathan Pue and then the narrator.*

Now, if our group of tenth-grade teachers used this list of what they noticed as skilled readers to plan their unit, they'd be right back to teaching the book. We want to help our students master what readers can do in *any* novel. Now it's time to generalize these observations so our students see what to do in their books.

For example, if we notice how Hawthorne uses setting to set a mood and hint at bigger ideas in the novel, we can ask readers to pay attention to setting in their novels, and why the author set scenes as he or she did. We might tell readers, "Authors don't just randomly choose settings for scenes and novels; they do so for a purpose. Today we're going to pay attention to this in our books." This way, we're using what we do as readers to allow our students to be mindful of the same things as they read.

## STEP 3: EXPAND WHAT YOU NOTICED IN YOUR CLASS NOVEL TO WHAT A READER CAN DO IN ANY NOVEL

Now we will rewrite our notes so they're not specific to our book but general so any reader can share in the same thinking.

Here are some questions to guide you:

- What thinking did you do that *any* reader can do?

- What was the bigger-picture idea that you noticed here?

- What overall reading move did you do?

Here are some *Scarlet Letter* examples using the list above:

*Tons of detailed description of the custom house and Salem.*

We can ask ourselves, "What thinking did you do that *any* reader can do?"

We can also say, "Setting is important. Pay attention to how the setting is described and make note of it."

That's how we'll help students transfer this bigger idea to their own book!

*I was tempted to skim this part but made myself slow down.*

We can ask ourselves, "What overall reading move did you do?" We slowed down to help ourselves understand. That is a reading move we can ask all of our students to do.

Here's what we can teach that readers can transfer to their own books: "We might be tempted to skim long stretches of description and narration that don't have lots of exciting action or quick-moving dialogue. Let's work today at slowing down and paying attention to the slow parts, too."

*It's already clear your reading of this book will be limited if you don't know about Puritans and their history.*

We can ask ourselves, "What thinking did you do that any reader can do?" We know historical context is essential to a meaningful understanding of the novel. Here was the focus lesson we generated as a result: "When we read about unfamiliar settings, especially historical ones, it's important to do supplemental research so we can read with understanding."

Now we noticed that a bunch of our notes all had to do with the narrator. We grouped those together and asked ourselves what kinds of things we were paying attention to.

*I found myself wondering who the narrator really is.*

*I wondered why he's so critical of the custom house.*

*There's already a conflict set up between the narrator and his Puritan ancestors.*

*I'm thinking about the purpose of the introduction, and why the story doesn't start right away with the story, so to speak.*

*How much of the narrator is Hawthorne? And can we even assume that they overlap?*

*The story is twice removed. We are learning about Hester Prynne's story through Jonathan Pue and then the narrator.*

Here are some possible focus lessons we created as a result that will help our readers pay attention to similar things in their own novels:

- Readers analyze the author's choice of narrator, considering the purpose and impact of that perspective.

- Readers are aware that a fictional narrator is distinct from the author but that the narrator may be a vehicle to express the author's beliefs.

- Readers know that there is a tremendous amount to pay attention to in the beginning of novels and that the point of view of the narrator is one of those essential components.

## STEP 4: NARROW IT DOWN TO A UNIT'S WORTH OF LESSONS

We already came up with six focus lessons, and we haven't even finished covering all the possible lessons that could come out of the first chapter of your chosen novel. You've seen the process, however, and what it means to take our thinking as readers from a classic novel that we love, and use it to help our students transfer that thinking to books they love. These steps are so important. We read, jot, share out, and make decisions all around how to help our students to be skilled readers in any novel.

Now it's time to streamline this process so we have a unit's worth of focus lessons and we expose our readers to parts of the novel from start to finish. When I work with teachers, a unit's worth of focus lessons is usually about sixteen to twenty total. That's about four weeks of teaching, considering the typical field trips, assemblies, holidays, and other events that shorten our weeks from five complete days of instruction.

Sixteen to twenty days of using our novel means we won't get to everything we love in it, and that's okay. It's okay because we aren't teaching students the novel; we're teaching them how to be skilled readers.

The classic is a vehicle to get there.

Besides, when we do close readings of excerpts without dissecting every chapter of the class novel, there's a decent chance some will want to pick up that book, all on their own!

> We won't get to everything we love in our classic, and that's okay. It's okay because we aren't teaching students the novel; we're teaching them how to be skilled readers.

Even though you'll easily have hundreds of margin notes you could share, we'll whittle them down. We'll also streamline them to four to five weeks to speed up our units. The old model of six to eight weeks on a novel means too little volume of reading and, frankly, a less engaging pace. We will get to volume by pushing it in students' independent books, but by tightening the pace to four to five weeks on our classic novel, too, we'll get invigorating movement.

Remember, we're not teaching them everything that's important to know in *The Scarlet Letter*; we're teaching them how to read well. We'll teach them how to read fiction well over and over again throughout the year, while they're building their reading muscles in novel after novel after novel, getting ready for the marathon-like stamina they'll need in college. This isn't our one and only chance to teach students how to read fiction well. We can save other lesson ideas for later units. The nice thing is, since we're building four- to five-week units, we'll return to this genre again at least once if not more! It isn't a matter of getting everything we know into students' minds all at once.

We don't have time to linger. Besides, when we do go slowly, the temptation to go back to the outdated model of teaching the book, not the reader, is greater.

## Tips for Narrowing It Down

- Take your most important thinking that happens across the novel. Look at your margin notes from across the book—make sure you have fairly equal notes from the beginning, middle, and end—and decide which of them are nearest and dearest to your heart. Remember:
  - We need to choose from across the whole text so students have a sense of closure, and also because what we do as readers varies greatly across a text.

- At the beginning, a lot of groundwork is laid out in terms of character, plot, and setting that we need to teach.

- Across the book, we need to look at the ways characters evolve, how theme develops, and what changes. If we only focus on one part of the novel, we'll miss teaching what readers do that is specific to other sections. For instance, it's hard to trace character change if we only look at the first half of the book.

- Use only the thinking that you modeled using the classic that most of your students can do in their own novels, especially in your first units of the year.

  - For example, I was working with a group of eighth-grade teachers using *The Outsiders* to create a fiction unit. They loved how S. E. Hinton used literary references and allusions throughout. But, we also knew most of our students' choice novels were unlikely to have literary references to outside texts. Therefore, we shelved it (for now). Likewise, any focus lessons specific only to the class novel you'll want to eliminate. Too little bang for the buck.

    - An exception to the rule is if your heart is tied to something in your classic text! Just because something won't translate to most of your students' choice books doesn't mean you have to abandon it. Sometimes our classic text showcases something so beautifully complex and rich and important that we show it to students anyway. It's admittedly hard to not teach Shakespeare's iambic pentameter, even though our students' books are unlikely to be formatted as such. Know you're showing them something important, or you can find ways to help them see it in a bigger, more transferable context. For example, "Shakespeare's use of iambic pentameter gives his text a flow, and the structure has purpose. In what ways did your author make the language flow?" or "In what ways did your author structure his or her text purposefully?"

For an example of a four- or five-week fiction unit for tenth graders, refer to **Resource 5**. It shows the focus lessons and text excerpts to model that thinking using *The Scarlet Letter*.

Now we've tried out looking at our chosen novels in a whole new way, as a way to teach transferable reading skills. It's time to craft a unit that will be fun to teach, empower all our students, and get them truly reading, not skimming from SparkNotes.

## How to Make Your Unit Pop and Avoid Potential Pitfalls

You've done important work already, getting to the essential reading work that will help your students be empowered readers of fiction. This is the groundwork that will help transform your classroom to a place where all students are engaged in meaningful reading. But we all know we learn how to make things even better through trial and error.

Consider this next section to be like the reviews on an Amazon product or the added notes on AllRecipes.com from those who have tried a recipe and tinkered with it, and want to share their learning curve to help you the first time. Here are some things that teachers and I have discovered to take these units to the next level, save you time and energy, and help eliminate little hiccups as well as full-on challenges.

### WEAVE IN LESSONS THAT TEACH READERS GOOD HABITS IN ANY GENRE

When I worked with middle schools in Garfield, New Jersey, to map out a unit on *The Outsiders*, we saved every fifth lesson to support students as readers in general, not necessarily addressing fiction or the class novel. We were working with students who came to reading reluctantly, for the most part, and they needed support in strengthening their habits as readers of any genre.

Do this to avoid the problems we faced. At first, we found ourselves constantly battling nonreaders and not getting to teach the smart lessons we had crafted. Teachers would show students a wonderful example of character analysis and send them off to try it with their own books. Instead of reading, however, students sharpened pencils, asked to go to the bathroom, had to go to their lockers to get their books, and did a host of other things to avoid reading.

Even those who were reading, kind of, were easily distracted. They struggled to find books they wanted to read. Some chose the first book they spotted that had eye-catching graphics on the cover, or they grabbed the shortest books (*Night* by Elie Wiesel, for example) only to discover those short books weren't necessarily easy to read.

We realized something had to change, and that something was teaching students how to be readers, period.

We thought about everything students needed to be able to do in order to read consistently in and outside of class. We knew students needed to find books that interested them and that they could read, to stay focused as they read, to know when to abandon a book that isn't a good fit, and to remember to bring their book home and back to school each day.

Then, we folded in those lessons throughout the unit. Sometimes teachers found themselves repeating lessons, replacing lessons on theme and setting with ones they had already taught on finding a book that's a good fit, and rereading to understand confusing parts. We found lessons that taught students the habits of good readers were more important, anyway. Until readers could go off and read, there was little point in asking them to do analysis.

Likewise, work with your colleagues to brainstorm a list of all the potential hiccups or challenges that your students might face as readers. After you show them what to do in a novel and ask them to read quietly and transfer those skills for up to thirty minutes, what are all the things students might struggle with? Remember, even though we feel middle and high school students should have mastered these fundamental habits, many haven't. It's worth addressing these so we set up everyone for success.

Here's a sample list of what I've found we need to do to support many middle and high school students so they're ready to read every day and transfer skills to their independent reading. You can borrow from here or generate your own list based on what you frequently remind your students to do or feel frustrated that they don't do.

1. **We need to reread to help us understand our books.** Whenever we're confused, we can go back to the part we last understood and reread from there. We can also reread little bits and pieces to remind ourselves about certain characters or settings or to answer questions as we go.

2. **We need to find books we love.** We can do this by listening to book buzzes in class; asking friends, teachers, and librarians; going on Goodreads.com, checking out lists on NerdyBookClub.com; and more. (This can be a list that you add to throughout the year to help readers find books they want to read. See Chapter 2, pages 41 and 61, for samples.)

3. **We need to set goals for our reading.** We can aim high in terms of page numbers, chapters, or minutes of reading. We can also set goals for when we'll stop in our book to jot down our thinking and what we'll pay attention to as we read (Serravallo, 2015).

4. **We need to change course, if necessary.** Reading a book that's right for us should usually feel like we can keep going and going. If the book feels like hard work because the topic isn't interesting or it's just really tough to read, we can find a better choice.

5. **We need to read everywhere.** It can feel hard to find time to read when school ends, but we need to take our book home and bring it back to school every day. Here are some ways we can help ourselves find time to read outside of school:

   • Put our book in a gallon-size Ziploc bag to help us know where it is and keep it handy

   • Use the "Remind" app on our phones

   • Put a sticky note in a spot that we know we'll see it, like our bathroom mirror or our pencil case

6. **We need to revise our thinking as we get new information in a book.** This can look like adding to our double-entry notes in a third column, putting in asterisks, or using sentence starters like "I used to think . . . , but now I think . . ."

7. **We need to stretch out of our comfort zones with our reading choices.** That might mean trying a new genre if we've been only reading manga, sci-fi, or contemporary fiction for a while, or we might read several books by one author if we always skip around.

8. **We need to use every minute of in-class reading time.** For this commonly needed reminder, teachers and I have generated an if–then list with students, listing all the things that interrupt reading time and what readers can do to reduce interruptions or distractions. For example, if your Chromebook battery dies or your pencil breaks, then sign out a new Chromebook or use a new pencil from a designated spot instead of using the electric sharpener. Once you're finished with your book, fill out your bookmark (see page 65 in Chapter 2 and **Resource 4**) and quietly find a new one, or have a backup book ready.

9. **We need to read a lot.** Volume counts. We can strengthen our reading muscles to read more and more by tracking how much we read and increasing that number all the time.

Save time and lessons to help readers transfer these essential reading habits and skills, just as we teach them reading for theme or any other literary awareness. If I want my students to be aware of *how* to reread, I'm going to put my own book on the document camera and read aloud a confusing part, showing them where I stop and reread. Likewise, teach these general reading habits by modeling how you do it, then asking students to try the same.

## USE A PREASSESSMENT TO SAVE TIME AND TO CRAFT UNITS THAT MATCH YOUR STUDENTS

Usually listing out what to teach is easy to generate—it comes from our old units, our class novel margin notes, and our new notes. Focus lessons also come from what we inwardly groan about on a regular basis that our readers are not doing, or what we see a few high flyers getting to and now want the rest of the class to get to, too. If these "need to knows" aren't readily apparent, or even if they are, it's a great idea to do a preassessment to see what your readers already know how to do within a genre and what they're ready for next.

Preassessments aren't graded; they're used to help us see what students are and aren't able to do. They're typically an easy, short common read with a few questions that address the type of thinking required for the upcoming unit. The text and questions are administered before the unit begins, when we still have time to adjust our teaching after seeing the results. Students' answers are a goldmine of information that lets us know what they know and what they need to learn.

An example of a simple preassessment before planning a fiction unit would be giving students a short story that is easy for them to understand. We don't want students struggling to comprehend the text, or they'll never get to show us their thinking about things like theme. We would ask students to read the story carefully and answer the following questions:

*What did you notice and think about in terms of character? Setting? Theme?*

*Use examples from the story to back up your ideas.*

We can make these questions more specific, but even these general questions elicit important information for us to use when we plan.

If many students already notice that characters are complex, for example, we don't need to teach that concept. If, however, most students rely on superficial observations such as physical characteristics to create ideas about characters, then we know to teach our class how to use what characters say and do to build their theories, and how to pay attention to minor characters as well.

The point is that doing a quick preassessment saves us time in the long run. We see what students do and don't know, and then we can plan and fine-tune our units accordingly. This isn't just a time saver, either. Preassessments let us meet the needs of our students.

## USE RESOURCES TO HELP YOU PLAN

In addition to what we collect from preassessments and spying on our reading selves, there are plenty of other resources to help guide our planning.

### Professional Books That Offer Excellent Suggestions for What to Teach Fiction Readers

There are many smart writers out there publishing books about what we do as readers of fiction. Their books are chock full of the thinking that we need to do and make transparent for our students. We can use them to get right to middle and high school–level reading strategies. Here are some of the books teachers and I have relied on and loved:

Beers, K., & Probst, R. (2013). *Notice and note: Strategies for close reading.* Portsmouth, NH: Heinemann.

Fisher, D., & Frey, N. (2015). *Text-dependent questions: Pathways to close and critical reading, grades 6–12.* Thousand Oaks, CA: Corwin.

Serravallo, J. (2015). *The reading strategies book.* Portsmouth, NH: Heinemann.

### Our Margin Notes in Class Novels

Find your dog-eared copy of *The Scarlet Letter*, filled with years' worth of scribbles and jots in the margins. Those notes are planning gold! Use your notes in your copies of class novels and pull out what you know is important to understand, think about, and pay attention to. Just remember that you'll likely have to whittle these down from hundreds of notes to include only the must-knows, what your students need most, and what aligns with the standards.

## The Common Core State Standards or State-Designed Equivalent as a Guide

Often a quick look at the standards will get us jump-started if we're stuck on what to teach. After looking at the grade-level standards for reading literature at CoreStandards.org, we'll say, "Oh right, let's make sure we work on getting to theme" or "That's it—they need to cite text evidence." And then we can use the standards' language to ensure we do grade-level work on theme and citing evidence.

**Aligning Our Units to the Standards.** Unless you teach in a mythical land that exists apart from standards-aligned curriculums, you'll need to be explicit in your unit plans how these focus lessons meet grade-level standards.

You can ensure that alignment by having the standards in mind while you comb through old margin notes in the class novel or read for text excerpts, zeroing in on thinking or sections of text that will help show ways of getting to the skills in the standards. In planning with teachers, however, I've found that we are able to first generate our lists of focus lessons and then find the standards that match up with ease.

One of the beautiful things about planning this way is that we're teaching reading skills and strategies, not the content of a novel. The language of our lesson's objective often mirrors what's right there in the standards for reading literature. Looking at the standards helps us, however, narrow down and group our lessons and adjust our language to make sure we're addressing what students need to know.

If we go back to the sample list of focus lessons from the first activity that helped us articulate what we do as readers, this is how that list would match the standards:

- *Readers pay attention to and can cite what characters do and say across a text to develop theories, and they can also compare theories about various characters to look at their similarities and differences.*

- *Readers notice how characters impact one another and if characters change as a result of others' influences.*

- *Readers use evidence from the text to show how characters are complex and may have contradictory traits.*

These line right up with two of the literature standards:

RL.9–10.1: *Cite strong and thorough textual evidence to support analysis of what the text says explicitly as well as inferences drawn from the text.*

RL.9–10.3: *Analyze how complex characters (e.g., those with multiple or conflicting motivations) develop over the course of a text, interact with other characters, and advance the plot or develop the theme.*

o *Readers pay attention to what might happen later on in the book and how authors might build our expectations about or create suspense with certain clues.*

This aligns with RL.9–10.5: *Analyze how an author's choices concerning how to structure a text, order events within it (e.g., parallel plots), and manipulate time (e.g., pacing, flashbacks) create such effects as mystery, tension, or surprise.*

Usually, a few focus lessons on our lists will line up with one standard. That's good—we want about three to four standards at most across a unit. There are ten anchor standards for reading literature for a reason. These are big-ticket items to teach, break down, and revisit, not one-and-done chores to tick off. If we break down those big reading concepts across several days, our students stand a good chance of really "getting it."

Now we can also do this same work of lining up our focus lessons to the standards for our non-genre-specific list of what good readers do. Those lessons may not count toward the three to four standards; they're what our kids need to do to be successful readers. We can often find matches to these focus lessons in an earlier grade's reading standards or in the writing, language, or speaking and listening standards. Even if we don't find an easy match, it's worth keeping them. Not everything worth teaching is in a grade-level standard. And because I've never worked in a classroom with 100 percent at-grade-level students, what readers *need* to be able to do is not always going to be in a generic list of what they *should* be doing.

Remember, these essential need-to-knows are something you'll never get from ready-made curriculums. Teaching isn't a fast-food restaurant where we can give every hungry customer a prepackaged meal. We're better off personalizing our instruction to individual tastes or, rather, what students didn't get and still need to become high-level thinkers and readers. Starting from what you want them to know and do will result in a genuine unit that impacts your students much more than anything you can find on TeachersPayTeachers.com or Pinterest.

## LAY OUT THE UNIT, DAY BY DAY

Just like in the model unit using *The Scarlet Letter*, we'll want to lay out our lessons across days and weeks. It may help to use a template like the one in **Resource 6**.

A few pointers as you go: Typically, mapping out the unit works best when we look at one standard across four or so lessons, or one week. Each week or so of lessons will concentrate on about one standard, fleshed out in three or four ways. These will come right from your list, grouped by standards. For instance, if we want students to really be experts at characterization, it will happen across at least several days, showing students multiple ways to become better at this concept. Take a look at the sample units in **Resources 5, 7, and 8** as examples of what this looks like.

Before moving on to Week 2 and to a new standard, make sure to address that essential list of what readers need that isn't specific to fiction. Some teachers keep these as Friday lessons, pulling students back to what it means to be a good reader before unstructured reading time over the weekend. Regardless, aim for one non-genre-specific focus lesson a week, for as long as needed, or until students are habitual and engaged readers. These lessons help our students grow in skills like focus and stamina and any other skill or habit that good readers use. At the end of **Resource 7**, a sample unit on *The Outsiders*, there are optional lessons outlined to support reading habits apart from a specific genre or reading standard. These lessons anticipate likely issues for the eighth-grade readers, but teachers can incorporate them (or others) as needed.

It also helps to think about which concepts readers can focus on right away in Week 1, and which are built up to in Weeks 2 and 3. For instance, theme isn't something we can teach on the first day, but characters and setting are logical places to start. (In the introduction to Serravallo's 2015 *Reading Strategies Book* there is an extremely useful chart showing the hierarchy of possible goals for readers, outlining what areas to focus on first, next, and so on.) First, readers need to understand what's happening in the book—it's the first standard in the Common Core for good reason. Then readers can do additional thinking and analysis of that baseline understanding. Our lessons will flow accordingly.

## CHOOSE TEXT EXCERPTS FROM YOUR CLASS NOVEL

To find great excerpts, we can go back to where we marked the text in the first place as a "spy on ourselves" text or where we marked up the margins in previous years' teaching. Or, we can comb through it anew. The great thing is that we'll typically find many examples for each focus lesson. If you're working with more than one teacher, you can divide this up to save time, each finding excerpts for different lessons.

## What to Keep in Mind as You Choose Passages From the Novel

1. **Go for a page or less of text when possible.** More than a page can muddy the focus of what we're looking for or run the risk of losing our listeners. When we want to show a reading move that happens over a larger section of text, such as character change, we can pull several short excerpts.

2. **Go for parts of the text that provide action, dialogue, and moments of tension** when possible, as opposed to long descriptions, inner thinking, or setting. Remember, every time we read an excerpt, we're essentially giving a little book buzz and selling this book. By choosing passages of rich writing and plot turns, we entice our students to want to see more.

3. **Go for easy-to-understand passages when read out of context.** Remember, we won't be reading the entire book, so it helps if this part of the text makes sense on its own. For instance, go for scenes with main characters as opposed to a peripheral character who only shows up once.

## CREATE RESOURCES TO HELP SUMMARIZE THE NOVEL BETWEEN EXCERPTS

Keep in mind that when we teach these lessons, our readers are getting isolated glimpses of the novel. Any time we sense these excerpts may confuse our students, we need to give them a quick summary of what's happened since the last time we looked at the book. One teacher I work with pulls up the SparkNotes whenever his readers need them. Instead of students secretively using these to get away with fake reading, the class uses them together to understand the plot of the book or refresh their knowledge of who's who. Then the teacher goes right into modeling what he pays attention to and thinks about as a reader, and students go to their choice reading to do the same.

We can also create resources to help students see these excerpts in context and prevent confusion when referring to our class novel. We can crib right from

SparkNotes if needed, but if we've taught the novel, we'll have this at the tip of our tongues.

Here are two examples of visuals to keep the class in on the major plot turns and character developments of the class novel:

## The Scarlet Letter: Key Events

| Chapter | Where? When? | Who? | What? |
|---|---|---|---|
| Intro | Custom House, 100 years after Scarlet Letter | Nameless narrator | Discovers docs. in scarlet "A"; begins to write "romance" |
| Ch. 1 | Outside prison door. 17th century Boston | Crowd of on-lookers | Symbolic rose growing in dreariness |
| Ch. 2 | same as Ch. 1 | Hester holding baby Pearl | Crowd is taunting Hester. Hester is in disbelief. |
| Ch. 3 | still outside prison at scaffold | Chillingworth, founding Fathers | C. doesn't admit to being Hester's husband |

## The Scarlet Letter: Key Players

### Hester Prynne
Protagonist. Wears "A". Married to Chillingworth. Affair with Dimmesdale. Passionate, strong, alienated

### Pearl
Hester & Dimmesdale's illegitimate daughter. Moody, mischievious. Wise beyond her years.

### Chillingworth
Hester's much older husband. He sent H. ahead to America and he was captured briefly by Native Americans. Now disguised as doctor. Vengeful. Bad guy.

### Reverend Dimmesdale
Secret father to Pearl. Former lover of Hester. Tormented by guilt. Deeply conflicted

These are examples of charts used about halfway through *The Scarlet Letter*. We created similar charts for what students needed to know in following chapters. It's worth noting that teachers created these charts, not students. The information on them isn't something students spend time copying down. The notes are there as a resource so students understand the excerpts easily, and they can put their energy into thinking about their own books.

Every time we use an excerpt that assumes knowledge of a significant plot turn or change in character or introduces a new character, we add that needed information to our charts. Then, before getting to that day's excerpt, we take a minute to refer to the chart and sum up any key events or character changes. This doesn't take more than a minute or two at most, even when students ask clarifying questions. And typically, they don't have questions.

Remember, we know and love this book. That's why we chose it. And while it's a bit heartbreaking for us, our students aren't usually desperate to know why Ponyboy keeps slipping out of consciousness, or whether Chillingworth is the father or not. On the plus side, it's a good thing students are ready for us to stop talking about our book—so they can get to the books they care about!

## PAT YOURSELF ON THE BACK

Congratulations. We have thought through a novel together so you can duplicate the process using your own class novels. When we do this again with nonfiction in the next chapter, the process will feel even more comfortable.

Once independent reading is happening and these plans are in place, we start seeing results in the form of authentic reading and growth. Students are immersed in books, and now we are able to teach what truly moves them as skilled and eager readers.

Now it's time to treat yourself and bask in the glow of your smart unit that gets to the highest level of teaching: transfer. What will that pampering reward look like? A bowl of M&Ms? A nap? I have a hunch it will be an uninterrupted hour with a great book.

Enjoy.

## CHAPTER FOUR

# BUILDING A BLENDED CURRICULUM FOR NONFICTION-BASED UNITS

In this chapter, we look at the autobiography *Narrative of the Life of Frederick Douglass, an American Slave,* and see how to create a unit that uses this text to help students transfer skills to other nonfiction texts. Similar to the planning chapter for fiction, we're trying out the process so you'll feel comfortable doing this work with any nonfiction book of your choice.

## Why Nonfiction?

I'll admit, as a voracious reader, my book choices weigh heavily toward story. Fiction or non-, my books are almost all narrative. I want to be sucked in by hardship and triumph; characters I love, envy, abhor, and admire; and the turns and journeys in their lives. In contrast, research- and fact-laden pieces can feel like work. But my husband reads sports statistics like I eat Reese's Peanut Butter Cups, and my older daughter subscribes to *Time* magazine and ignores the young adult (YA) literature I put in her Christmas stocking. I've had countless students with the same fascination for what's "real," for facts and information, for curiosity-satisfying explanations. Regardless of our own tastes toward "the truth," we need to teach it.

In fact, as Kylene Beers and Robert Probst (2016) remind us, we must teach our students to determine what, indeed, the truth is when reading nonfiction. And if we want our students to immerse themselves in nonfiction, we need to make that a thoughtful part of our lessons. Jeffrey Wilhelm and Michael Smith show the way in *Diving Deep Into Nonfiction* (2017). This book sets up a thoughtful framework for unpacking nonfiction, providing explicit instruction on how to read it well, and then helping students transfer their learning to new texts.

Such popular resources show that we can't leave the task of helping our students become expert nonfiction readers to other content areas. Gone are the days when English class is for literature and literature alone. According to the Common Core and equivalent state-designed standards, it's our job to teach our students to be confident, skilled readers and writers of nonfiction as well. In fact, by senior year, students' reading across the school day should be 70 percent nonfiction and 30 percent fiction. This makes sense. Unless they are English majors in college, the bulk of our students' future reading and writing lives will be characterized by immersion in nonfiction texts. Everything from the dense textbooks on their college syllabi to the reports from their bosses will be nonfiction, so we must set them up to navigate this world of informational texts successfully.

We also need to teach our students to be skilled readers of nonfiction because our world is inundated with information. Every day, a staggering 2.5 quintillion bytes of data are produced (*VCloudNews*, 2015). Former Google CEO Eric Schmidt tells us that we produce the same amount of information every two days as we did from the dawn of mankind until 2003 (Siegler, 2010). Our students are swimming in a sea of digital content, and if we want them to be empowered citizens of the world, they deserve to have the tools to read it critically.

We live in a world of information, and the skills needed to be fluent readers of that content are different from those required to read fiction. Just because we sail through novels and analyze them with ease doesn't mean we can transfer those same strengths to editorials, data reports, textbooks, manuals, or even narrative nonfiction. Strong readers of nonfiction build on their fiction skills but also use entirely new skills. Even as lovers of literature, we need to embrace nonfiction and the skills to read it well, too.

This chapter will help you plan units that show what good readers do with one nonfiction text so that students can transfer those same reading moves to nonfiction texts of their choice.

# What's Important to Know About
# Planning Nonfiction Units Before Diving In

This chapter assumes you've tried out the fiction planning work from Chapter 3 and that you understand the process and what's helpful to know when planning for transfer to independent reading. There are a few additional issues to be aware of, however, specific to planning nonfiction units.

## NONFICTION IS A BIG UMBRELLA GENRE

When we go into Barnes & Noble, visit our local library, or browse the Kindle store, we don't see one huge section labeled only "Nonfiction." It's a massive overarching umbrella that covers everything from biographies to editorials to true-story accounts to oral histories to manuals to textbooks. The skills we need to read a narrative nonfiction book like *Unbroken* by Laura Hillenbrand differ from those we need to read a warranty for our new iPhone. Both are nonfiction, but that's about all they have in common!

Likewise, our units need to be specific about what kind of nonfiction we are teaching students to read well, what skills are unique to reading that genre alone, and what skills are universal to most kinds of nonfiction. Beers and Probst (2016) define nonfiction as "that body of work in which the author purports to tell us about the real world, a real experience, a real person, an idea, or a belief" (p. 21). They knew it was important to define this broad wide-spanning genre and to be thoughtful about what we do as nonfiction readers that is so vastly different from what we do in fiction. Indeed, this book is a wonderful planning resource. For now, keep in mind the importance of going deeper than nonfiction and naming your unit with what kind of nonfiction you're helping your students to read well.

## YOUR READING IDENTITY PLAYS A PART

While we know we need to get our students up to speed with nonfiction, it's important to consider how comfortable we are reading nonfiction, too. It may be that your love of literature, novels, plays, and poetry led you on the path to English teacher, and therefore you don't feel highly knowledgeable about teaching research-based units. Or, perhaps you're used to teaching only fiction and leaving all the other stuff to the content-area teachers. That was the role I assumed for years. There are also those of you with nightstands and Kindles loaded up with nonfiction. That passion will be contagious!

Regardless of where you fall on the spectrum—from a voracious, competent reader of nonfiction to an occasional, intimidated consumer of it—your identity will play a part. If you are less comfortable in this genre, it is good to be aware of that so you know to shore up those gaps. You can incorporate more nonfiction in your pleasure reading, call on your knowledgeable colleagues in and out of your department, rely on some helpful resources when planning, and be more conscious of what you do when reading (even avoiding!) nonfiction. That awareness will help you reach all of your students, who of course represent all kinds of nonfiction readers, too.

## CHOOSE A CLASS TEXT FOR MODELING YOUR THINKING AS A NONFICTION READER

It's likely that you can't go to your book room and find shelves filled with nonfiction books. You probably didn't teach class texts using nonfiction like you did with class novels. You also tend not to think of the classics in terms of nonfiction. Most of us think of literature as fiction. On the plus side, this opens up our choices when we find a book to teach our students how to read nonfiction well.

### Some Ways to Find Nonfiction Texts for Your Focus Lessons

- Immerse yourself in nonfiction reading! There is a wealth of beautifully written content out there. Whether it's *Field & Stream*, *Cook's Illustrated*, podcasts, *The New Yorker*, biographies, or *Sports Illustrated*, find nonfiction you love and want to share.

- Do an interest survey on what your students care about. Then find matching publications so they're hooked on content while you model how to read it well. You can unearth good writing on everything from skateboarding to veganism to the creation of anime to tattoos to cell phone plans to sibling studies.

  ○ Some groups of teachers I work with keep a shared Google Classroom folder where they stockpile and share texts of possible interest. There are links to articles, podcasts, pdfs, transcripts, YouTube videos, and more that teachers know have been vetted and are of potential interest to their students.

- Look at the Common Core State Standards (corestandards.org) or state-designed equivalent to determine what specific nonfiction genre you'll need to include. Some grade-level standards will clarify certain genres you'll want to teach at some point in this grade band.

  ○ For instance, in Grades 9–10, teachers are required to find important documents from U.S. history to use when modeling their thinking as readers: Analyze seminal U.S. documents of historical and literary significance (e.g., Washington's Farewell Address, the Gettysburg Address, Roosevelt's Four Freedoms speech, King's "Letter from Birmingham Jail"), including how they address related themes and concepts.

  ○ Then, in Grades 11–12, that specification becomes more precise: Analyze seventeenth-, eighteenth-, and nineteenth-century foundational U.S. documents of historical and literary significance (including the Declaration of Independence, the Preamble to the Constitution, the Bill of Rights, and Lincoln's Second Inaugural Address) for their themes, purposes, and rhetorical features.

- This is not to say that all nonfiction units need to address primary sources from history, however. There is also room to look at narrative nonfiction, biographies, autobiographies, memoir, pop science, and more. The important thing is to be clear about what kind of nonfiction you're looking at, what skills you need to read it well, and how students will try it in texts of their choice.

- Find longer nonfiction works on best-seller lists, at NerdyBookClub. com, and in Appendix B of the Common Core, which lists text exemplars by grade level for English language arts. These lists include shorter texts such as essays and speeches, as well as longer works like Maya Angelou's *I Know Why the Caged Bird Sings*. You may also consider winners of the National Book Award for Nonfiction and the National Book Critics Circle Award for General Nonfiction.

- Check out this Oklahoma school's website (www.woodland.k12 .ok.us/217497_3) for pdfs of literature and nonfiction works for all levels, including middle and high school.

- There is an overwhelming wealth of nonfiction texts to choose from. When in doubt, go for works that you love. That passion will be contagious.

## What to Do When Your Students Are Choosing to Read Novels and It's Time to Teach Nonfiction

Here we are, ready to embrace nonfiction and plan units that address all there is to know as nonfiction readers. But we just barely got our students reading, and more than likely, they're reading novels. Or, as discussed in Chapter 3, you may have dealt with this issue already in a fiction unit with nonfiction fans. How can we set up our classroom routines so students see how we read nonfiction, transfer it to texts of their choice, and still *want* to read?

It may feel like nothing short of a miracle when you look around your classroom, and all of your students are quietly immersed in books of their choice. Indeed, the most important thing is to establish their habits of reading in whatever genre they choose. If they're already reluctant readers and we narrow their choices, we might set up even more resistance, which is tough on them and on us.

You are the best judge of what your students can handle in terms of choice. Some teachers encounter little resistance when asking students to limit their choices to books that follow the genre of the class text. As Mary Haile, a high school teacher in South Carolina, reminds her students, this is "highly negotiated choice reading," and they don't seem to mind. The idea that there is autonomy at all still feels fresh enough that even a narrowed set of choices is appealing.

The following page shows a snapshot of a unit that outlines the class texts and the corresponding choice of independent reading books students will need to make. Throughout this teacher's curriculum, choices are often limited by genre or even more narrowly: "coming of age" novel, biography of a non-American twentieth-century revolutionary (loosely defined as anyone who pushed the thinking of the time), contemporary book of poetry by one author, and more. This teacher met little resistance, although her students lean toward highly motivated and eager to make the grade. This teacher also provided support with book title suggestions and media center visits.

Consider the following options if you're nervous that you might lose readers by confining choice to the genre of the class text:

1. **Keep copies of the class text on hand for strategy practice.** A way to compromise and let students choose what they want, be it graphic novel or YA or narrative nonfiction, is to give them a copy of the class text you are using to model reading strategies, or another book

| Unit and Focus Skills | Essential Question | Class Texts | Choice Texts |
|---|---|---|---|
| Unit I: Characterization and Tracking Multiple Themes Across a Novel | What individual desires and societal values define what it means to be an American?<br><br>How can tracing a character's search for identity help us to understand themes in a novel?<br><br>If complex novels portray multiple themes, how does the reader evaluate text evidence to determine which is the most important theme? | Chang Rae-Lee, *Native Speaker* (excerpts)<br><br>Jhumpa Lahiri, *Interpreter of Maladies* (excerpts) | Your independent reading choice book must be a novel written by an author from the late twentieth or twenty-first century. The novel needs to explore issues of navigating identity within multiple cultures.<br><br>A complete list of suggested texts and recorded book talks from last year's readers is on the class website, or ask the teacher if you have a choice not on the list. |

in the same nonfiction genre, to try out the reading moves you model. Trying out the reading strategy using that text might take students ten to fifteen minutes, and then they go back to their choice book.

This is where you make decisions based on the resources at hand. Do you have, or can you get, a class set of *Narrative of the Life of Frederick Douglass*? If so, your students who are reading fiction can try out the work with a copy of that book.

2. **Get students into books that align with your class text before the unit begins.** Provide a list of suggestions with titles that match the mentor text in terms of features and characteristics, do some book talks on them, and let your students choose in advance. Is there a school librarian who can help you check out a rich array of autobiographies, biographies, and memoirs? That is a great option because you'll allow students some choice, and they can transfer what you teach them to a new book, one that might be easier for them to understand than Douglass's work. Remember, the goal is to set up your instruction so that students see you do important thinking and noticing, then try to transfer that same work to a different section of the book or a new book entirely.

3. **Provide a text set.** Another option for setting up transfer of reading skills in some nonfiction units, which requires some legwork, is to provide shorter versions of the genre. You'll pull a few short articles, essays,

or excerpts from longer works into a set of texts for students to choose from. This packet is called a text set. It's just that—a preselected set of texts. Students choose from this set if they're not currently reading a book in that genre.

A resource for finding excellent, short nonfiction texts is *Text and Lessons for Content-Area Reading* (Daniels & Steinke, 2011). It is a collection of gems—short, student-friendly nonfiction texts, along with smart reader strategies. While of course you may want to find your own, this kind of resource is there to save you time and sanity.

## COLLECT HIGH-INTEREST NONFICTION TEXT SETS FOR YOUR STUDENTS

In order to provide a good collection of short texts for students to try out the work of nonfiction readers, keep some things in mind so students can success-fully transfer what you're doing with the class text to these other choices:

1. **Be clear what specific kind of nonfiction your class text is written in**, and what you want students to be able to do with that text and any other similar text. This will help you select shorter texts that are comparable. The short texts don't have to look similar in terms of content, but rather should be similarly structured.

   a. For instance, let's say you are planning a unit around *The Boys in the Boat* by Daniel James Brown, a narrative account of nine boys in the western United States who overcame all the odds to beat the German team rowing for Adolf Hitler. You've decided this is a great model for teaching how the author unfolds a series of events and how readers can determine the connections between them. Now you'll need four to five shorter pieces of narrative nonfiction that include series of events tied together by overarching ideas and connections. Those shorter texts will likely be journalistic accounts of other events and people in history, but the era or events are not as relevant as the structure.

   b. Plan ahead so you have lots of time to read for high-interest texts that will make your unit come to life. When you're clear what you'll be teaching well in advance, you'll have plenty of time to fine-tune your reading eye to any good reads that are similar. Suddenly, you'll be tearing pages out of the newspaper, bookmarking links, and asking certain reader friends for recommendations. The more time you have, the easier it will be to gather a pile of great texts to choose from.

2. **Find texts at your students' reading level.** Even if you don't know the exact Lexile level, you have a decent sense of who your students are as readers, what their background knowledge is, and what they'll feel comfortable reading. Err on the side of easy. Remember, we want them to feel successful and like they've got this! Success will breed motivation and the desire to do and read more. Also, we don't want them struggling to understand these texts. If students struggle with knowing what the text is about, they definitely won't be able to learn reading skills such as tracking main ideas or determining an author's point of view. Your text sets should ideally include a range of texts from challenging reading for your high flyers to easier reading for those still learning the English language.

3. **Find high-interest texts.** Remember, it isn't your job to make sure your students are experts in certain areas of history or culture. It is your job to empower them as readers in any content area. You might as well sweeten the pot of this reading work by giving them texts they want to read. If you find two well-written editorials—one about land rights in another country and the other about video games and violence—opt for the video games, a subject relevant to students' lives. Relevance is a credible determining factor.

   a. Podcasts are a guaranteed hit with resistant and eager readers alike (Godsey, 2016). There are transcripts for popular nonfiction podcasts such as *Freakonomics*, *This American Life*, and more. You can also find transcripts for educational and public radio podcasts, in addition to lesson ideas, at Listenwise.com.

4. **Rely on databases and websites to help you find appropriate texts.** Several websites allow you to organize texts based on topic as well as reading level. Two popular ones are Newsela.com and Tween Tribune.com. There are also many text resources available at ReadWorks .org and ReadingA-Z.com.

   a. Don't forget about your media specialists! If you're lucky enough to have one at your school, capitalize on his or her expertise. If you give these professionals enough prep time, they are likely to provide you with extensive choices that are great matches for your class text.

## REQUIRE SPECIFIC GENRES FOR
## CHOICE READING ONLY WHEN
## READING HABITS ARE WELL ESTABLISHED

Before long, you may find your students are reading their choice books consistently and with ease. Your classroom libraries will fill up with intoxicating choices, and you'll see your nonfiction selection grow. If these prerequisites are up and going, you can consider guiding students to a nonfiction choice book before your nonfiction unit begins. No text sets necessary!

It can be amazingly fruitful to model something in your own nonfiction class text, and then have all your students transfer that same skill to their choice reading. The logistics, however, ask a lot of you all, so do this only if you're ready to recommend a wealth of appropriate nonfiction books in that genre, if students can easily access those books, and if their reading habits are well established so that they can grapple with a book or genre that may be outside their comfort zone. Save assigning choice books in a specific genre for when you, your library, and your readers are really ready.

## How to Plan a Nonfiction Unit
## Based on Your Class Text
- - - - - - - - - - - - - - - - - - - - - - - - - - - - - - - - - - - - - - - - - - - - - - - -

Just as we collectively read the first chapter in *The Scarlet Letter* to try out the planning process for fiction, let's see how it works when reading the first parts of *Narrative of the Life of Frederick Douglass, an American Slave*, which are a preface and letter.

Remember, if you have previously written nonfiction units, much of this work may be done. The concepts, understandings, and reading strategies embedded in those lessons are fodder for your planning. Those old lessons may simplify this process and provide you with ready texts that you already know.

It's important to try this work with a colleague, using any nonfiction work of your choice.

### STEP 1: SPY ON YOURSELF AS A READER

As we read the preface by William Lloyd Garrison and letter from Wendell Phillips, we keep pens in hand and make notes of our thinking. Similar to how we framed our thoughts using a work of fiction, we'll keep the following sentence starters in mind: "I'm thinking . . . I'm noticing . . . I'm surprised . . . I wonder . . ." This helps track our thinking as we read.

Likewise, we could do this with the first chapter of any nonfiction book, or with an article, a speech, or another nonfiction text. It will help illuminate what we think about as nonfiction readers so those same thinking processes can be accessible to our students.

## STEP 2: SHARE OUT WHAT YOU NOTICE

Once we finish reading the preface and letter, we share our notes. Our jottings likely include thoughts and questions like the following:

*Right away we get the time frame, as Garrison says he met Douglass in 1841 at an antislavery convention.*

*I'm thinking that he has a great deal of respect for Douglass, and exudes an enthusiasm and reverence when he repeats the word and punctuation "fortunate!" almost a dozen times in the second paragraph when referencing Douglass.*

*We're getting a ton of information here about Douglass, as told through Garrison's eyes. I'm trying to get a handle on their relationship, and it seems like a strong and long-lasting one. The respect is clear when Garrison recounts rising after Douglass's speech and declaring it a better speech than that of Patrick Henry during the American Revolution.*

*Garrison seems influential in Douglass's national presence at the time. He recruits him to be an antislavery promoter.*

*I'm wondering if Garrison was White or Black. Would Douglass have been able to achieve status without a White benefactor? But maybe Douglass didn't need that access to White culture to get others to listen. I'm thinking about who held power at the time, and what it meant to have a voice inside or outside of that power circle.*

*This preface is almost like Garrison is giving Douglass's narrative his blessing. He also vouches for its authenticity when he says that Douglass wrote it on his own. This seems important. I'm wondering what function prefaces have, and if this approval of sorts is the primary use.*

*I'm thinking that Garrison's purpose is to get others to believe in, read, and support Douglass's views as a credible and honorable source of wisdom that they might otherwise not consider as such.*

*Garrison cites cases of White men killing slaves in Maryland, as well as other instances in Douglass's work. He uses these facts to drive a point home to readers: that they must join Douglass in support of victims of slavery.*

*At the end, Garrison uses readers' faith in God to convince them to agree with and support Douglass's views. Knowing how strong a part religion played in people's lives at that time, this was a crucial persuasive move to urge them to do what was right. It's like he's calling on a higher authority to convince the reader.*

All of these shared noticings will be possible examples to use in our teaching. They are models of what readers do when they read narrative nonfiction and, in this case, a preface to a personal account. However, they won't enable our students to transfer important reading skills unless we first frame them within more generalized concepts of what readers do.

## STEP 3: TRANSFORM YOUR TEXT-SPECIFIC NOTICINGS INTO UNIVERSAL LESSONS ABOUT NONFICTION

We want to ensure that we don't teach Douglass's work, per se, but that we use this book to show our students ways they can read nonfiction works, including prefaces and personal accounts.

By taking our initial thinking about this section of text and generalizing it to what a reader can do with any preface, we are empowering our readers to transfer important reading skills. First, let's consider questions that will help us transform our thinking about the preface, as well as general questions to help guide us:

- What thinking did you do that any reader can do?

- What was the bigger-picture idea that you noticed here?

- What overall reading move did you do?

For example:

*I'm thinking that he has a great deal of respect for Douglass, and exudes an enthusiasm and reverence when he repeats the word and punctuation "fortunate!" almost a dozen times in the second paragraph when referencing Douglass.*

We can pay attention to word choice with single words but especially when words are repeated for emphasis. What is the author's purpose in repeating certain words? Why one word and not another? What is its significance?

*We're getting a ton of information here about Douglass, as told through Garrison's eyes. I'm trying to get a handle on their relationship, and it seems like a strong and long-lasting one. The respect is clear when Garrison recounts rising after Douglass's speech and declaring it a better speech than that of Patrick Henry during the American Revolution.*

What comparisons are made? What is the difference between these two things, and why does it matter (Beers & Probst, 2016, p. 121)?

*Garrison seems influential in Douglass's national presence at the time. He recruits him to be an antislavery promoter.*

Readers of nonfiction can carefully consider the relationships between the author and subjects in a nonfiction text. Who has influence over others? What impact do they have?

*I'm wondering if Garrison was White or Black. Would Douglass have been able to achieve status without a White benefactor? But maybe Douglass didn't need that access to White culture to get others to listen. I'm thinking about who held power at the time, and what it meant to have a voice inside or outside of that power circle.*

It's important to consider who is writing, and what power or status they have. Whose voice is being represented, and whose voice is not?

*This preface is almost like Garrison is giving Douglass's narrative his blessing. He also vouches for its authenticity when he says that Douglass wrote it on his own. This seems important. I'm wondering what function prefaces have, and if this "approval" of sorts is the primary use.*

We can look at how a nonfiction text is structured, including all of the "extras," such as prefaces, blurbs, afterwords, and appendices, and their purposes. For instance, what comes before and after the main text? What purpose do those additional sections serve?

*Garrison cites cases of White men killing slaves in Maryland, as well as other instances in Douglass's work. He uses these especially brutal facts to drive a point home to readers: that they must join Douglass in support of victims of slavery.*

Readers of nonfiction can carefully examine what kinds of evidence, facts, or statistics the author chooses to cite. Why those facts and not others? What is the author's purpose?

*At the end, Garrison uses readers' faith in God to convince them to agree with and support Douglass's views. Knowing how strong a part religion played in people's lives at that time, this was a crucial persuasive move to urge them to do what was right. It's like he's calling on a higher authority to convince the reader.*

We can study the craft of nonfiction authors by looking at how they order their arguments or points. Often, writers will end with what they predict will be the most compelling thinking or their strongest point. We can analyze what authors choose to leave their readers with, and why.

## STEP 4: NARROW IT DOWN TO A UNIT'S WORTH OF LESSONS

It's clear that just with the preface, we can generate many important concepts worth teaching our readers. We can spend weeks on the preface alone. By selecting just a few key concepts and moving on, we'll prioritize our teaching, keep the pace moving at an engaging clip, and keep our unit focused.

Even though you won't be able to use all the thinking generated by working together on one section of text, it's worth going through the process to understand what it feels like to spy on yourself as a reader and make that kind of reading transparent and then transferable to your students.

Now it's time to condense the process so we can put together a cohesive unit of about fifteen to twenty focus lessons from our model text.

### Tips for Keeping What Counts

1. Just as in the novel unit, we need to **select excerpts from across our text**. While we don't expect our students to read *Narrative of the Life of Frederick Douglass* from cover to cover, we do want to expose them to the entire scope of this work. What we do as readers at the beginning, middle, and end of nonfiction works varies, and we want to empower our students to access all of those kinds of thinking.

2. **Choose focus lessons that your students will be able to transfer** to whatever text or choice of texts you are providing. In this instance, perhaps it is a text set of other personal accounts in diary form, or a copy of *Narrative*. But if there are no prefaces to the texts students are using for transferring their new knowledge as readers, don't use a focus lesson on prefaces.

3. **Use the standards to help narrow down your possible focus lessons.** They are a useful guide to help you see what big concepts and ideas need to be modeled for each grade band.

    a. For example, when planning a nonfiction unit for ninth and tenth grade, look at standard RI.9–10.2: *Determine a central idea of a text and analyze its development over the course of the text, including how it emerges and is shaped and refined by specific details; provide an objective summary of the text.* This work around central ideas is essential for us to support when shaping our lessons within the class text, and in helping our students get ready to transfer powerful reading to their own texts.

    b. Using the standards to guide your lessons will also help you avoid unnecessary repetition and ramp up the level of thinking across grades. If we follow the same standard for Grades 11 and 12, we'll see that readers now have to determine two or more central ideas across a text. This attention to the specific language in the standards can inform our lessons in meaningful ways so we are always getting our students ready for what's next.

4. **Give a preassessment to find out what your readers already know, and what they're ready for next.** (See page 110 for a more detailed explanation.)

You will find an example of a four- to five-week nonfiction unit for eleventh grade in **Resource 8**. It shows the focus lessons and text excerpts to model that thinking, using *Narrative of the Life of Frederick Douglass, an American Slave*.

## How to Make Your Unit Pop and Avoid Potential Pitfalls

You want your unit to engage students and to flow beautifully. Here is a list of resources that teachers have found help them avoid pitfalls and streamline their planning, as well as two brief explanations of strategies to help make your units seamless.

## USE PROFESSIONAL BOOKS THAT OFFER EXCELLENT SUGGESTIONS FOR WHAT TO TEACH NONFICTION READERS

It would be foolish not to rely on the amazing resources out there about how to help our nonfiction readers. These books brim over with smart strategies that will benefit our teen readers, and they will help you plan lessons that make skilled reading moves transparent.

Beers, K., & Probst, R. (2016). *Reading nonfiction: Notice and note stances, signposts, and strategies*. Portsmouth, NH: Heinemann.

Fisher, D., Frey, N., & Anderson, H. L. (2015). *Text-dependent questions, grades 6–12: Pathways to close and critical reading*. Thousand Oaks, CA: Corwin.

Serravallo, J. (2015). *The reading strategies book*. Portsmouth, NH: Heinemann.

Wilhelm, J., & Smith, M. (2017). *Diving deep into nonfiction, grades 6–12*. Thousand Oaks, CA: Corwin.

## USE A PREASSESSMENT TO SAVE TIME AND TO CRAFT UNITS THAT MATCH YOUR STUDENTS' NEEDS

You are doing important thinking about what to teach and how to teach it. Make it all count by starting with what your students need! You can figure out what they need by giving them a preassessment. This isn't graded—it's used to informally assess what they know and what they need to know, and to help you focus your units on those essential focus lessons.

A preassessment usually looks like a very short version of what your unit will be asking of your students, but you ask them to do it cold, without any guidance from you, to suss out what they know and don't know. For example, in this unit, we can give them a personal account in diary form that we feel most of them can read fairly easily. We can give them time to read it and tell us what they notice and think about as they read.

We can ask them to answer these questions:

1. What do you pay attention to as you read this?

2. What do you notice?

3. Write a short summary of this text.

4. What is important to question/think about/pay attention to as you read a nonfiction text?

You'll collect students' writing and look for patterns about what they are able and not able to do. This will help you focus your lessons.

## CREATE RESOURCES TO HELP
## STUDENTS UNDERSTAND THE CLASS TEXT

When you use a fairly short nonfiction text (less than ten pages), you'll be able to essentially read the entire thing with your class. Students are unlikely to feel lost because you'll show them the text, piece by piece, and they'll follow along.

If you have a longer work with chapters, however, you may need to give your class some context before diving into close reading of excerpts. Just as we looked at examples of plot and character charts to familiarize students with a novel, we can do something similar for nonfiction texts. Instead of plot and character, this unit's charts might bullet the main ideas, text features, or the who/what/when/where/why, or simply provide an ongoing list of what students are learning.

## Narrative of the Life of
## Frederick Douglass: An American Slave

**Nonfiction readers read well by thinking about / paying attention to:**

- all information provided in addition to the authors words and asking what we're learning & why this is provided
- the historical & cultural context in which it was written
- traits of characters & relationships, just as we do in fiction
- nuanced evidence in the text, not just explicit information
- how the author develops ideas through structure

A classroom chart detailing what nonfiction readers pay attention to, added to after every close reading lesson using *Narrative of the Life of Frederick Douglass*.

It's helpful if these resources can be posted in the room, as well as in students' Google Classroom folders, so you don't need to spend time each day familiarizing them with the model text. Instead, you jump right into what you're doing as a reader, and what they can do, too.

## Why What You Just Planned Is Important

Think about the last time you did an Internet search for anything, be it what hotel to stay in on vacation, the etymology of a word, a political candidate's position on an issue, or what brand of toothpaste will whiten your teeth. The amount of information at hand is staggering. Never before have we had access to so much knowledge, and it's expanding exponentially all the time.

Then there's the fact that unless our students go on to be English majors, the bulk of their assigned reading in college (and later, in careers) will be in nonfiction. And for right now, in middle and high school, they are steeped in nonfiction in all of their content classes outside of English. You are setting them up to navigate that reading with new confidence and skill.

Our world is saturated in information, and you are empowering them to access it, use it, and perhaps be not just bystanders but creators of such important knowledge and content to share with others.

## CHAPTER FIVE

# WHAT TO PLAN FOR DAY TO DAY

I spent my first year teaching at an English language middle and high school in the Dominican Republic by planning each day's lessons one night before-hand. Here I was, in a Caribbean paradise, but most evenings I would spin my wheels, flashlight in hand (electricity was spotty), trying to figure out what to do the next day. The following year, teaching at a high school in Connecticut, I still relied on nightly mad dashes, pulling lessons together by calling teacher friends and family, sorting through piles of books, and even looking through notebooks from my high school English classes. And this was before Pinterest and TeachersPayTeachers.com could tempt me for hours with lesson ideas.

The beauty of having a plan that consistently relies on us as readers and a book we love is that we don't have to reinvent the wheel each unit or week or day. And, we don't need to Google the latest way to make Shakespeare enticing or find graphic organizers to help our students read *The Odyssey*. Just think of all those hours we can now devote to reading for pleasure, not to mention grading and Netflix. Pinterest can become your go-to resource for kitchen redecorating or personalized basketball shoes, not rubric sleuthing and lesson plan ideas.

# Crafting Daily Lesson Plans

In the last two chapters, we worked through planning fiction and nonfiction units, essentially relying on our thinking as we read a book we love. Congratulations— you have eliminated the need to ever sift through other people's lessons, download attachments of handouts, or earmark countless books for possible ideas that just might work. You've got a system that can be replicated again and again without losing its luster.

The formula that these units rely on doesn't get old because the spark comes from your students—they are discovering new worlds every day in their reading and thinking. It's not your job anymore to provide the enticement. Students get there on their own, blazing individual paths as readers, similar to the way they are creating identities as young adults. Your job is to guide them on that path with a set of daily reading routines.

As a new teacher, I remember feeling as if I had to shake it up. In the staff room, teachers would collectively complain about our students' short attention spans— about the pressure we felt to do cartwheels to keep them from mentally clicking a remote control on us, changing the channel when we got stale. I assumed that keeping things unpredictable and new on a consistent basis would draw in my students.

The problem was that the more I shook it up with group projects, readers' theater, inquiry circles, and Socratic seminars, then rotated back to old-school rows and worksheets when things got chaotic, the more my students and I flailed. They didn't know what to expect, and as a result, many shut down. Students weren't taking risks in their reading, writing, and thinking because their energy was consumed by figuring out how to operate within the class.

There's a reason, I realized, that pro athletes have regimented training routines, toddlers do best when naps and meals function like clockwork, and successful innovators and businesspeople often adhere to highly ritualized schedules.

"Be regular and orderly in your life," Gustave Flaubert said, "so that you may be violent and original in your work." I wanted genuine work happening, not rotating activities that produced a weak blend of chaos and apathy. So, I stuck to routines and told students exactly what to expect on a daily basis. I wrote one agenda on the board that stayed up because only the content and tasks changed, not the template. The result was work: when students were freed up to concentrate on the job at hand—instead of what was coming next, what I expected of them, or how long an activity would last—they performed.

Students shone; I basked. As a result of consistent routines, there was a newly found space for me, too. I focused more clearly on my students, listened to who they were and what they needed, prepared better lessons, and gave them more thoughtful feedback. Sometimes I even had a little energy left over on a Friday afternoon to meet friends for happy hour. Win-win.

Let's take a look at the consistent daily routines and rituals that will help your unit fall into place and allow your students' risk taking, reading, and thinking to come to life.

## Breakdown of the Period or Block

Whether you teach within a forty-five- to sixty-minute period or a longer block schedule, reading instruction should feel about as familiar as brushing your teeth. Here's a breakdown of how the timing can look in either scenario:

| Timing | 45- to 60-minute period, every other day | 90+-minute block |
|---|---|---|
| 10 minutes | All together.<br><br>Teacher-led instruction. You model a strategy that students can use as readers, working with a text excerpt to illustrate your thinking. | All together.<br><br>Teacher-led instruction. You model a strategy that students can use as readers, working with a text excerpt to illustrate your thinking. |
| 25–40 minutes | Independent work, usually.<br><br>Students read books of their choice, trying out the thinking, questioning, and writing about reading that you modeled in their own books. The bulk of this time is spent reading, with a smaller percentage spent documenting their thinking. Students are working hard to become better readers.<br><br>Sometimes students talk about their reading in pairs, in small groups, or as a class.<br><br>You are circulating, talking to students about their reading and thinking. | Independent work, usually.<br><br>Students read books of their choice, trying out the thinking, questioning, and writing about reading that you modeled in their own books. The bulk of this time is spent reading, with a smaller percentage spent documenting their thinking. Students are working hard to become better readers.<br><br>Sometimes students talk about their reading in pairs, in small groups, or as a class.<br><br>You are circulating, talking to students about their reading and thinking. |
| 5 minutes | All together.<br><br>Class ends not when the bell rings, but by taking a few minutes to come back together and reinforce the focus of that day's reading work. | All together.<br><br>Class ends not when the bell rings, but by taking a few minutes to come back together and reinforce the focus of that day's reading work. |
| Writing instruction | Every other day, rotate writing with reading. | In the second half of the block, transition to writing after reading. |

Of course, many of your days may look entirely different, with book clubs, in-depth writing work, student presentations taking over, or maybe even a bunch of excited readers giving book talks! Find routines that work for you and that support your readers' growth and engagement and of course, be flexible.

The critical thing is consistent and substantial time for students to read choice texts and for you to talk to them about their reading. Engaged students are learning. So, while you may adapt this template, the components outlined here will protect the essentials: you model moves of good readers in mentor texts, and students try those in books they want to read.

Let's take a closer look at what happens during each of these chunks of time, the rationales behind the structures, and practical tips to make it all go smoothly, or at least avoid the big potholes in the road.

## Ten Minutes of Focused Teacher-Led Instruction

Remember *Dead Poets Society*, where Mr. Keating, played by Robin Williams, magically inspires his students by lecturing on classical poetry? But we aren't Robin Williams, and our students aren't actors. I remember what happened when I tried this Hollywood version of teaching in an actual classroom. The polite students, the grade grubbers (bless their hearts), and the completely checked-out didn't give me grief when I talked for long stints and read aloud from works they didn't care about. But they weren't learning. Then, there was the bigger, openly hostile group who checked out completely and goofed off, went on their phones, or talked to one another (and not about the text). This shouldn't be a surprise.

The average adult attention span is just five minutes (Fisher, 2013). TED Talks, attended voluntarily by curious professional adults, are capped at eighteen minutes for a similar reason. A study by Microsoft declared the average human attention span to be shorter than that of a goldfish (McSpadden, 2015). Of course, we can teach for as long as we want, and because most students have been taught that listening is their primary job, they will sit there. But it doesn't mean they are learning; they're just passive. So we might as well stop talking.

Apart from our human tendency to have short attention spans, teachers also need to stop talking because the more we talk, the less students read. Remember the research that shows that the more students read, the better they do academically? Unfortunately, it doesn't work to expect that reading to happen outside of class. Lisa Delpit (2012) shares that it is reading *in* class that works to help students become "crucially literate." We need to save time for this important work with us by their side.

Students' worlds are filled to the brim with sexy distractions like video games, iPhones, Instagram, and hanging out, plus commitments like chores, sports practices, piano lessons, and part-time jobs. It's unrealistic to think books can compete with all these distractions before students have well-established reading habits. For most of them, even the go-getters, reading is an "extra" they'll get to when there's time. And there is never time.

We need to use class time to help them with what's hard, which is real reading. The more time we devote to reading, the more our students know we value it, and the easier it will be for them. We all like to do things that feel easy, or that we feel good at. So, reading will beget reading. Spending time reading in class is actually the best way I know to ensure time is spent reading outside of class.

One of the highs of teaching is standing in front of a group of students and knowing they're with us, responding, sometimes laughing, and hanging on our every word. It's such a lovely ego boost, and many of us are tempted to keep that high going by talking more! Resist the urge. That's what I tell myself, anyway, when I notice people's eyes glazing over, even though they were laughing at my goofy joke just moments before. Sometimes I even catch these signs before that point and stop talking. Never once has a group of teachers or students said, "Oh, please, Berit, keep going!"

So, let me stop going on about this and give you practical tips for keeping it short, because it's easier said than done. I should mention, if you believe yourself to be an outlier who doesn't talk that much, ask a friend to record you while you teach. Just a warning—it will be painful. I've done this with many amazing, heartfelt, passionate teachers who were convinced they didn't talk that much. Even with me there, camera in hand, each and every one spoke for the majority of class time. Save yourself the agony of watching yourself go on and on, in addition to seeing that your favorite pants aren't quite as flattering as you thought, and try these tactics instead.

## HOW TO KEEP YOUR TEACHING SHORT AND FOCUSED

### Plan it in advance

Be ready with your text excerpt, what you're going to teach students in a pithy sound bite, and what you'll ask them to do to show you whether they "got it."

Write out any notes or thinking you want to show ahead of time, and have everything ready to go on the document camera or SMART Board. Twenty plus years into teaching, I still never wing it. The more prepared I am, the shorter I teach.

## Warn them

You're not insulted when your dentist engages you in a completely one-sided conversation because you knew your mouth would be occupied; nor are you insulted at church during the sermon when your job is to listen. There are perfectly appropriate times when life is not a conversation, and this is one of them.

Likewise, your students will be okay with not chiming into your lesson when you let them know in advance. Whenever I model a lesson, I tell students right away, "This is my only time on stage. I'm going to talk for the next ten minutes, and if your hand goes up, I'm not going to call on you. You can write down your thought on a sticky note, and I'll read it afterward, or we can talk about it later. But for right now, it's just me." This may sound a little top heavy, but it's necessary to protect what matters most: their reading. Plus, some students call me "the happy lady," so you know I say all this with a friendly smile.

If you don't tell them ahead of time, you're going to feel compelled to call on those raised hands. One student comments that her friend had something just like that happen to him, then another says he's going to Six Flags next week, and another . . . Just cut it off at the pass.

## Time it

I've been teaching for years, and still, ten minutes in my head is usually more like fifteen or even twenty out loud. Now I rely on a watch or the timer on my phone. I tell students right away, "It's 10:20 right now, so I'm going to be done talking by 10:30." This holds me accountable. If I forgot my phone or think I might forget to check my watch, I ask a student to set a timer on his or her phone. Students are pros at politely telling me to stop talking.

## Put it on a bumper sticker

I find the best, most compassionate teachers struggle with keeping it to one thing. They take their job seriously, and they know how much they need to teach in a short amount of time. This happens to top-notch teachers of English language learners, strugglers, students with special needs, and mainstream students, as well as high-powered achievers. We want to pack in a lot to help students get up to grade level and give them a competitive edge. That compassion (or panic) leads us to overload our teaching.

I've learned students are highly unlikely to take away more than one key learning point or concept in a period. Remember, our class is one of seven, eight, or nine blocks in the day when our students have to absorb new ideas from different people and push their personal learning curve. And that's just before 3 p.m. We want to set up our students for success by keeping our goals challenging but tightly concentrated, and resist the urge to cover lots of ground all at once. When I keep the focus of my lesson to just one thing that will help most readers improve, I stand a good chance of teaching that one thing well and having students get it. When I try to squeeze in just one more little point, I risk losing those who most needed help with *any* of the points I taught.

My unscientific litmus test is to try and fit my focus lesson's main point on a mental bumper sticker. When I find myself stretching it out to anything longer than a driver could read from twenty feet away, I know I'm doomed. Here's the bumper sticker I keep in mind: "Today I'm going to teach you how readers . . ." *Period.*

Notice the absence of *and*, *in addition to*, or *while you also*.

I once had a principal who didn't evaluate me by watching me teach. Sounds great, right? Nope. Instead, she randomly pulled a few students into the hallway and asked, "What are you learning today? Why? How are you going to show that you got it?" They needed to answer consistently, too. She put the fear of God in me, and she taught me to remind students what they're learning to do in a sound bite, over and over and over again. And guess what, they still didn't always answer the questions consistently! So, keep your teaching short and sweet, and say the main point like it's on repeat.

> Here's the bumper sticker I keep in mind: "Today I'm going to teach you how readers . . ." Period.

## WHAT TEN MINUTES OF TEACHING LOOKS LIKE

Here's a sample script of what I might say when teaching a focus lesson about character in less than ten minutes. (By the way, five minutes of teacher-led instruction is not half as good as ten; it is probably better!)

*I'm setting my timer for ten minutes, so you know I'll be done talking by 1:30, okay? All right, today I want to pick up where we left off. Yesterday we paid attention to what characters say and wear and do, and how those details provide us with evidence for our theories about characters. I want to keep looking at characters today, too.*

*Today I want to show you how readers can pay attention to ways that characters are complex. In the kinds of books we're all reading, characters are not totally predictable, all one way or another. Sometimes they're brave and they're weak, or they're loving and they're spiteful. Kind of like us, right? I like to think I'm a pretty caring person, but my kids, other drivers on the freeway, and robocallers would probably tell you that's not always the case. We all have multiple traits, good and bad. Let's take a look at* Of Mice and Men *to see how characters are complex. You remember Lennie and George, the main characters who are close friends. I'm going to show you a part of text where I really thought these characters are not just one way or the other. They have qualities that even contradict each other. Characters are complex.*

*Here's a conversation between Lennie and George on page 23.* [This page is displayed on my document camera.] *They just met the boss at the farm where they have a new job as farmhands. George is mad at Lennie for almost "giving it away" that Lennie is mentally disabled by talking to the boss. Lennie feels badly that he forgot not to talk, and now he is looking for some reassurance that George still loves him. Lennie asks George if he was really kicked in the head by a horse. George replies viciously, "Be a damn good thing if you was." Ouch. There's nothing kind or compassionate to that conversation at all, even though we've seen George protect Lennie and take him under his wing. So, even though George is almost parental in his caring for Lennie, he's also cruel. These qualities make him complex. Even though protective and cruel feel like contradictions, these complex qualities are what make characters authentic and real.*

*When we read, we can pay attention to ways that characters are complex. We can note how they have certain qualities at some times, and contradictory qualities at other times. Characters are complex, and that's what makes them feel genuine, because people are complex, too.*

*Today, as you read, keep notes on ways that the characters in your book are complex. Jot down all their qualities and what parts of the text made you think that, and jot down the ways in which your characters are complex.*

*1:29. Time for me to stop talking and for you to start reading!*

Even with an unexpected phone call from the office, a student coming in late, and my fidgeting with the document camera settings, this takes under ten minutes. I still managed to say what I want my students to take away about ten different times—which from experience seems to be about right if I want most of them to remember it: characters are complex. Students pay attention to the whole thing because they know they just have to hold it together for ten minutes. That feels doable, so they hang in there and listen. Then, when it's time for them to read, they know that's coming, too.

## Transitioning Into Reading Time

Keeping our teaching short and sweet might be new for us, but we can get there fairly easily. After all, we're 100 percent in control of what we do. What happens for the next big chunk of the class can be a little tougher. It's dependent on students reading for a long time, and as we've discussed, they might not be good at that yet.

Having all students quietly read for over half an hour might present challenges at first, but that's no reason to avoid diving in. This isn't like getting a vaccine with a long needle, where you'll muck through it with gritted teeth because you know it's good for you. This is more like taking Driver's Ed: it's not a ton of fun at first, it's a little tricky to keep track of all the moves, there's a lot that can go wrong, but then it all clicks and . . . Yahoo! Freedom! Joy behind the wheel! Beautifully focused reading!

I'll explain how to avoid a lot of the potential hiccups. Rest assured that you *will* get to that kind of California coast, convertible-driving experience where everyone is reading. Two of my recent school visits confirmed that it feels like magic when it falls into place. At a middle school on my way to another class, I saw a teacher through the glass window in her door. She waved me in, then put her finger to her lips. In a second, I saw why she was beaming. Twenty-two eighth graders, mostly boys, eighteen of whom had individualized education programs, or IEPs, were quietly reading. All you could hear were pages turning. And this was half an hour into independent reading time! They worked up to this, and now they read every single day. For at least thirty minutes. And they're *all* doing it.

## HOW TO GET STUDENTS TO ACTUALLY READ

Maybe you'll work with a group of students who spent time doing independent reading the year before. When you ask them to find books and read, they probably will do just that. If that's the case, you should go find their last year's teachers and hug them or take them out for dinner. They did a lot of heavy lifting, so now you don't have to. You get to go talk to readers (and skip to the next section).

If, however, your students are used to fake reading a class novel for a marking period, plan to spend time helping them learn to find books they want to read and how to stay focused for long periods. We discussed things you can do to help students find books and build reading stamina in Chapter 2. Those are worth revisiting as much as needed.

Check out the next two pages for some more things you can do to manage a successful transition into reading time.

### Give students breaks.

Give them little breaks as soon as they start to lose focus. When you notice heads coming out of books, pencils being sharpened, or bathroom requests being made, call a break. This doesn't have to be like a cigarette break where everyone chills and nothing happens. Take just a minute or two to share out something great from students' notes, give them another example from the class novel, model your reading or thinking on the document camera, ask a question to help guide their thinking, or, most helpful of all, give them a strategy for staying focused. Jennifer Serravallo's *Reading Strategies Book* (2015) suggests explicit strategies for staying focused in reading. If your students are not yet readers, they'll benefit immensely. After a minute or two of coming out of their books, send them back. Keep up the reading time interspersed with breaks as long as needed.

### Set timed goals.

Students may respond well to a little competition. "My Period 7 class is up to eighteen minutes of quietly reading. Think we can beat that?" Or, just time them for how long they quietly read, and put that number on the board. It might be painful, but put it up and celebrate it even if it's just three minutes! Remember, that's three minutes more than they were doing with SparkNotes. Let them know you'll be adding a couple of minutes every day to the timer, using their baseline time as a starting point. I know bribery is an amateur teaching method, so I would never suggest donuts for the class that gets to twenty minutes first . . .

### Use silent management.

Every time you call out across the room to say, "Devon, your book is upside down. I can tell you're not reading" or "Michaela, please get out your book/put away your phone/stop talking to your friend," you pull everyone out of their reading. If you use your supersonic teaching voice to manage the class, students will see this as time to talk. Treat reading time like time in church or in a snooty spa, and never talk above a whisper. They'll follow your lead.

### Keep a stack of sticky notes in hand.

When someone is off task, write a short message (*Read!*) on a sticky note and put it on the student's desk as a reminder to get back on track. I know one teacher who laminated a bunch of index cards with a drawing of an eyeball and a book on each. She quietly places them on students' desks like a waiter dropping the check at a fancy restaurant. It reminds them: eyes on the page.

## Remove the easy temptations.

Students are so smart. They are pros at avoiding what they're not good at or don't enjoy (usually the same thing) and will sharpen pencils, look through books on the shelves, ask for paper or to go to the bathroom, sneak peeks at their phone, and more. Until reading routines are solidly established, let them know that the only pencil sharpening happens before class starts, and after that it's get a pencil from a designated spot or do without. Or, put the sharpener in a drawer. Same with limiting bathroom breaks. Phones go in the shoe holder at the door. The only time to abandon a book is before class starts.

This teacher knew her students felt like a limb was being lopped off if she kept phones at her desk. Plus, she knows there are purposeful ways to occasionally use phones in class. For these reasons, she put these holders on each desk. Students know screen side faces away during all times other than when she approves their use. Notice she also gave visual reminders on a laminated card to remind them what they're working on as readers.

## Eliminate reading avoidance.

Think of the apps that get us to pay money to keep us off the Internet in order to get our work done. I'll often pick the dead leaves off my houseplants before getting work done, and I don't even like my plants. My goal is to end the useless time I spend checking Facebook, sales at J.Crew, or the long-range weather forecast, and just . . . work. If we struggle to focus, why shouldn't our students? Take a few days to see all the ingenious ways they avoid reading, then shut them down. Eliminate as many ways to avoid reading as you can. One simple solution, for instance, is to provide back up reading material so there's no legitimacy to the excuse: "I forgot my book."

## Help them with what is hard.

As readers, this all feels so easy to us. We know the utter joy of getting totally lost in a good book. My fantasy is someone booking a fancy hotel room for me and . . . no George Clooney, no bubble baths, no filet mignon room service. Just reading. I don't have to check out until I've finished a stack of my favorite books. When you aren't familiar with that feeling of getting lost in a great book, that fantasy feels like a torture chamber. Empathize with students who avoid reading, because they don't know how to do what good readers know how to do. Then show them. Pull groups of readers together who struggle with the same thing, and show them what they can do. I can anticipate right now that the majority of your avoiders need help finding the right books, so start there. Know it might demand many times of helping them before they get good at this, but when you show them you're on their side, they'll get there faster.

## Hold them accountable, too.

Keep a clipboard or iPad handy with a class roster. Let students know that you are keeping track of who is reading and who is not. Don't call out anyone's name or even let students know whom you're monitoring. Just put a symbol next to the names of those who are and aren't reading every few minutes and show them individually at the end of class. (Show them privately, as there's no need to humiliate anyone.) Use this information to figure out who needs help, and also to show your students that this is an easy way to get or lose points in your class. I work with several teachers who used this clipboard technique in September and gave bonus points to anyone reading for a certain amount of time. They also assigned small tasks such as library organization to those who didn't. By October, one teacher told me she didn't even have anything on her clipboard. She'd just have it in her hand, and suddenly everyone's eyes were on books.

## Praise.

Mother Teresa said, "Kind words can be short and easy to speak, but their echoes are truly endless." If you've tried all these things and your students are still driving you bonkers, check how often you've praised them for what they're doing well. Show a little love. Teens can get the short end of the stick with praise. We might assume they don't need it, but I'd argue that teens crave praise, have a harder time trusting it, and respond to it more than any other age group of students. Make it genuine, because they smell BS a mile away, and then say it over and over again. "Love to see you reading." "You've come so far." "I'm so proud of this class." "Seeing you all read makes my heart sing." And, it will be true.

## What Students Are Doing in Addition to Reading: Writing, Thinking, and Questioning

A room full of students reading is a marvelous thing. When you get them there, remember that is a massive accomplishment. Celebrate it, take pictures, call your friends, email me, and get a fancy coffee to toast yourself.

But of course, we need to take it to the next level. Our classrooms are not just for delicious pleasure reading, but for growing our thinking about books and continuously lifting the level of how we read. Reading a lot is one (very big) piece of it.

We need to be careful not to overload the work part of reading at first, because for many of our students, that is all they associate reading with: a chore. But we do need to show them that the joy of reading and then the work of thinking, questioning, and reflecting are not mutually exclusive. And if students are going to think about, question, and reflect on their reading, they'll need to show us by writing and talking about it. What does that writing about reading look like?

Let's take a closer look now at how to set up that writing about reading so it is inviting to readers, doesn't get in the way of their reading a lot, and pushes them to get better and better at reading.

## Teach Readers to Demonstrate Their Thinking About Reading: Modeling

Each day we model something we know how to do as readers, and then we ask our students to try the same thinking using their own books. In order for us and for them to see that transfer, students have to write down their thinking, not just think it!

The more specific we are in what we ask them to do, especially in the beginning, the easier this writing will be for them. When I model noticing the ways that characters are complex by charting the main characters, the qualities I see in them, and the text evidence that supports that, I'm going to ask students to do the same in their reading notebooks that day. Inevitably, students will tweak the way they write to fit their own style, which is fine. But they have a model and a structure to use to the degree they need it.

Here are some examples of the writing and note taking that students do after seeing the teacher model a focused lesson using the class novel.

### SPECIFIC PROMPTS THAT GET TO TRANSFER

As a resource, I've put together a sample set of prompts that you can offer to students to help get to a transfer of skills from a class novel to a choice book. Some teachers ask students to choose a certain variety of prompts per category (theme, symbols, character), and other teachers just ask for a total number of written responses to the prompts per marking period (see **Resource 9**).

## Multiple Conflicts in We Were Liars

The central conflict in We Were Liars is Cadence, struggling to find out what happened during her accident at her family's private island (She hit her head during the accident so she doesn't remember). However, there are multiple underlying conflicts such as Cadence fighting to keep her sanity throughout the haze of medications she has to take since her accident. Also, her picture-perfect family turns out to be not so perfect, as the trust fund money is running out and the way their family interacts is dysfunctional. For example, the aunts fight over the different houses they inherited and are all money-greedy. Also, Cadence who comes from a wealthy family wants to be with Gat, who is Indian and has had to work his way out of poverty, but Gat feels Cadence doesn't understand what it's like to come from a poor family. Cadence tries to keep the relationship going, but the 2 social classes just won't merge.

After seeing the teacher look at multiple conflicts in *Of Mice and Men*, this student looked at a central conflict as well as underlying conflicts in her book, *We Were Liars*.

Remember that as long as you are teaching the skills of strong readers, almost any of it can transfer. One teacher modeled asking essential questions about her own book, which she then went on to answer in her writing. Students generated similar "big idea" questions about their novels and then answered them. The possibilities for how to get your students transferring skills to their own books and showing you that transfer in their writing are endless.

## SENTENCE STARTERS

Sentence starters are a useful method for framing students' writing about reading for the day. These unfinished sentences provide a gentle easing into the writing I'm asking students to do. Here are some examples. You'll see how simple it is to adapt a lesson into the beginning of a sentence that almost guarantees students will try out the thinking we want them to do.

### Lesson on complex characters:

"I'm noticing this character is complex because he has these different qualities . . . as shown in the text by . . ."

### Lesson on inference:

"This isn't said outright in the book, but I can assume the author wants the reader to think . . . because . . ."

### Lesson on theme:

"The main character learns that . . . And, therefore, I think the theme of this book is . . ."

Obviously, you'll want students to elaborate and write more than one sentence, and you'll model that, too. But these sentence frames are ways for all students to enter into the work and get started.

## CHARTS, NOTE-TAKING STRUCTURES, AND OTHER WAYS TO SHOW THINKING

With or without sentence starters, another way to help your students take notes is to model your thinking in a chart or table. Basically, you're creating a graphic organizer while they watch instead of handing one out. Having students draw their own similar organizer has several advantages, but the primary one is that students now see this as way to organize their thinking as a replicable strategy, not something they do only when a handout is distributed. Plus, you don't need to worry about whether there's toner in the copier or how many preps to spend making handouts.

Model as many note-taking frameworks as possible (double-entry notes, bullets, tables, illustrations, Cornell Notes, etc.) so students see a wide variety of structures for organizing their thinking. Our personal preferences may not suit our students', so it's worth it to stretch ourselves out of our own comfort zones when we model writing about reading. For example, I feel like a bit of a fraud doing artistic notes with illustrations to remind me of character detail, but I'll force myself out of my comfort zone (or ask my daughters to help me out) so certain students see that as an option.

Here is an example of a columned set of notes that teachers modeled and students used to document their thinking as they read.

### Memoir, El Deafo chart

| Others who influenced him/her | Challenges s/he faced | How s/he impacted the world around them |
|---|---|---|
| - Batman Batman influenced her because she was a lot like batman - solitary, Batman also had superpowers, and Cece learned she, too had them. Her hearing aids connected to the teachers' microphone would allow her to hear whatever her teacher was doing in the building. - TV TV also influenced her confident side when she saw a deaf kid on TV getting bullied and called "Deafo". Cece took this as a strength, and started calling herself "El Deafo". | - Deaf This is the most obvious one - being deaf. Being deaf causes her to not fit in, and frequently isolates herself for fear people will judge her. Also, some people treat her differently due to her disability which Cece doesn't like. Such as people act condescending towards her, even with her aids on. | She allowed other deafs to not feel insecure and also sent a message to people who have deafs in their community - to not underestimate them, treat them like regular people (Because they are), and to be kind. |

This student charted her thinking about the subject of the memoir *El Deafo* into three columns after seeing the teacher do the same with a biography on Harriet Tubman.

## STICKY NOTES

Most student writing about reading will go in a notebook, a binder, or, increasingly likely, a Google Classroom folder. Ideally, it all goes in one place so you can assess it (more on this in Chapter 7) and so students can see patterns and reading habits across a long stretch of time. But we all know that "real" readers do highly informal and quick jots about their reading, too. We tuck scraps of paper into the pages of our books to mark lines we love, jot notes in the margins, or track lines with our Kindles. It's good to allow your readers similar methods of jotting quick thoughts as they read.

Not every note-taking entry needs to be formalized in pages filled with elaborate thinking. In fact, quick jots that hold your thinking without losing the momentum of reading can be a useful strategy. Decide if you'll invest in bulk-sized packets of sticky notes or ask students to bring them for supplies, because many will love using them to hold their thinking as they read.

There are phenomenal ways readers can organize their notes so they can elaborate on that thinking later on. Here are some great resources to check out to explore some of those methods:

- "The Power and Possibility of a Post-It": https://chartchums.wordpress.com/2011/10/24/the-power-and-possibility-of-a-post-it/

- "Post-It Note Strategies to Improve Understanding": http://712educators.about.com/od/teachingstrategies/tp/6-Post-It-Note-Strategies-to-Improve-Understanding.htm

- "From Post-Its to Theories in the Reader's Notebook": http://onceuponateacher.blogspot.com/2013/09/from-post-its-to-theories-in-readers.html

## MAPPING AND ILLUSTRATIONS

Not all entries need to be paragraphs of writing, either. Visual representations of characters and settings can reflect detailed thinking about reading. I recently saw a student's mapping of the districts in Panem, the setting of *The Hunger Games*. She incorporated an incredible amount of detail, using that map to better understand how characters traveled, the relationships between the districts, and how the Capitol kept control. She spent far more time creating this map based on text evidence than she did creating any other entry.

Allowing students to illustrate entries creates buy-in and reinforces the reading strategy of keeping an image in our head as we read.

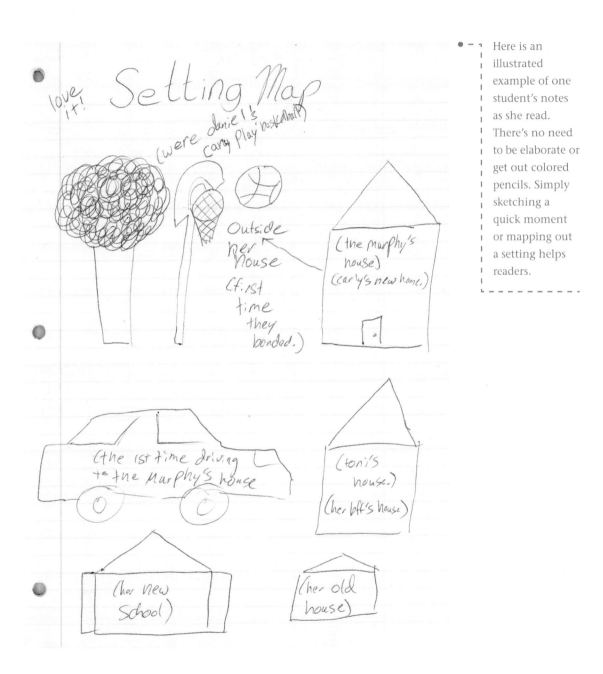

Here is an illustrated example of one student's notes as she read. There's no need to be elaborate or get out colored pencils. Simply sketching a quick moment or mapping out a setting helps readers.

After the teacher mapped her personal reading across a marking period, along with page numbers and connecting themes between her choice reads, a student took that and created her own connections between her choice books, including the total page number to celebrate volume.

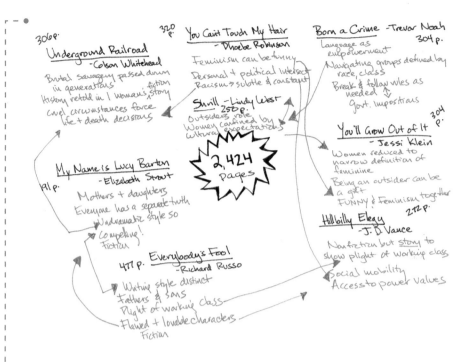

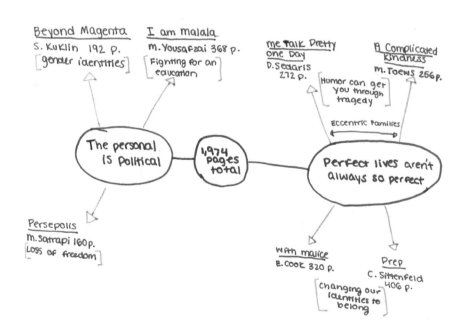

## DIGITAL OPTIONS

Some middle and high schools are one-to-one with Chromebooks or other tablets and laptops. If you're teaching in one of them, consider yourself lucky. There are so many ways students can collect, organize, share, and reflect on their writing about reading when it's all online. Of course, you'll have to navigate how to keep them from YouTube when they're supposed to be reading. (Desks in a *U* facing you so you can always see screens? Loss of laptop privileges if you see their history includes anything other than Google Docs? Screens only open for the last five to ten minutes of reading time?) The upsides of gentle supervision are endless!

Here is an example of a digital notebook entry using Google Classroom as an online organizational and sharing tool:

Shift in Tone 3/22

Just like the tone shifted in the article in class today, the tone shifts in my reading, too. "Non-profit 3-D prints a $100 arm for boy in Sudan" starts off by stating the grim circumstances of trying to create a prosthetic laboratory in a developing country. It then shares a highly emotional example of a young boy who lost both arms in a bombing attack. The details are stark, and the reader is pulled in by the description of a war-torn country and the loss of resources.

The tone shifts in the seventh paragraph, with a sentence that stands all on its own: "Not Impossible's mantra is 'to help one to help many.'" This short declarative statement signals a change from the dire, almost hopeless images of a war-torn country to the idea that innovations can offer miraculous change.

The image attached to the text, that of a prosthetic arm holding hands with a human, reinforces the hopefulness that the article projects in the second half. There is no image of a war-torn country, a limbless boy, or the harsh circumstances of a country without resources. Instead, the reader is left with the sense that innovative technology is the answer to the world's more challenging problems. This shows substantial shifts in tone within a relatively short article.

## HOW MUCH TIME STUDENTS READ
## VERSUS WRITE AND TALK

Students writing a lot about their reading can look great, but it can also serve as yet another smart avoidance technique. When we see them generating pages of notes, it might be a red flag that they're more comfortable writing than reading.

I've heard Jennifer Serravallo suggest to a group of teachers that they aim for about one minute of writing time for every ten minutes of reading. This ensures that the bulk of reading time is spent doing just that. This is another case of not letting students pick the dead leaves off their houseplants, so to speak, instead of read. If writing a lot or too much has become a crutch for any of your students, help them by

- Reminding them of the suggested 1:10 time ratio

- Setting page count goals versus pages-of-notes goals that support it

- Providing sticky notes instead of paper

Just as reading needs to be emphasized over writing, be conscious of how much time students spend talking about books instead of reading them. Chapter 6 will share multiple strategies for getting meaningful talk happening about choice books, but discussion needs to be thoughtfully paced in relation to how much reading students are doing.

If students are reading at high volumes inside and outside of class, then talking about reading can happen frequently, such as the first twenty minutes of reading time every Wednesday and Friday. (More about how this talk time will be highly structured, however, appears in Chapter 6.) But if students are still coming reluctantly to reading, then the biggest payoff will be time in class to read when you're there to help guide them.

Start off with small opportunities for students to talk in assigned partnerships for just a few minutes at the end of reading time a few days a week, then build up to longer blocks of time, say twenty minutes every Friday. Getting rid of fake reading is a process, just as it is to get rid of fake talking about reading. By building up in increments, you'll help students get to meaningful discussion that stays on topic for longer and less scaffolded chunks of time.

## What to Do With Students' Writing
## About Reading: Assessment and Differentiation

These jottings and sticky notes are gems for us as teachers. Reading them is our chance to peek inside students' reading brains to see what they're getting and what they need from us.

I remember reading a student's notes on his book. He summarized the events, pulled out words that were confusing, and had fairly detailed notes, but it was all so . . . flat. There was no picture of what was really going on, and certainly no joy. When I followed up by asking him what he imagined in his head when he read, he admitted he didn't see anything. He saw the words on the page. Naive me assumed all readers had a movie playing the whole time they read a novel. When I realized this student didn't have one playing, I had better ways to help him. His notes helped lead me to this conversation and discovery.

## WHAT TO DO WHILE THEY'RE READING

What you might be tempted to do, for good reason, is read while they read. After all, we are modeling ourselves as readers, right? As nice as it would be to teach by curling up with a good book, that would be a lost opportunity. When our students are quietly focused on their books, there is so much we can do. Talking to them individually or in small groups will move them in profound ways.

This is your time to put additional differentiation into action. You're talking to them one-on-one or working with small groups to ask questions about their reading and find ways to help them grow. Chapter 8 will go into detail about what one-on-one conversations can look like, questions to ask, practical tips to make these conversations productive, and why this is likely to become your favorite part of the day. Here, we'll focus on grouping students to offer needs-based instruction.

Taking a holistic look at what students are and aren't doing, based on their notes, is a go-to assessment in terms of teaching me what readers need. Because of this, I also use students' writing to guide my decision

- To change my next day's whole-class lesson to pinpoint just what students need

- To group students for a focused lesson with others who struggle with the same thing

- To suggest books that will be a better fit

Student writing about reading is powerful evidence of what stuck and what didn't for each student. We can use students' notebook entries and sticky notes, as well as the notes from our conversations with readers, to tell us things like who needs help getting to more reading, who needs help choosing the best evidence to support thinking, and who needs to be acknowledged for taking a risk in reading or thinking.

Use all the information available to you, including what students do with class reading time, bookmarks, note writing, stickies, and what they say about their reading to form needs-based groups. Once you have identified students with a similar need, use class reading time to pull them for a focused lesson to help them master the concept or skill. You can use needs-based groups once or twice a week (or more, if needed) to pull small groups of readers to ensure everyone has an opportunity to succeed.

For example, after Monday's lesson on paying attention to minor characters, let's say you skim through students' writing about minor characters on Google Classroom. You notice a few students struggled to differentiate between main and minor characters. Then another handful of students were succeeding in paying attention to minor characters, but their text evidence didn't back up their thinking. Yet another small group of students were successful at analyzing the role of minor characters in their books. They seem ready to compare similar qualities across different characters, perhaps even in other books they've already read.

A powerful move will be pulling each of those groups for ten to twenty minutes across the next few days while everyone else is reading in class. You'll talk to them about what you noticed in their work and make suggestions for how to take it to the next level. You might quickly model a way to improve with your own short writing about minor characters in the class novel, then reteach your lesson in a new way (your prior lesson didn't work for these students) and have them practice the skill or understanding. This differentiated instruction not only saves you time from repeating a similar concept over and over; it saves your students from falling behind. Left unaddressed, students' lack of understanding will accumulate over time, and for some students, this can translate into an inability to meet grade-level expectations.

Regardless of when or how you address gaps or needs, the notebook responses are an essential way to determine what those needs are.

We'll discuss grading these notes, because I know we all need a grade, in Chapter 7. But for now, consider these notes to be like an extensive (or minimalist, which also tells us a lot!) portfolio of how students' brains work when they read.

Remember, too, you'll often need to manage this reading time by keeping the class focused, providing mental breaks and redirection tips, helping students find a better book choice, and more. This will play a bigger part in the beginning, or if your students have never read their own books in class, and will take up less and less time and energy as you go.

When the management is fairly solid, you can start talking to your students about reading. If you're ready, head to Chapter 8!

## Closing Out the Class

Here's how my class often ended when I first started teaching:

"Briiiiiiing!" The bell would ring, students would be cramming binders and books into their backpacks, and I'd yell out a reminder about the homework.

I know you do better than that, so let me suggest a routine way to close out each class that will feel consistent without being boring. Plus, it will be much more peaceful and productive than the bell.

The last five minutes of class, or of the reading half of your block, is a chance to pull everyone together and reinforce the focus of the lesson, which helps students as readers.

Maybe you

- Reinforce that day's teaching by sharing out an example from someone's notebook on the document camera

- Champion someone's amazing analysis of symbolism that day

- Have students share the best example from their notes that day with their neighbor and why it is a good example

- Have students trade notebooks and circle the most interesting thing their partner wrote

In any case, use this time to cement some important learning, to ensure your students leave with that nugget of reading wisdom. And then, of course, remind them to do their homework.

## Training Ground for Readers

All of this building up to long stretches of reading, in addition to writing and talking about reading, is like training for an athletic event. Just as a practice session for any sports team is primarily spent with the athletes actually doing the sport, so it should be with your students in your classroom. If we want them to get good at reading, they need to read a lot with us there to coach them.

And because I'm not a jock, so I'm overcompensating with sports analogies, I'll compare it to cooking, too. You'd never teach someone how to make a chocolate soufflé or a Bolognese sauce by having him or her do it alone at home, then analyzing it verbally the next day. Trust that this is the way we learn: by doing, by getting guidance and feedback from an expert, and by doing it some more.

Your classroom is becoming a training ground for readers, not to mention a haven in the midst of their often frenetic challenging lives. Protect that time and space for reading, and know that it is going to build communities of readers.

Teachers are tough on themselves. The outside world can be pretty hard on teachers, too. So, occasionally, remember to look around your room of students reading and soak it in. If you have a co-teacher, give him or her a wink or a pat on the back. Then, give one or two to yourself!

## CHAPTER SIX

# BRING TALK INTO YOUR BLENDED READING CLASSROOM

Your classroom is becoming a Zen-like zone for quiet reading. Students are racking up page counts and immersing themselves in a life-changing habit: consistent voluminous reading.

Maybe your blood pressure has dropped, and a yogi demeanor has emerged as you listen to pages turning for long blocks of time. It's a little like babies taking a nap—of course, you adore their gurgly smiles and babbling, but quiet time is bliss. Middle and high schools can be tiring loud places. They're filled with big people with big voices and big energy, and we're nurturing these oases for readers.

But, reading isn't always a hushed solo endeavor. Our classrooms also need to be a home for another aspect of reading—the social conversational one. There's a lot to teach our students about how to talk about books, even if the first step is getting them to read.

When I taught in the Dominican Republic, I worked at a school with all Dominican teachers who had families and lives and commitments to occupy their weekends. For the first couple of months, I was beyond lonely. I used to get my hair done just for a little human contact. On weekends, I'd sneak into a hotel pool with a stack of books. Eventually, two women working in the Peace Corps befriended me and mentioned they'd seen me reading. A lot. One said, "You know, there's such a thing as reading too much," then darted off to join her boyfriend for an evening of merengue dancing. I saw her point, put down the books, and put on my own dancing shoes, so to speak.

Of course, reading too much isn't the issue. We'd all love to work with that problem! But our readers and nonreaders need to know that reading isn't always, and shouldn't be, an isolated act or a way to escape. Books bring people together and establish profound connections. If we never talked about our books, we'd never have the chance to grow our thinking, to hear important new ideas, or to have our own ideas validated and built upon.

## Why We Need to Teach Our Students Ways to Talk About Books

In Donalyn Miller's wonderful book *Reading in the Wild* (2014), she encourages us to teach the habits of "wild" readers in the real world, not just what readers typically do in classrooms, so that our students can go on to be independent lifelong readers. Part of that "wild" reading, she says, is talking about books and sharing our ideas with others. We need to teach this social part of reading so readers know it's an essential component—and so they can do it well.

### IT'S HOW REAL READERS READ

After all, as readers, we know we can't keep our mouths shut about our books! How many times do we say in conversation, "In this book I'm reading . . ." or, when we see a friend, "You've just got to read this book!" And how often do we talk about our books in book clubs or on Goodreads, Twitter, and Facebook? I know there are times, even, when my own children talk *too* much about the books they're reading. I'll be thinking before breakfast, "Please don't give me the twenty-minute 'summary' of why Snape from the *Harry Potter* series is good *and* bad until I've had coffee."

Readers are hardwired to want to share and discuss what they're reading. We want our students to access this habit, and in teaching the habit of talking about books, we also grow the communities in our classrooms.

## TALK DEVELOPS NEW THINKING AND GROWS COMMUNITIES

Books have powerful ways to shape us. We fall in love with characters, see new worlds, empathize with people who are like and unlike us, and get our emotions pulled in a million directions. If we never share that with others, we stay in a flat relationship with the books we read. By opening up the conversation, we feel connected to others, lay paths for community building, and grow layered perspectives about our books.

A former teaching colleague used to tell her students, "You shouldn't leave any discussion with the same thinking you had when entering into it." Talking about books is a way for our students to push their thinking, instead of keeping it stagnant. By incorporating talk into our classrooms and showing our students how to do it well, we teach them to have discussions that truly expand their minds, instead of just showcasing their opinions.

Teens need to know how to truly interact, listen, and share ideas with others, not just through texting. We can use their reading to help grow them as citizens in our classrooms and in the world.

## TALK ABOUT BOOKS EXPANDS OUR BOOK CHOICES

When readers talk about big ideas in their independent books, they're also giving unintentional book commercials for those same texts. Without even being the end goal, these discussions have the fringe benefit of pushing readers' book choices out of their comfort zone. When a friend or classmate keeps mentioning a book, students are hearing it sold to them, over and over.

I've been amazed to see a book run like wildfire through a classroom after a student talks about it in discussion, not even giving it a hard sell. Having firsthand knowledge of a popular book becomes a club others want to enter, and the ticket in is to read the book. One New Jersey high school teacher shared with me, in awe, that she now catches her students talking about books outside of class. She thought it was a prank until it kept happening, and somewhat bittersweet, they never even noticed their teacher eagerly listening in. They were too busy talking about their books. These delicious eavesdropping moments are in your future, too. But it will speed up the process if you do some explicit teaching around why and how to talk about books.

## TALK ABOUT BOOKS GETS STUDENTS READY FOR COLLEGE, LIFE, WORK, AND CITIZENRY

Getting our students ready for college by reading at high volumes is a priority. But after they read those books, students will need to talk about them, too. Even huge, freshmen intro classes have breakout discussion groups. Professors and teaching assistants are paying attention to those who talk, and talking becomes a key way to be part of the class, not a distant bystander.

We want our students to feel empowered to join the discussion in formal and informal academic environments. Imagine them marking up a text and taking it to office hours to talk to their professor, starting a study group with friends, posting about it on online discussion forums, or continuing a conversation with a classmate as they leave class. Teaching our students how to talk, listen, and build on others' comments helps them get ready for the big leagues.

The benefits of teaching our students how to talk about books won't end in class. After sharpening discussion habits in our classrooms, our students will use the same speaking and listening skills in interviews, work meetings, and everyday conversations with friends, family, neighbors, and colleagues. Knowing how to respectfully challenge someone else's thinking, to invite others into a conversation, to build on others' thinking, to listen as opposed to simply waiting for one's turn to talk—these are life skills, not just what we do in English class. We want to instill these talk habits because they are the moves of thoughtful conscientious citizens who know that their ideas aren't the only ones that matter.

## WE CAN'T ASSUME STUDENTS KNOW HOW TO TALK ABOUT BOOKS

The first times I had my high school students work in discussion groups, my classroom looked like a dysfunctional family dinner. Every group had the token alcoholic uncle, the eye-rolling cousin, the hostile cook, and the timid little brother. My students weren't even looking at each other, and still they managed to monopolize, sabotage, provoke, or avoid the conversation. Just as I learned the hard way not to assume they all knew how to read by high school, I couldn't assume they knew how to hold a good discussion.

My choice was to avoid having them talk or to teach them how to do it well. Since even my quiet-loving self needs to hear voices now and then, I taught them. For more on *how*, see the discussion later in this chapter.

## TALK CAPITALIZES ON WHAT STUDENTS CARE ABOUT MOST: EACH OTHER

Just pick up any student's phone to see how much teens talk via texting. Long, seemingly endless and inane conversations—these dialogues are their lifeblood. Disappointing as it may be, even if our students love us as teachers, they love their own voices and care about their friends' opinions more. Why not use that to our advantage? Discussion with their peers, even about books, has a built-in motivation.

## TALK ABOUT BOOKS BUILDS ON BEST PRACTICES

Anytime I look around a classroom and see students engaged rather than passively listening, I know that learning is taking place. Book-based discussion is one of those times I know I'm off the stage, and students are front and center.

Students have to be engaged to learn, and engaging in talk about books is a great learning tool. Brain research tells us that talking helps move information to our long-term memory. Emotional experiences (both positive and negative) enjoy the highest probability of reaching permanent memory storage. It is the amygdala–hippocampus connection that fosters the development of our most memorable moments in life. In the classroom, emotions determine what students pay attention to, which impacts what students will later remember (Wesson, 2012). Why not tap into that easy way to access both engagement and memory?

Class discussion also shows us if what we are teaching and modeling is transferring. I can ask students to put their thumbs up, sideways, or down to show me if they understand a reading concept, and I'm lucky to get any honest feedback. Or, I can have students talk about that concept with others, and hear firsthand if they truly know and understand what it means and how to apply it to their books.

I'll share more ways to see if transfer is happening in the following chapter on assessment, but know that talk provides a great check for understanding. Even the writing students do to get ready to talk, the notes they take during discussion, and the reflections they write after talking will provide you with ample evidence of whether transfer of reading skills happened. Melissa Calamari, an eighth-grade teacher in Morristown, New Jersey, has her students provide substantial written evidence of their discussion about character, themes, and conflict in the class novel and their book group novel. See **Resource 10** for a sample assignment that asks students to take notes for book club discussion and, using those notes, write an analytical essay on their choice books. Talk is a great practice for students' writing about reading, and all of it helps us see what our students are and aren't "getting."

## How to Bring in Talk in Meaningful Ways

Even if we're sold on using talk in our classrooms, it doesn't mean that it's easy to make dynamic deep conversations happen overnight. As adults, we know that our book clubs can consist of messy conversations that quickly go off topic. How many times have I stayed up late to finish the book so I can talk about it the next night at book club, only to show up for a boozy evening of kid and husband gossip, not literary conversation? Not that I suffer too much, of course.

But our students don't need more time to gossip and get off track. They need a place to grow their thinking in focused conversations about books. So, how do we get there?

### STRUCTURE TALK AND LEAVE OUT WIGGLE ROOM

We wouldn't dream of telling our students to just go off and "write an essay." And we shouldn't tell them to go "talk about their books," either. Left to their own devices, a few will talk, a few will listen, and many will check out completely. They need guidelines.

I'm no Martha Stewart, but I know etiquette for fancy dinner parties exists for a reason. Successful hostesses (according to my Emily Post guide) are thoughtful about having couples sit separately, inviting good conversationalists, staying informed on current events, tossing out a slightly controversial topic, keeping the courses moving, and using all kinds of moves to subtly foster conversation among all their guests. Most meetings I attend in school have formal structures, protocols, and norms so no one monopolizes and everyone respectfully listens to one another. If adults benefit from this preparation and strategic planning, we can expect teens to need a little help, too.

### Easy Methods So Every Student Talks and Listens

We can set limits for the quick thinkers and frequent talkers who tend to dominate. We can also set up entry points for the shy hesitant students who get lost in the shuffle. We can give them talking points, model what we're looking for, and give them frameworks so good discussion feels possible, even easy.

The advice listed below appears in order of what to try first so students can get good at discussion in small ways before launching into big class-based conversations. After all, if they aren't using talking time to talk well, they're better off reading.

I. **Assign a prompt and additional talking points at first.** Discussion, to start, may consist of students simply stating their opinion as they go around the circle. "We're done" is a common refrain after about forty-five seconds of "discussion." Posing an open-ended question that readers need to write off of first can help push discussion past a quick whip-around. Try giving the class five to ten minutes to prewrite on a question such as "What was the most important decision a character made in your novel, and why?" or "Consider what writing techniques your author used to catch the reader's interest. Go back into your book and look for examples to share." Giving students time to think and write off a prompt will help everyone prepare to contribute.

Prompts give students something to talk about and focus on for more than a minute or two. Provide a few follow-up questions as additional support for those who need to keep conversation going. For instance, if students were first given the question about the most important decision in their books, you could follow up with "What would be the potential impact if the character had made the opposite decision?" and "Which, of all your groups' examples of the 'most important' decision, was the most pivotal, and why?"

2. **Arrange students in pairs, not groups.** For some reason, we have adopted the image of four desks together as the pinnacle of a student-centered classroom. But why not two desks versus four? Paired conversation produces the benefits of group work while eliminating potential landmines. At least half the group is talking at all times, so you know that at a minimum 50 percent of your class is completely on task. Put them in fours, and it's down to 25 percent.

Give students extra opportunities to practice, plus the safety of an intimate conversation, by structuring paired discussion. When students get good at paired talk, up the numbers in the groups. Keep track of what students are ready for when talking about books, and try not to jump too far ahead to talk that they can't independently manage well. If you notice you've asked students to do more than they're ready for, no big deal. Just backtrack to a place where independent discussion is set up for success.

One way you can set up pairs for success is to assign partnerships. You'll protect students from potentially awkward, even humiliating risks of being left out or more. Some teachers ask students to jot down a few people they'd like to work with and someone they would struggle to work with, and do their best to honor those preferences.

If you've been getting to know your students by talking to them about their books, you'll likely feel comfortable partnering them with someone they can work with. For instance, putting an English language learner who is self-conscious about her verbal skills with another English language learner speaking the same language may be a comfort to both. They can go back and forth between their languages if they choose, allowing them to participate freely. Pairing students will save time and energy and put the focus on moving right into smart discussion, not reinforcing social rankings.

If you do work up to having students pair up on their own, make sure you discuss in advance what that responsibility entails. For instance, if we are teaching our students to be citizens of the world, don't we want them to know to look around them and make sure everyone found a partner? I was asked to find a partner recently in a workshop for adults, and afterward, the workshop leader asked if anyone had looked around to help others, too. Shamefully, we had all congratulated ourselves on simply finding a partner in a group of strangers, rather than looking out for the community at large. If professional adults need this reminder, surely students will, too.

This pair of students can speak comfortably and at length about their books. They're ready to go because they've already formulated some ideas on paper first. All the benefits of group work happen in pairs, but with a greater percentage of time on task. Start here.

**3. Encourage online discussion.** Invite students to take part in informal chats online with their classmates about their reading. It's a good way to use what students are doing already—being online—to your benefit.

Katy Daly, a middle school teacher I work with in Orange, New Jersey, has her students decide on a mutually convenient time to do online "discussion" on a Google Doc. They can share their thinking in the live document, and Katy knows what time to pop in to ensure everyone is "present" and adding to the written dialogue. She can pepper in with comments and questions, guiding the discussion without shaping it more than necessary (or more than her own time allows).

Not only is this similar to the kind of collaborative discussions students will do in college and careers, but it puts teens in charge of the conversation and provides the buy-in of peer interaction after hours. Also, whether you chime in or not, you have an online record of who said what, due to the revision history on Google Docs. Katy can quickly do a spot check of student contributions without any guesswork.

Other teachers ask students to discuss readings using Skype calls or Google Hangouts, and they can again join in to spot-check their discussion. Or, students record their conversation on their phones and send the audio to their teacher. Just knowing that the teacher may listen in is highly effective in keeping the talk on point. I'm suggesting not that you actually listen to them all, just that students know there is the possibility of you doing so!

Getting teens to collaborate in discussion using technology is also a great way to prep for college and career. Many college courses will ask students to "team up" using Google Hangouts, Skype, and other online discussion tools. Many professions, too, conduct meetings through conference calls and require collaborative online planning. Our classrooms should reflect these tools from the "real" world. Plus, having students talk online means you'll save class time for what many teens struggle to find time for: reading. And you'll assign evening work for what they gravitate toward naturally: online chats.

**4. Assign groups.** You don't need to stay up late doing the kind of agonizing charting that engaged couples do for rehearsal dinner seating, trying to finesse each group so there's a talker, a struggler, etc., etc. But, you will be better off not leaving groups to chance. Again, it would be great if teens treated one another with kindness, generosity of spirit, and empathy, even toward those who are not their friends. But that's not always true for everyone, so let's give our students as many advantages as possible.

Even if you simply have them count off as they walk into the room—say by eights if you have thirty-two students—then go to their number table, you'll provide structure and eliminate painful cliques and jockeying for position. The randomness ensures most students will be working outside their immediate friend group. Or, knock yourself out and consider each group carefully, being mindful of dynamics and who broke up with whom and creating safe spaces for every student. That's lovely, too. Then, will you please come teach in my children's schools?

5. **Set clear expectations.** Set them up for success by saying exactly what you want (and don't want) to see. Even though we think teens should know these things, tell them anyway that you're looking for eye contact, physically turning their bodies to face each other, asking questions, nodding and showing that they're listening, avoiding yes-or-no questions or answers, and aiming for an even exchange. Compliment them when you see them doing these things. "I like the way you are asking follow-up questions, Jessica," or "I like the way everyone is getting a chance to speak in this group." Even teenagers like positive attention from the teacher.

6. **Use sentence starters and take time to think first.** The difference between nontalkers and talkers is often having something to say so they won't sound

The writing students do to get ready to talk, the notes they take during discussion, and the reflections they write after talking are ample evidence if they are able to apply concepts and skills to their own books. Talk can be a great check for understanding and transfer.

dumb. *We* know they won't sound dumb, but many students live in fear of exposing their ignorance, and the older they are, the more likely they've ingrained some of that fear. Providing everyone with some thought-provoking sentence starters often lays the path toward participation. These can be very concept-specific, but you can also start with some universally applicable ones. Keep them posted on an anchor chart where students can always see them:

> "I think the author is trying to . . ."
>
> "I notice that . . ."
>
> "I wonder . . ."
>
> "I'm confused when . . ."
>
> "The big idea here might be . . ."
>
> "This reminds me of . . ."
>
> "I'm picturing . . ."
>
> "I'm surprised by . . ."
>
> "I hope that . . ."
>
> "I used to think . . . , but now I think . . ."

When I worked at a high school in the Bronx years ago, there was a lovely young man in eleventh grade who just refused to talk. He faced the triple whammy of being an English language learner, shy, and dyslexic. He had learned years ago to disappear in class. I finally started meeting him in the hallway before a lesson and telling him a question I'd ask, then giving him an index card with the answer on it. And it worked. He began by sticking to the exact words on the card, and built up to occasional comments on his own. If your objective is to get everyone participating, why not give your students as much scaffolding as possible?

Before having students join a partner or group to talk about a concept in their books, give them time to write. You can have them write questions, elaborate off of sentence stems, choose a favorite thought in their notebooks to share, leaf through their books for an example of the concept, and more. This is like letting them make a cheat sheet before talking. This conversation prep ensures they don't just blab the first thing that comes to mind. Taking time to write first gives them a chance to root their thinking in the text and even revise that thinking. Group members can even exchange this written work and write comments to each other before launching into discussion, getting further ready to talk with a short preconversation on paper.

**7. Model it.** After explaining what you're looking for in discussion, show them. Ask a friend to come to your class during her prep, invite the principal, or ask a student to join you. Then, model a top-notch conversation with both people looking at each other, listening, asking questions, talking at length, and staying on one topic instead of bouncing around a ton of ideas that never go beyond surface-level.

While you're modeling, have students take note of what they see you doing. Likewise, you can model a lousy conversation. Channel that disastrous Thanksgiving dinner or awkward first date, and show students what *not* to do while they take notes and share out. Those become your class's guidelines for what discussion does and doesn't look like.

When you spot students in the midst of good discussion, get out your phone and take short videos. Those become powerful visual tools for modeling what you want to see and celebrating your students at the same time. Students are well acquainted with this way of celebrating special moments.

**8. Use talk tokens and time limits.** Harvey "Smokey" Daniels shared a phenomenal and simple tool in a presentation I attended a few years ago: poker chips. This is particularly useful when you graduate past paired talk, although it's a great scaffold when starting paired discussion, too. Every student gets the same number (try four or five) chips to "spend" each time he or she talks. When students' chips are gone, so is their ability to contribute by talking. Daniels jokes that you'd think the frequent talkers would ration themselves, but they don't! I've now tried using chips enough times to know this is true: confident quick thinkers love to talk. And thank goodness—it's what gets the conversation moving. Then, when they're out of chips, there is this space for the others' voices to emerge. And they do.

Placing limits on how often students can talk is helpful, and so is placing limits on how long the group (or pair) talks overall. So often I witness great instructional strategies devolve simply because students were left with too much time to try out the work. Paired talk can happen effectively in incredibly short bursts, such as one minute at the end of reading time, during which they share out their most important noticing from that day's reading.

Of course, you'll want to offer longer times, too, in which students can build off of what their classmates say. But longer can mean five minutes, three days a week, at the end of class; ten minutes, twice a week, in pairs; or two to three times a week, for fifteen minutes, in book clubs. Those might feel like very short segments, but remember, getting our students to read is the primary goal. Every time we prioritize anything other than eyes on the page, we are taking away from what most of our teen students need most: developing the habit and skills of "real," not fake, reading.

Listening to students talk lets us hear firsthand if what we are teaching and modeling is transferring. Plus, they like to do it. Talk builds on what they want to do anyway, so let's focus that talk around books.

## WHAT TO DO WHEN STUDENTS ARE TALKING

Just as you will circulate among readers when they read, you should rotate among them when they talk. At first, you may notice pairs or groups fall silent as you approach. But just stay there, quietly expectant. They'll soon learn you're there to listen in, not direct conversation.

Your role is to listen more than speak. As soon as students know that we will rescue dying conversations, urge them on with a new question, or redirect their talk, they learn they can depend on us to fix their conversations. We want to set them up for success on their own, not just when we're standing there. So, practice listening and then simply walking away for a month or more, if needed. Trust me—it takes an iron will not to chime in. At the end of class, you can frame suggestions to your students as a whole, or just celebrate great things you heard and save the teaching points for the next discussion day's lesson.

Eventually, you can build up to listening in on conversation, acknowledging what's going well, and then offering one quick suggestion for taking it to the next level. But for now, rest assured that having an adult listen rather than fix or talk will both shock and spur them on.

## STUDENT-LED BOOK CLUBS

Structuring ongoing conversations about reading in book clubs is a powerful teaching tool (O'Donnell-Allen, 2006). Usually made up of four to six students, these groups are prearranged by reading level or interest and stay together for at least the unit, if not longer. While it might be tempting to jump right to book clubs, I encourage you to try paired discussion and prompted group discussion with online Google Docs or audio "transcripts" first. These will allow for more structured practice and for you to gauge how they're doing more easily.

When you see students mastering the moves of strong discussion in those formats, then dive in, and keep these things in mind.

1. **Plan ahead for a whole unit based on a book club that meets regularly**, at a minimum twice a week. Let students know when they'll be meeting so they can prepare with notes, questions, ideas, and discussion starters.

2. **Allow for in-class time to talk and time to get ready to talk** by reading and taking notes on their reading. It helps to give specific time frames for time to talk and time to get ready to talk by reading: "A" days might be ten minutes reading, twenty minutes talking, and "B" days the reverse when they are in book clubs. Just don't let go of reading time entirely unless students are reading robustly on their own outside of class.

3. **Avoid roles like "Connector," "Question Maker," and "Recorder."** In strong discussions, all students interchangeably take on all of these roles. We don't want a great question to go unasked just because it wasn't on that student's task card.

4. **Put them in charge.** Ask students to generate the questions and do the prewriting about those questions *before* discussion days. To craft thoughtful open-ended questions, students will need modeling and explicit instructions. Helping students get good at questioning and answering on their own will mean that eventually you will be able to simply facilitate, while your class is leading the way to great discussion.

Here are a couple of examples of what book club members wrote in advance of discussion days on their group's selected text, *Columbine*. The group formulated the questions in advance, and members spent time at home getting ready by answering them on paper first. Their prediscussion writing work shows they took time to go back into the book and find examples from the text, and then they elaborated on their answers to the questions. This is still a starting point, however, as discussion will take this thinking further.

Riya Gavaskar
Sheller PD 4

# COLUMBINE CHAPTERS 14-23

Why is Eric's childhood and upbringing so surprising?

What was the effect of the media covering the aftermath of the shooting?

Does religion play a positive or negative role in the process of healing? Consider Reverend Kirsten vs. Reverend Marxhausen.

"The detectives conducted five hundred interviews in the first seventy-two hours. It was a great boost, but it got chaotic. Battan was worried about witnesses, who were growing more compromised by the hour from what they read and saw on TV." (p. 110)

Due to the constant media attention, the police had trouble collecting evidence for the investigation. This brings up the controversy surrounding the media coverage of disasters. Although news stories about terror attacks and murder are important, the surveillance of false information can impede and even redirect the investigation. The police in this situation are trying to interview students after a period of mourning, but their anecdotes are compromised because of the media. Instead of trying to analyze information themselves, the media should report solely on the facts and work to help officials conducting the investigation.

"The pastor walked through Clement Park and sniffed the air. Satan. The pastor could smell him wafting through the park." (p. 117)

I believe religion played a very important role in the aftermath of the Columbine Massacre. Littleton was always a very religious town, but the citizens of Jefferson County really embraced religion as a method of healing. There were two ways the church pastors dealt with this horrible event. Pastors like Reverend Kirsten preached about Satan attacking the school, while Reverend Marxhausen chose to analyze the situation as it unfolded; two teenagers attacked the school. Reverend Kirsten's method of claiming that Satan is in Littleton makes me feel frustrated that the church puts the blame on a religious demon. I understand that some may find solace in thinking that this was the

*(Continued)*

(Continued)

evil work of Satan, but reality needs to set in, and people need to realize that this was a calculated attack. It's delusional to take shock victims and tell them that Satan attacked the school. The church in this situation should act as a place of clarity and comfort, not preach untrue statements.

"Wednesday morning, Fuselier entered the ghastly crime scene. The hallways were scattered with shell casings, spent pipe bombs, and unexploded ordnance. Bullet holes and broken glass everywhere. The library was soaked in blood; most of the bodies lay under tables. Fuselier had seen carnage, but still, it was awful. The sight that really stunned him was outside, on the sidewalk and the lawn. Danny Rohrbough and Rachel Scott were still out there. No one had even covered them." (p. 108)

This passage really embodies the "after" part of a chapter titled "The Before and After." The author describes the wreckage after—damages to the building, corpses on the ground, and blood everywhere. But the corpses outside that weren't even covered were what kept haunting him in the future. The author does a really good job of painting this image in our minds and effectively makes us uncomfortable.

"Fireworks, he remembered . . . Explosions, thunderclaps, the whole sky on fire. 'I remember running outside with a lot of other kids,' he wrote. 'It felt like an invasion.' Eric savored the idea—heroic opportunities to obliterate alien hordes. His dreams were riddled with gunfire and explosions. Eric relished the anticipation of the detonator engaging. He was always dazzled by fire." (p. 111)

This passage depicts a part of Eric's childhood that is interesting when thought about. Eric wrote about being fascinated but afraid of fireworks, and he would see it as the whole sky on fire as if it were an invasion. He also describes dreaming of shooting up all the aliens. Perhaps this is part of the psyche that built up in Eric.

## Questions:

1. What of Eric and Dylan's past do you think most contributed to their decision to go through with "Judgment Day"?

2. What do you think of Eric's fascination with Nazi Germany and Dylan's Jewish history?

3. Do you feel pity for Dylan's family after seeing them seeking spiritual solace with the pastor? Or, like many in the community, do you feel calling them the "loneliest people on earth" is simply incorrect?

5. **Give students time to set goals and reflect on their progress.** Even if they don't start out with phenomenal discussion, foster growth from where they start. With book clubs, you can't be the only one assessing their work, so involve them early and often with marking that progress.

For example, you might pose the following questions to pairs or groups for the last five minutes of discussion. Students will add their strengths and goals to their Google Classroom folder (or hard-copy notebook) for reference before their next discussion.

*Think about the following areas we have focused on in terms of improving the level of our book club discussions:*

- *Using the text to back up our thinking*

- *Coming prepared with juicy questions and prewriting about our thinking*

- *Having everyone in the group participate at length*

- *Prompting one another to refer to the text by saying, "What in the text made you think that?"*

- *Inviting other group members to join in by saying, "What do you think about what this character is saying?" or "What would you like to say about this topic?"*

- *Staying on one topic for a while instead of jumping around from idea to idea*

*What did your group do well? Think specifically about ways you have grown from the last set of book club discussion. You might jot down a quick success moment.*

*What can your group do better next time? Be specific in your goals. For instance, "We will each refrain from jumping into discussion a second time until everyone has spoken at length at least once" or "We will elaborate further on our prewritings to two paragraphs per question each, so the level of our discussion starts off high."*

## SOCRATIC SEMINARS

If paired talk is a step above calling a best friend to talk about a book, then larger groups with online or teacher-prompt structures are next, student-led book clubs are after that in terms of ramping up sophisticated talk, and the next step up the ladder is Socratic seminars.

Socratic seminars are formal discussions that typically involve the entire class and, ultimately, are designed to be student led. A structured way to help students connect their thinking about books to others' ideas, the discussion model allows students to transfer knowledge to bigger concepts and universal ideas. Fisher, Frey, and Hattie (2016) say the purpose of Socratic seminars is to "understand a text deeply by linking it to other ideas and values" (p. 123).

These are inquiry-based discussions in which a facilitator begins (you to start, then eventually students) with open-ended questions. The facilitator can create these questions and share them with the group in advance, so seminar members have time to mentally mull over their thinking and jot down evidence from the text.

Speaking of text, Socratic seminars *traditionally* revolve around a shared text such as a class novel, but they don't have to and, for our purposes, shouldn't for the most part. My personal experience (and that of many teachers I work with) is that Socratic seminars around a class novel can be an exercise in making vague generalizations based on fake reading. Students know just how to craft a fluff comment off of the blurbs on the back of the book, from a quick skim of the text while others are talking, or by simply building off the comments of the one or two kids who actually read.

Just listen in on a traditional Socratic seminar and wait for the comments like "I agree with so-and-so because [restates the exact comment]" or "This all really represents the theme of good versus evil/the American Dream/overcoming challenges in life . . ." The last thing we want to do is waste class time helping our readers craft mini fake news stories about their reading. We have enough of that online!

Let's look at how to use the structure of Socratic seminars without necessarily falling back on fake reading habits. Students still call on one another as they explore the question or idea posed by the facilitator. They are responsible for keeping the discussion going, building on one another's thoughts, and backing up their thinking with the text—powerful but challenging skills for all of our teens to get to, not just those headed off to college classes. Even more powerful is eliminating fake reading reliance by basing discussion on choice books. This way, we set students up for authentic reading. It will be hard if not impossible to SparkNote their contributions to discussion, and they probably won't want to, either. Being able to talk about books they want to read makes our students feel like an essential piece of the conversation. They will be the only ones who can say what they have to say. They will see how much, indeed, each of their voices matters.

## If They're Not All Reading the Same Book, What Are Students Talking About?

Maybe all of this talk about talk is old news for you. You already do paired, group, and whole-class discussion and have solid ways to structure those groupings so everyone participates and grows his or her thinking. You've got some excellent teaching chops, by the way. Now the big question in your mind is how to do all of this talk if students are no longer reading the same text. You might be worried that this is like plunking down thirty people who speak thirty different languages and hoping they'll magically communicate.

Let's look more closely at how students can take part in discussion when they're not reading the same text—and how this can be an asset, not a hindrance.

### DISCUSSING READING CONCEPTS THAT EXIST IN *ANY* BOOK USING EVIDENCE FROM STUDENTS' INDIVIDUAL BOOKS

Instead of discussing one book and hoping to build to critical thinking concepts, this discussion model relies on concepts evidenced across texts. Students are asked to look at a big idea or question in class and in their texts. For instance, maybe they are all paying attention to minor characters and how those characters move the plot forward. Each group member has taken notes on his or her book's minor characters and done some thinking in advance. When the group discussion begins, one member talks about how there is a subtle line between main and minor characters in her book, *Grasshopper Jungle*, and how seemingly minor characters shift into main characters by the end, essentially taking over the driving plot lines. Another group member comments that his minor characters in *All the Light We Cannot See* didn't drive the plot as much as the central themes, and yet another group member went through every minor character in *An Abundance of Katherines* and saw that the plot simply could not have existed without the key players on the side. Each reader is staying on topic regarding the role of minor characters, but supplying evidence from different books to support those ideas.

The beauty of this kind of discussion is that students are building toward bigger understandings of concepts that cross all literature. They're transferring one idea throughout many complex texts, instead of seeing it as specific to one class novel. This kind of transfer is evidence that they truly understand a concept because they can apply it anew.

> The beauty of this kind of discussion is that students are building toward bigger understandings of concepts that cross all literature. They're transferring one idea throughout many complex texts, instead of seeing it as specific to one class novel.

Even if not every student has mastered how to transfer concepts from the class novel to his or her reading, it's okay. Simply by trying out that work, all on their own, and with the support of the shared effort in their group, students are doing so much more than typically happens during the discussion of a shared text. Those independent attempts are powerful—they help our readers feel in charge of their own learning, and that this is something they can do, all on their own.

Talk about a concept that applies to everyone's books is powerful, too, because applying this concept anew will ramp up the level of discussion. Discussion will be better because students won't be able to participate if they haven't read their books. Each student will be the only resident expert on his or her book, and that unique perspective will matter more than when everyone is speaking of the same text. It also ups the accountability, as it will be harder for discussion members to adapt someone else's point, rephrasing it slightly just to get points for contributing. Discussion members will have to offer an original perspective that connects to their own choice book.

The discussion is also inherently more interesting. Think about when you grade eighty-plus essays on the same novel. It's rare for someone to really surprise you with a comment by the end: you're reading endless versions of the same analysis. When everyone is contributing examples from different books, the thinking about the concept can go deep, but the evidence is fresh.

> When everyone is contributing examples from different books, the thinking about the concept can go deep, but the evidence is fresh.

To that end, students are also hearing about new books and getting plot references, character explanations, and more guidance to help them if they choose one of their classmates' books. It's kind of like when we read an excellent review of a book prior to the book itself: it orients us, giving us some heads-up and opinions we might seek to affirm or disagree with, but it doesn't make reading the book less engaging.

If this still feels nebulous, let's take a look at some sample questions that would frame the discussion. These are adapted from Glenn Powers, who runs roundtable discussions every week with his students as they discuss sophisticated concepts, using their independent books as evidence. Each question has the potential to sustain an entire conversation.

Here is an example of how this looks in Glenn's classroom:

After a focused lesson on the characteristics of genre, Glenn has his students do two paragraphs of writing on the concept. They use their current book to supply evidence in one paragraph and examples from their previous reading for an additional paragraph.

But first, he provides a model of this kind of writing on his own book, focusing on the characteristics of genre, so that students know what kind of writing they will need to do in turn:

> The genre of *Moribito* by Nahoko Uehashi is a martial arts–centered fantasy because of the combination of kung fu–based battles combined with magical powers and monsters. For example, in Chapter 6, there is a large battle that includes detailed descriptions of kicking, hitting, and weapons that I know are used in martial arts. The weapons include shurikens, spears, and short swords with decorated tassels. The descriptions and weapons show how Uehashi wanted to set the novel within a kung fu setting because all of these items and described moves remind me of kung fu fantasies like *Crouching Tiger, Hidden Dragon.*
>
> Another example that shows more of the fantasy side is how the lead character has to fight an egg-eating monster, Rarunga, and engage magical water, forest, and earth fairies. The egg-eating monster follows them throughout their journey to deliver a magical egg to a water spirit. This shows all of the traditional elements in fairy tales and fantasy. Rarunga is not a Western monster, like a dragon, but follows a Chinese traditional mythical monster.
>
> The elemental fairies in *Moribito* are similar to the nymphs in Greek mythology that show up in Rick Riordan's series, Michael Scott's books, and Brandon Mull's *Fablehaven.* All of those books are fantasy, and I think because of that Uehashi's book is, too. This shows me that different cultures may have different ways of expressing a fantasy using monsters, myths, and magic that come from that tradition. So a fantasy in Uehashi's culture, filled with Chinese ideals of heroic acts and monster myths, may look different than one from Rick Riordan who draws from more Western Greek myths.

Then, students bring in this kind of prewriting on their own books so they are ready to talk and share examples in discussion. No more off-the-cuff comments or discussion dominated by one confident quick thinker. Everyone has something thoughtful to contribute.

## Questions for Roundtable Discussions

1. How do you know the genre of a book? What are the defining features of each genre?

2. How have writing styles and author's craft changed from the kinds of books you're reading as a [tenth] grader versus those you read in middle school?

3. What do authors do to create effective lead characters?

4. Do lead characters need to be admirable? Why or why not?

5. Who is the antagonist in your book? How does the author use this character to challenge the main character? What impact does the antagonist have in creating change in the main character?

6. How does an author draw you into a book? What types of leads are there? What does an author do to write an effective lead? What are the types of leads for the various genres?

7. What was the moment of truth in your book? What happened? What types of moments of truth are there, and how does the genre affect it?

8. How does an author build up to the moment of truth?

9. What is the problem of your book? What makes a problem compelling?

10. Why does an author use a particular narrative point of view?

11. How do authors write effective endings? What makes an ending of a book satisfying?

12. How does genre affect a problem? How are problems created by authors? How are problems resolved?

13. How does an author balance dialogue, description, and reflection in the book?

14. How have you changed as a reader?

15. How does the author move the story along? What was the shape of your books' plots?

16. How do you know a book is good before you read it? How do you choose books to read?

17. Which is most effective: first-person narrators or third-person narrators? Why?

18. How has a book affected you emotionally? What books, characters, or plots do you have a hard time forgetting? Why?

*Source*: Glenn Powers, personal communication, September 11, 2016.

Here is a summary of a discussion in Glenn's class after a lesson that asked readers to consider *the difference between a character's goal and his or her problem:*

- One student references *The Secret Hum of a Daisy* to show that the main character's mother dies and she has to live with her grandmother. That is the problem. The goal, however, is that she has to solve a treasure hunt her mother left behind.

- Another student adds on to this to say that characters are often pulled into problems—their goal might be living a normal life, but they are pulled into the problem.

- A student adds on that in her book, *Cress* by Marissa Meyer, the problem is different from the main character's goal. The problem is that Queen Levana will marry someone to give her power, but the goal is to have freedom.

- Another student says the problem and the goal are always different, and the goal is often created by the problem. For instance, the problem in *The Hunger Games* is the games themselves, and therefore the goal is survival.

- The group continues to make distinctions and connections between characters' goals and problems in their books, using *One for the Murphys*, *Lucky Strike*, *The Truth About Forever*, *The Meaning of Life*, and more to supply evidence for their theories.

**Assessment/Reflection:** Glenn has students give feedback to one another using a score sheet like the one on the following page. He also uses this to assess students, along with the prewriting that they generated before discussion.

These kinds of discussions, using evidence from individual books to support a common question or concept, are as sophisticated as any I participated in during college English. And the beauty is every reader comes to the table as an expert in his or her book, with something only he or she can offer.

## Time for Shared Texts, Too

Most English teachers I know love a rich class discussion. It feels dynamic, sophisticated, and close to their favorite memories of college English when the class discussed a shared text. There can still be (occasional) room for that in our classrooms, not only because teachers and students enjoy it from time to

## Round Table Discussion Score Sheet

### Discussion rules:

1. Think before you speak.

2. Refer to the text.
   Provide *evidence* for your ideas.

3. Refer to previous question/comment.

4. You may disagree;
   you may not disrespect

5. Everyone has a voice.
   Monitor how much you speak.

Name: _____   Date: _____

Topic: _____   Reading: _____

| Name: | Positive | | | | | Negative |
|---|---|---|---|---|---|---|
| | Speaks thoughtfully | Refers to previous comment | Refers to the text | Asks a question | Makes a thoughtful connection | Interrupts, gets off topic, behaves distractingly |
| | | | | | | |
| | | | | | | |
| | | | | | | |
| | | | | | | |
| | | | | | | |
| | | | | | | |
| | | | | | | |
| | | | | | | |
| | | | | | | |
| | | | | | | |

Notes from the Roundtable:

Warm feedback:

Cool feedback:

time, but because it is still a structure in some college English classes. I should mention, however, that, anecdotally speaking, many college students I talk to say this is much less a standard practice than it was years ago. And, so few of our students will become college English majors that this shouldn't be a driving factor.

Remember, whole-class discussion around one book is in our comfort zone because we were taught that way, not necessarily because it's what works for the greatest number of our students. In fact, when and if you do try it, you may notice that instead of stimulating discussion, only a few students may be talking, and you may be tasked with a lot of prodding, prompting, and heavy lifting.

There *is* something admittedly satisfying in knowing everyone else knows the book you are talking about. If you choose to incorporate discussion around common texts, you can still validate students' independent reading style with a short reflection, written or verbal, on how the concept extends to their independent reading. Again, go for the highest level of learning and see the transfer. Asking them to apply these ideas and skills to all the books they read is too powerful to skip, even then!

And remember, discussion around a shared text doesn't have to happen as a whole class. By putting students in pairs or groups of four, we raise the chances that more voices will be heard.

As for how often you should structure discussion around the class novel, I suggest giving it an occasional role, such as no more than once a marking period, and even then, only for Grades 11 and 12 when students need to get ready to discuss shared texts in college. Using this any more than as an occasional chance to close out the class novel will make it tempting to fall back into old patterns of discussion in which few have a voice. No matter how vibrant and thoughtful these discussions are, they still involve students listening for the bulk of class as opposed to talking or reading. High engagement is simply more likely in smaller groups.

When you occasionally opt for the traditional Socratic seminar around a shared text, frame questions so that readers will be thinking about concepts that apply to almost any book in the genre. For instance, you might pose the following questions specific to *The Scarlet Letter*, but relevant to any novel:

- Considering the narrator of our stories is important. What role does the narrator play in this book? How does his telling of the story affect our sympathy for the other characters, such as Hester, Dimmesdale, or even Chillingworth? Feel free to use examples from the narrator in your own book to expand on your thinking about a narrator's impact.

- We've spent a lot of time considering repeated images and symbols in our books. How does Hawthorne use repeated images to represent bigger ideas in *The Scarlet Letter*? What is the significance of those images? How does an author's use of symbols strengthen (or weaken) a book? Refer to your choice reading as well if you choose.

Having the opportunity to look at the class text as a group may provide a closing to the unit and an opportunity to solidify a place for that "classic" in your students' memories. It may end up as a rare addition to your class routines, however, as rich discussion emerges more and more around choice texts in paired, small, and whole-class groups. The power of these discussions, when there's little chance of fake reading, may make going back to the old model feel less and less important.

## How Often We Incorporate Talk Into Reading Time

Until reading habits are well established, keep talk minimal and in pairs. You'll save yourself a lot of management headaches if you get independent reading in place first. Prioritize getting students' heads into books, and then consider what routines you'll establish for talk.

Will you do paired or group discussion every Friday? Every other week? The first fifteen minutes of independent reading time every other day? I stress routine because again, when students know it's coming, they tend to do much better. They mentally prepare and come in with things to say.

Just as you built up to longer periods of focused reading, monitor how long they're actually staying on topic in discussion. It's almost always less time than I expect or think they're actually doing. By middle and high school, they might look very engaged after fifteen minutes of group discussion, but the actual content of their conversations is no longer about their reading. In fact, sometimes a lot of high-volume engaged talk is a clue students are focused on anything *but* the book. You be the judge, and if they are struggling to sustain the conversation, do one of the following:

1. Move right back into independent reading, and take note of how long they stayed on task so you know to help them do a bit more next time.

2. Pull their focus, briefly, back to you for a reminder of how to stay on topic or ask questions, or share something great that one group did. This reminds them that you're paying attention as well as gives them a new focus for pushing the reset button on their talk. Or, give them a new task or question to consider.

3. Send them back to their books, briefly, to find more evidence. Or, send them to their notebooks to write again before moving back into discussion or to exchange written notes instead of verbal ones. A beautiful example of how to help students do prewriting before out-loud discussion is "Write Arounds" (Daniels & Daniels, 2013).

4. Have them write a quick reflection on how they got off task and what they might try next time to avoid it.

While it takes some practice, so does anything worth doing. Through consistent opportunities to talk, students will get better and better at keeping comments rooted in the text, staying on one topic for a sustained time, and opening their minds to new perspectives.

## Why Talk Boosts Our Teaching

Just like looking out over a room of students quietly reading will move you and make you want to flag someone down in the hallway to say, "Come! Look at what's happening!" so will a room filled with students talking with gusto about those books.

You will be a bystander to dynamic conversations and a guide to move that talk onward and upward, instead of the one doing the talking and urging them to participate. This is going to buoy you as a teacher and leave you with energy in the reserve tanks. Even with the necessary dinner-planning prep to facilitate these dynamic discussions, you'll be energized by putting students in charge of their own learning and talk, using their own books to explore big ideas.

Using talk will also provide you with immediate feedback on how well they're understanding what you taught and modeled. No huge stack of essays—it's right there (or not) coming out of their mouths. Having that instant knowledge of how well they are grasping these reading skills will allow you to make smart decisions about what to teach, right then, to lift their reading to the next level.

## CREATING A COMMUNITY

Every middle and high school I work in now has to confront reprehensible behavior done via texting, Instagram, Snapchat, and so on. The worst bullying, ostracism, racism, and sexism is done not face-to-face, typically, but through social media. When we help our students speak to one another in considerate ways, listening and building off of one another's thoughts, we nurture one of the most important skills they need to learn: how to communicate face-to-face.

> When we help our students to speak to one another in considerate ways, we nurture one of the most important skills they need to learn: how to communicate face-to-face.

Real people emerge and surprise us; crude assumptions and stereotypes fall away. New voices will be heard.

I've seen two seventh-grade boys, one a shy student the size of a ten-year-old with learning disabilities and the other a confident strapping star of the soccer team, form a connection over the *Warriors* series in a paired discussion. I don't know how they treat each other in the hallways, but in class, the shy guy visibly lit up during animated passionate discussions about reading. The soccer star listened, high-fived his partner, and started reading his partner's books.

I've seen a group of high school girls start their own book club outside of school after a core group of them was assigned to talk together in class. They latched onto this identity as readers and decided to let their book nerd flag fly high, posting notices around the school to welcome others in, too.

I've seen books traded, conversations continue into the hallways, and passionate talks about reading go on in sustained meaningful ways, long after I suspected students had moved to gossip or sports chat. I've seen puffed-up readers, proud to be the resident expert on their book. No one else has the answer but them, and they take that responsibility seriously. All these things feel like a little mark in the plus column for boosting teens' sense of self, in a world that often erodes just that.

Every teen needs a community, or two, or more. They will find their tribe in some way, and if teachers provide a place where some of those connections emerge around books instead of what they wear or what they post, we expand their communities in hopeful ways. By talking, sharing, and listening, we're also upping the chances that our students might sit next to someone at lunch, wave hi in the hallways, and simply see one another as real people with thoughts and emotions worth protecting.

## CHAPTER SEVEN

# ASSESSING READERS

## Grading That's Useful and User-Friendly

What would I do before sitting down to grade? Floss, reorganize my Tupperware drawer, clean out my freezer, scoop the cat litter . . . Maybe there's a teacher out there who enjoys grading, but I don't think I've met one.

Yet we must grade. It's part of our job, parents want to know, there's a grade book to fill, and students are asking us "what they got." There are even more hopeful rationales: that grading can celebrate our students, mark progress, help them set goals, and let them know areas to shore up. I'm afraid our current grading system isn't set up to celebrate growth as much as highlight deficits, but it's what we have to work with, so we do what we can.

Let's look at ways to grade what you've been teaching readers to do, which is reading, as well as writing and talking about reading. We'll go through tried-and-true ways of giving readers meaningful feedback and of producing needed numbers for the grade book. None of these methods will drive you to clean out the freezer in avoidance, either.

## Formative Ongoing Assessments
## That Won't Make You Hate Your Job

We want reading to feel like a warm welcome to our students. We risk sabotaging that invitation to read if we also ask students to do a ton of work around reading. After all, would you send out invites to a party and in fine print explain that your guests are responsible for cleaning up afterward? We spoil all the joy of reading if we ask students to do lots of work surrounding the reading itself, proving that they have read.

We'll get to the big assignments you might do from time to time, but the bulk of your grades should assess what we want students to do the most: read.

You don't need to assign copious outside projects about reading. The following are things you can grade frequently (thereby lowering the stakes), without much fuss, and still put the act of opening and reading a book at center stage.

### VOLUME OF READING

The single most important thing students need to do to read well is to read a lot. If we want to hold them accountable for anything, then, it should be for how much they're reading. We probably tried to do this when teaching the class novel by giving chapter quizzes and the like, but those are easy to fake and serve as more of a "gotcha" than a way to empower readers. Those quizzes also started about the same time our suspicions were sparked that they weren't reading: in others words, too late.

Now we'll tell students from the get-go that we'll all be assessing how much they read (they will be assessors, too) because it's an ongoing goal to read a lot, to read more and more, and to read increasingly varied and challenging books. Building up reading stamina is the essential piece to the puzzle in helping our students be better readers. It's what will help them successfully navigate the demands of college and carve a path to a lifetime habit of reading. The data, then, around how much they're reading are worth tracking and counting as a grade.

Tracking and assessing for volume is also a beautiful equalizer. It is a demanding requirement, but it allows everyone—from the English language learner reading graphic novels, to the high flyer immersed in the classics, to the sports fanatic devouring athletes' biographies—entry on the path to success. Readers are inherently differentiating goals based on where they're at, not on a uniform benchmark, because their texts are right for them and their corresponding volume goals will be manageable.

So, how do we assess reading volume? Let me save you some grief by telling you what many others have tried, adapted, and settled on as systems that work.

## Penny Kittle's Reading Rate

Penny Kittle has a beautifully simple but effective system whereby students calculate their reading rate in a book they've chosen, then use that number to establish how many pages or books they will read in a marking period. This rate serves as the data for both reader and teacher. Again, it is at once beautifully simple and incredibly effective. It allows students to personalize reading goals starting from where they're at, giving all a chance to feel successful. It also gives them the freedom to try longer and more challenging books because they can slow down with harder texts.

Essentially, readers set a goal based on their reading rate for every new text they choose. Once students know how fast they read, they use it to establish a concrete reading goal for volume. Here is the formula for calculating a reading rate:

1. Read your book for ten minutes

2. Write down the number of pages read at the end of ten minutes

3. Multiply that number by twelve to see how many pages you will theoretically read in two hours

4. Multiply that number (what you should read every week) by the number of weeks in your semester to see approximately how many books you will read if most books are about two hundred pages

5. Do this with each new book so you aren't discouraged from taking on longer books or books that take more time to read, such as dense nonfiction

The two-hour page number becomes students' reading goal for the week. The number of books is their marking period or semester goal.

Kittle's book about getting her high school students (all of them!) to become readers, called *Book Love* (2013), should be required reading for us all. It is one of my most dog-eared, margin-filled, sticky-note-decorated books because she truly walks the walk of a teacher who transforms students into book-loving readers.

She also has a wonderful system for pushing students to read increasingly complex texts, called reading ladders, which is worth checking out. The goal there is to push not only volume but also challenging books, still chosen by the reader. Ladders and reading rates are phenomenal tools for putting our students in charge of growing their reading skills and lives.

## Reading Bookmarks, or Personalized Reading Calendars

We introduced bookmarks in Chapter 2, but let's look more closely at how this system works.

Some teachers found that readers were short-changing their book choices by intentionally choosing short books they could easily finish in a few nights. So, teachers changed the completed book requirement to *page numbers* students had to complete every two weeks. This still allowed for differentiation in that struggling readers could get to the page count but in easier books. For example, 250 pages of *Harry Potter* is different from 250 pages of *Unbroken*, though both are engaging quality texts.

This takes a small effort to set up, and it is beautifully simple in its execution. Every reader is expected to finish a book, or a certain number of pages approximately equivalent to a book (say, 200 to 250 pages), every two weeks. Every second Monday, students start a new book or continue on with their longer one, with a new bookmark, and lay out their reading calendar for the next two weeks.

There's yet another way to use the bookmark. Have students negotiate their own volume goals entirely. Encourage them to go for volume but to set a deadline that works for them. Some readers might give themselves a month to finish a particularly challenging book, while others might plan for six weeks as their dyslexia prevents them from churning through titles. Still other readers might give themselves just a few nights to finish a reread or an "easy" read.

Just add multiple rows to the bookmark and tell students to pick an end date they think they can meet, then have them create nightly reading goals to get to that self-appointed timeline. If we want to empower our readers with independent, lifelong reading habits, this is a great way to start.

A blank template is available for your use in **Resource 4**.

Remember that the expectation for volume can gradually increase. Grade levels might gradually increase the page numbers that equal a book, or they might decrease the amount of time to finish a book. Remember, if students go to college, they will be asked to read hundreds of pages a week, so by twelfth grade, they should be trying out that volume with you. Similarly, life and work will be richer and more productive for all our students, college bound or not, if they have well-developed reading habits. Literacy is empowerment. We want all our students, especially those headed straight to work lives, to share in the benefits of lifelong reading.

The two-week requirement to finish a book might be appropriate for lower grades in middle school, and then the expectation can move to eight nights of reading to complete a book, then to five. Page numbers can go up, too, by grade and also be differentiated for various readers. Use the bookmark as a template and put your own stamp on it to make it work for you.

How to give it a grade? Students' reading bookmark goes on their desk as they read. You can easily spot-check to see if their book is open to a page within their suggested reading calendar. They're marking *Y* or *N* if they did or did not read. The number of pages for every reader will be different—students are reading at their own pace in books of their choice—so whether they meet the reading calendar set in their bookmarks is a demonstration of whether they're meeting their personalized goals. If they complete their reading calendars on time, they get full credit. It's an easy grade to calculate, and you're assessing what counts.

> ### Side Note: Bookmarks
>
> You may be worrying about fake reading with the bookmark. What savvy teen won't just put Ys all the way down and hand in a bunch of counterfeit bookmarks? This hasn't been an issue in the many, many classes that have tried this system. It's hard to fake when students are opening their books right there in class every day. You'll see them actually reading or not. This is a much harder system to game than SparkNoting the class novel. Most students resist faking it pretty quickly. They're too busy reading.

## Book Checks

That said, fake reading is what we're seeking to avoid, so by all means work to eliminate it entirely. If you worry, as many teachers do, that your students will game the system and fake choice reads, too, you'll be reluctant to fully commit. Admittedly, we'd probably all speed more often if we didn't worry a police car with a radar gun was around the corner. It's okay to instill accountability for your readers, too.

Many teachers I work with have adapted a tip I heard from Kelly Gallagher in a presentation at the 2016 National Conference of Teachers of English conference in Atlanta. He said that in a test on an occasional whole-class read such as *Romeo and Juliet*, he'll pull a random passage and ask students to explain it as a way to check whether they actually read or not. I also heard a high school teacher share how he does this for his readers using choice books. Then teachers and

I created a rubric for grading similar spot checks. No more wondering if students really read or not!

A form you can use to spot-check if students are really reading their choice books appears in **Resource 11**. Essentially, you sit with the reader during class time. This can be announced or not—it won't matter because the only way students can "cheat" or prepare is to read! You hold the student's book, read a paragraph or so from a random page, and ask the student to explain the relevance and context of that passage.

If the student is unable to explain the passage, you can reschedule his or her assessment. On the reschedule date, you will pull a different passage and ask the student again to explain. This gives students an opportunity to save face, go home and read, or simply redo the exercise if the passage you pulled was legitimately hard to place.

## Side Note: Reading Logs

Many teachers have a bad taste in their mouths with reading logs, and students have similarly sour experiences. You can find endless examples of reading logs on Pinterest, and many require lots of inputting of information: title, author, page numbers, minutes, signatures, strategies used, and more. What I love about the reading bookmark is that it requires a simple Y or N. That's it. Similarly, Kittle's reading rate puts the reader in charge of getting to volume.

## Goal Setting and Reflections

We are not the only ones in charge of assessing student growth as readers: they are monitoring their progress, too. One of the best ways to facilitate this is to have them set reading goals and reflect on how well they are meeting those goals. Goals should include not just volume and stamina but also book choices and reading habits. An example of a student's reading goals appears in **Resource 3**.

If students are not meeting their volume goals, address that area first. I've had countless conversations with readers about what's getting in the way of them reading regularly and what they can do to get over that hump. Sometimes it's as simple as setting a regular time each afternoon and doing it first thing, not last; sometimes it takes some real finessing of schedules; and sometimes it's right back to the bookshelves to help them find a book they want to finish. Helping your students set and meet goals is putting them in the driver's seat of a reading life.

How you assess their personalized reading goals will be up to you, but know that holding them accountable will move each and every one of your readers. Model it with your own goals to help you see what's realistic and better understand the process. Then, ask students to document how they've met, approached, or neglected their goals. This can be in the form of a reflection at the end of each marking period. Students might collect bookmarks, calculate pages read, share screenshots of Goodreads posts, create a podcast, send a link to self-created book buzzes, or simply write about what they accomplished and where they're going next. This allows you to give credit to the "nonreader" who discovered and read three books in a series, in addition to the already voracious reader who challenged him- or herself to reading multiple books by international authors and creating buzzes about them. If we are nurturing readers, meeting these kinds of goals deserves credit and a notch in the grade book.

Logs can feel tedious, a lesson in forging signatures, if required. If you do use logs, and certainly many teachers do so successfully, I suggest keeping them as simple as possible. Logs can serve as useful data, but not if they're faked. Like any of the assessment tools noted here, honesty is essential. Otherwise we're grading who is best at manipulation or downright deception—not what we need more of in this world.

## NOTEBOOKS

If the most important thing students are doing is reading, then the second most important thing is noticing and thinking as they read. The best place to see evidence of that thinking is their notebooks.

### Reading Notebook Rubrics

The standard protocol for assessing notebooks is a rubric that outlines clear expectations from the start and that students can use to self-assess, too. Again, there are countless examples on Pinterest, but here are some guidelines for making a rubric an effective tool and guide for helping students grow skills in thinking and writing about reading, not a discouragement for them or a time-suck for us. Sample notebook rubrics are provided in **Resources 12–14** for your reference.

> **Side Note: Book Buzzes and Book Talks**
>
> Grading book buzzes (or commercials, or talks) defeats the very purpose of getting readers interested in reading books. I can attest to this after seeing a student stand at a podium, note cards in hand, talking for seven deadly minutes about characterization and plot sequence about a book his fellow classmates might have actually enjoyed had they not been falling asleep trying to listen. If you must grade students who have done a book buzz, either they do it or not, but there's no incentive to make it long or detailed or, basically, boring.

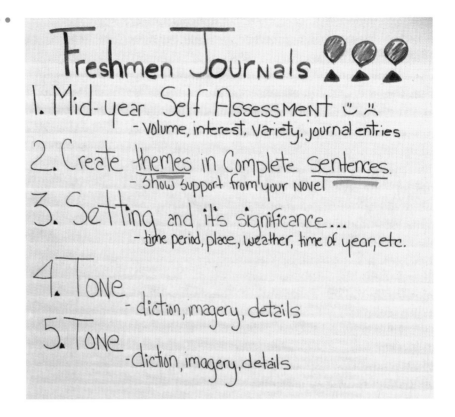

Freshmen Journals

1. Mid-year Self Assessment
   - Volume, interest, variety, journal entries
2. Create themes in Complete Sentences.
   - Show support from your novel
3. Setting and it's significance...
   - time period, place, weather, time of year, etc.
4. Tone
   - diction, imagery, details
5. Tone
   - diction, imagery, details

**Share the rubric right away.** Show students exactly how they'll be assessed, and remind them frequently so they're not caught off guard. Every once in a while, show how your own models for note taking and reflections in your notebook would stack up against the rubric so they see what it means to do well. Have them self-assess frequently, too, so this is not a "gotcha" but a way for both of you to track progress.

**Keep it simple.** The best rubrics in terms of clarity and sanity for grading are very simple—not a lot of columns or rows, and not a lot specified in the boxes. Assess only what you've explicitly taught, and only what really matters. This makes the rubrics user-friendly for both you and your students, and helps you pick your battles for what you care about most.

Rubrics can be unit specific, depending on what reading skills and concepts you've emphasized, or assess in more general terms. Here is a sample rubric that students used to self-assess; afterward, the teachers used it as well.

## Reader's Notebook Rubric

| Notebook Quality | Yes (2) | Sometimes (1) | No (0) |
|---|---|---|---|
| Every entry lists the title of the focus lesson, date, and page number. One entry is recorded for every day of class. | | | |
| Entries show practice and understanding of the strategies, applied to the reader's own book(s). | | | |
| Entries have examples of text evidence, such as relevant quotes including page numbers. | | | |
| The reader connects the focus lesson not only to the current choice book, but to previous choice books and/or the class novel as well. | | | |
| One out of every five entries elaborates in detail, filling up at least two pages in the notebook. | | | |
| Total points out of 10: | | | |

## Talk About Reading Can Go in Notebooks

We'll get to other ways you can grade talk by listening to actual talk, but notebooks are a place to assess how well students are talking about their books. A few teachers I work with have students record conversations; then the teacher does spot checks. If you do this, don't get stuck listening to every conversation. That's time-consuming and a bit boring. But knowing you'll likely choose a random spot to see if they're on topic will provide accountability.

Another option is to have students reflect in their notebooks after discussions, writing how the conversation pushed, expanded, and challenged their thinking. They can cite group members' points as evidence. These notebook entries can get assessed like any others.

## Self-Assessment With Notebook Rubrics

If we are the only ones grading the notebooks, then we are teaching our readers to be wholly dependent on us to let them know how they're doing. By middle and high school (and even before), they should share in that responsibility. We're getting them ready for the world of college and jobs where they will be asked to perform and not necessarily receive a ton of feedback on that performance. Therefore, include a section on the rubric for self-assessment. Your grade goes alongside theirs. For any big discrepancies, let them know you will meet to discuss. Students typically want to avoid that meeting, so they are tough on themselves, as you will be, too. And the meeting is always a joy when you're showing them why, in fact, they deserve more credit for their work than they thought.

## Staying on Top of Notebook Grading

You're starting to open your freezer door, or unspool some floss, as you imagine all these notebooks piling up, along with your Netflix queue untouched, dinners unmade. Here's what you can do to avoid an onerous pile of grading:

1. Collect notebooks on a rotating basis, taking home a few each night (relatively painless).

> **Side Note: Notebook Entries**
>
> Be careful of over-rewarding lots of high-volume writing about reading. Of course, we want students to elaborate on their thinking, but for a slow writer, writing can start to replace reading time. Emphasize quality over quantity for most entries and then, if you like, require one long entry a week that asks them to make longer connections and elaborate on their thinking, using text evidence to back it up. That way, you can ensure students are capable of writing at length about a text, without letting writing become a way to avoid reading.

2. Grade students twice, or even once a marking period, or have students grade themselves more frequently.

3. Do spot checks in class when you meet with students to talk about their reading, and let them know if you see trouble ahead (especially for any you suspect are falling through the cracks).

4. Don't read every entry, but have students preselect an entry that best shows their application of a concept—a great task to have them assess which entry that is. (For quality control, you randomly select one other. I've been known not to be *completely* random in my choices, but that's up to you.)

Look at Chapters 1 and 5 for sample entries by readers who applied a concept to a book teachers may be unfamiliar with. The application of the concept is the point, not the book itself.

## USE OF CLASS TIME TO READ

You've granted students a gift: time to do the most important work in class with you by their side. Instead of treating reading as an extra to get to if they have time that night, you're walking the walk of valuing reading by showing them this is what we do right here, right now. If students aren't using that time, you can hold them accountable and try to help them get back on track.

As referenced in Chapter 2, have a list of names with as many days of the marking period afterward in rows. Every day, take twenty seconds to scan the class at random and check off who is (or who is not) focused on reading. If students forgot their book and have to borrow one, that can be a minus as well. Tallying up these points can result in easy credit for most students. And for those who are off task, you're using the data to pull them into groups and help them find the right book before the end of the marking period so they can get back on track, too.

Side Note: Grading

If you're wondering how you'll grade entries for accuracy when you haven't read the book, you're not alone. Many teachers fear that once again, they'll be duped by fakers who aren't reading but are just spewing out words like synthesize and symbolism to make their entries look smart. Rest assured that (a) we couldn't tell any better before with the class novel, (b) it's harder to fake when SparkNotes are less likely to exist for your book, (c) you'll be constantly reminding them that faking only hurts their progress as readers, (d) the ones who aren't reading are usually the ones too lazy to fake it, (e) it's surprisingly clear if they got the concept, even if you haven't read the book, and (f) you can always ask them to write a brief summary of the book as their first entry to orient you, or remind them to write for a reader who hasn't read this book.

## TALK ABOUT READING

Assessing how students talk about their reading can be done through written reflections after discussion. They reference group members' ideas and comments and how their thinking changed as a result of the talk. But you can also grade by listening in on the talk itself. You can ask them to submit recordings of those conversations for additional accountability, but don't listen to them all unless you need an insomnia cure. Instead, have them record their conversations and then select a one-minute excerpt that best shows a specific reading strategy or concept (changed thinking, text citations, attention to setting, building off of one another's comments). It can be powerful for students to listen back to their conversations and then set goals for their next talk so they can do even better.

You can also grade talk when it occurs. There's nothing to take home, and you have an authentic assessment because you're listening in on your students. At first, it might feel slightly stilted, but if you just linger, listening, they learn quickly to carry on. In fact, it's a bit humbling how fast they ignore our presence and dive into their discussion.

On page 185 is an example of a note-taking sheet you can use when circulating among paired talk about reading. You can let students know you'll be listening for a specific discussion skill, or provide a general set of goals to work on.

Once again, we are not the almighty judges of discussion, the only ones capable of deeming if a conversation is hitting the mark. We can invite students to reflect on how well they did, to set goals, and to get better next time.

## PROGRESS ON READING GOALS

Reading goals likely go in students' reading notebooks, but they can serve as a separate grade to assess what counts: their personal improvement in reading. It's not enough to set goals—they need to meet them! If readers aren't meeting those goals, they can work on adjusting them, as well as strategize about how they'll get there. Just as high-caliber athletes develop training regimens and alter them slightly to better meet specific goals, our students should study their own data, too. If they aren't meeting volume goals, for instance, how will they find more time outside of school to read? On the bus to track meets? By setting a reminder on their phone? Or, if they need to do more listening in discussion, how will they help themselves meet that goal and know if they've met it? Ask a friend? Assign themselves two comments only?

## Paired Talk Note-Taking Sheet

|  | Student A | Student B |
|---|---|---|
| Evidence of thinking about today's focus lesson (*multiple conflicts in a story*) |  |  |
| Evidence of thinking about other focus lessons |  |  |
| Talk habits |  |  |
| Next steps |  |  |

Reflections on reading goals can serve as a vital assessment that helps students mark progress, readjust habits, and steadily work toward getting better and better. Whether you assess these as a written grade or in a conversation with them is up to you, but know that revisiting goals is worth your (and their) attention.

## A POWERFUL ASSESSMENT TOOL FOR ANY READING WORK: LEARNING PROGRESSIONS

Learning progressions look similar to rubrics, but instead of the deficit language often employed in rubrics ("more than four grammatical mistakes"), learning progressions lay out what a particular skill looks like when done at varying levels of expertise. Each level of the progression builds up one notch to an expert understanding, treating each step along the way as a necessary valid link toward gaining that expertise.

Learning progressions, also sometimes referred to as learning ladders, are my favorite tool for co-assessing what we value in our classrooms. They give every student an entry point, show them explicitly how to get better, and make what we're looking for perfectly transparent.

Here is a simple example of a learning progression for reading volume, showing what a novice-level reader might do when working to establish habits in reading for volume, with slight gradations toward what robust readers are able to do. Notice the language is in positive terms and allows everyone to see what it means to go up a notch.

### Reading Volume: Phase I

| I | 2 | 3 | 4 |
|---|---|---|---|
| Book is always brought to class. In-class reading is about ten pages each reading day. | Book goes between home and class on weeknights. In-class and out-of-class reading is about twenty pages most days. | Book goes between home and class all week. Total reading is about thirty pages every night, including weekends. | Book is always on the person. Student reads habitually during any free moment and averages at least three hundred pages a week. There is always a backup book ready to go. |

You can create learning progressions for notebooks, reading goals, or reading stamina, and you can ask students to go up at least one level every marking period. For yearlong reading habits, make these harder each period. By November, for instance, take off Column 1, shift everything to the left, and add a new set of expectations for the furthest column on the right, ensuring even the top readers are pushing themselves.

## Reading Volume: Phase II

| 1 | 2 | 3 | 4 |
|---|---|---|---|
| Book goes between home and class on weeknights. In-class and out-of-class reading is about twenty pages most days. | Book goes between home and class all week. Total reading is about thirty pages every night, including weekends. | Book is always on the person. Student reads habitually during any free moment and averages at least three hundred pages a week. There is always a backup book ready to go. | Reading is done habitually during free time, and reader averages at least three hundred pages a week in increasingly complex texts. Genres are intentionally varied, going outside the reader's comfort zone. Reader is promoting favorites through frequent book buzzes. |

Frayer Model for genre of memoir

Definition in my words:
A genre that is a true account of particular events in the author's life.

Characteristics:
True
Events are life-changing
Reflection on the events
First person
Author comes to some new understanding
There's a theme (s)

Memoir

Examples:
A Long Way Gone, by Ishmael Beah
The Glass Castle by Jeanette Walls
Rock 'N' Roll Soldier by Dean Ellis Kohler

Non-examples:
Night, Elie Wiesel ?
The Autobiography of Malcolm X
I am Malala

Example of a notebook entry showing the student's understanding of the memoir genre.

These assessments are fairly easy to create by looking at what your struggling readers are doing, articulating what that looks like in nonjudgmental language, then moving upward to the next level, all the way to your strongest readers and making sure they have a way to improve. This allows everyone to go up a notch. Learning progressions are amazing tools for self-assessment and goal setting.

## Summative Assessments

It's likely that we still feel the need for a few heavily weighted grades toward the end of the marking period: the reading test, the literary essay, the big book project of old. But now, instead of getting those assignments all on the same book (deadly to grade!), you're getting fresh glimpses into individual reading lives and minds—much more interesting to read and assess.

### LITERARY ESSAY

The literary essay is similar to the essays we assigned in our previous teaching model. We ask students to think critically about the book (except this time it's their book) and write about certain concepts such as symbolism, character, setting, or whatever concept we emphasized and modeled in this unit. But instead of SparkNote interpretations, we get to read a rich variety of their interpretations of these concepts in their own books.

The common fear is often that it is hard to grade these essays without having read each of the students' books. My advice for you, and for them, as you first try this out is to remind them what it means to write for a reader who hasn't read the book. They will benefit from seeing your own examples (or even book reviews from the *New York Times* Book Review or from online resources such as LibraryThing.com or Biblionasium.com). Remind students to provide some background or context before launching into examples or references to character or plot interspersed throughout.

By including a brief summary of the book, students are also addressing a key core standard, writing objective summaries of a text. Now they have an authentic reason to do so: orienting the reader of their literary essay who has not read the book.

Another concern is whether students are applying the concept correctly. After all, when they write about symbolism in *The Scarlet Letter*, you know if they got it "right" because you have predetermined ideas about symbolism in that book. Now, you can't grade them on whether they got to *your* interpretation of symbolism. You have to suspend that basis for assessment, and instead evaluate how clearly they are expressing their interpretation and whether it is plausible. Once we are able to suspend that need for control of the "correct" interpretation, the beautiful thing is that we are letting them explore these concepts without SparkNotes or us to guide them. And indeed, it will be clear how well they are doing this work. Their evidence and explanations and thinking are right there, and if they write and speak clearly and with appropriate evidence and elaboration, they get credit. This is not a cushy grade, or a worrisome reward for faking it—they are taking on the real work of critical thinking as readers.

Examples of a literary essay assignment, rubric, and outline template for choice books appear in **Resources 15 and 16**. These high school students applied reading skills modeled in excerpts of *Great Expectations* to their choice books, then wrote essays showing the application of that thinking.

## BLOGS, PODCASTS, AND STUDENT WEBSITES

We don't need to limit big displays of thinking about books to essays. All kinds of digital publishing modes engage students, tap into their technical fluency, and allow them to creatively show their thinking.

The wealth of examples online is both inspiring and overwhelming. You might provide one digital option per marking period, slowly building up a repertoire for students to showcase their knowledge. Or, dive in and see what students are able to master. As a small example, I once suggested to a classroom that we try emaze presentations to show students' thinking. The teacher was reluctant as she had never used this method. She bravely said they could try it, anyway, and within ten minutes most of her students could have given us a tutorial. It made them feel great to be ahead of us for a change! Trust that they are so expertly fluent in digital expression that this will be not daunting but a welcome invitation.

I recently saw a playlist created by a middle school reader to align with his choice read. Each song had an in-depth explanation of why it connected to the book. The student's musical knowledge shines, and his evidence-based writing reflects thoughtful connections to his book.

Here's just one excerpt from five in-depth writings this student did connecting lyrics to the memoir by Chris Herren, *Basketball Junkie*:

# "UNDER THE BRIDGE" BY THE RED HOT CHILI PEPPERS

The song "Under the Bridge" relates to how connected Chris Herren was to his hometown of Fall River, Massachusetts. Chris was a big-time high school basketball player who was getting recruited by many Division I college programs. He could have gone to any school he wanted to, but instead, all he wanted to do was stay in Fall River. Chris wanted to stay in Fall River for as long as he could.

Chris was the face of Fall River. He was a basketball superstar in a basketball-crazy town. Basketball was the most important thing in Fall River. It was the only thing people in the town cared about. Chris was a big part of that. He was a part of that basketball-crazy town. Chris lived and breathed Fall River, and he never wanted to leave the town he loved. Chris felt like Fall River was its own world, and he never wanted to leave. When the time came for Chris to decide on a college, he chose Durfee, his high school. It was like he was in denial about ever leaving high school and moving on with his life. The book states . . .

> At the end of the three-part series I was asked what college I was going to.
>
> "I'm going to Durfee," I said.
>
> The Herald News wrote an editorial about it, praising me for living in the present tense, for realizing that you're only in high school once and making the most of it.
>
> If only they knew. (p. 70)

Chris did end up going to Boston College, but only because he was a top prospect and was expected to go to a top basketball program... But, in his heart, Chris wanted to stay at Durfee for as long as he could. The song "Under the Bridge" has the same theme of not being able to leave the city. Like Chris, the character in the song wants to stay in the city for as long as he can. The song states . . .

> I drive on her streets
>
> 'Cause she's my companion
>
> I walk through her hills
>
> 'Cause she knows who I am

She sees my good deeds

And she kisses me windy

I never worry

Now that is a lie

Chris and the town are almost like friends, as it says in the song lyrics. Chris and Fall River know each other. Chris is comfortable with the city. He never has any worries in Fall River. Chris and the city have a special relationship, like the song has with the artist. Because of this special relationship, it causes Chris to love the city too much, and he is too afraid to leave it and break out of his comfort zone.

When we free up our students to showcase their thinking about choice reading in new ways, they will surprise and delight us over and over again.

## INFORMAL BOOK TALKS

While I mentioned not grading the informal book buzzes or book talks—little snippets when a student holds up a book and briefly "sells" it to other readers—you might assign writing to go with it. The purpose of the book buzz is to help readers find new titles, and the danger of grading those is censoring them entirely or making them so thorough and evidence based they become a snore fest. However, you can have it both ways: ungraded, highly encouraged informal book buzzes to start off class; and then, once a marking period, a summative assessment in video or written form that "sells" the book to readers *and* a write-up with further explanation and evidence of close reading.

Consider the video book talk done by an eighth-grader on *Code Name Verity*:

The video all on its own is a beautiful resource for fellow readers. They can watch for two minutes and see if this is a title that piques their interest or not.

Eighth-grader book talk

In addition, the formal write-up provides a thorough summary, an explanation of directorial choices, and evidence-based reflection on the book's mood, theme, and more. Check out the following to see an example of a reader's book talk write-up. The Works Cited page alone is evidence this choice reading assignment is anything but "fluff."

Katie Baskin
Independent Book Project
Period B6

# CODE NAME VERITY
## BY ELIZABETH WEIN

## Summary

*Code Name Verity*, in its entirety, was a very creative story. The book took place during World War II in various European countries, based on what was happening in the story. The stories are told in two parts: *Verity* and *Kittyhawk*. Two pilots flew into German-occupied France as spies, but the plane crashed and one of the girls, Verity, was arrested by the Gestapo. The book is told through a first-person point of view, each part told by a different character. In *Verity*, the story is told through confessions from one of the pilots (who is referred to as either Queenie, Verity, or Eva and whose true name is Julie) who narrates the story through physical writing while imprisoned in a hotel-turned-prison called the Château de Bordeaux. In the prison, Julie is given only two weeks to live, and is guaranteed to be executed at the end of that time. Meanwhile, she is given the choice of revealing everything she knows about the British War Effort or being tortured until the minute she dies. Being intelligent in her decision, she decides to cooperate, knowing that being killed at the end of her disclosure will be satisfying. She knows she will be killed by her own people for treason if she makes it out alive anyway. In her detailed explanations of what she is being asked to write about her occupation, she creatively weaves her confessions of the air force with stories of how she came to know the other pilot, Maddie, in the first place. Unexpectedly, there is a second part to the story, called *Kittyhawk*. It is narrated after finding out that Julie has been executed; however, it is meant to be written during the same time period in which Julie is writing her confessions. *Kittyhawk* is told through the perspective of Maddie, Julie's best friend and the other pilot. It starts after Maddie wakes up after the plane crash and Julie is gone. Maddie logs her experience in her pilot's notebook, given to her for her job. Through Maddie's confessions, not only is more revealed about her, but even more is revealed about Julie as well.

## Theme

The foremost theme conveyed in the book *Code Name Verity* is that even the thought of having a friend is enough to be hopeful, and that friendship is very important. This is because the two girls, who became inseparable best friends through their jobs, were still friends even after being separated for months. On their flight into France, when Maddie realized the plane was shot, she trusted Julie to be confident enough to jump out, and Julie trusted Maddie to land the plane safely. After this incident, when Maddie went into hiding and Julie was taken by the Gestapo, they would never stop thinking about each other, and thinking about whether or not the other was safe. In the end, when Maddie and the family she was staying with ran into Julie and her leaders, Maddie did something that she knew Julie agreed with, and Julie trusted her to make that decision (I will not say what she did, for it is the best and most surprising part within the book). Quoted from Maddie, knowing that Julie is in captivity, "It is HELL not knowing what has happened, or what is happening, to Julie . . . Incredible what slender threads you begin to hang your hopes on" (p. 237). This quote shows that even the thought that her best friend might still be alive, and that she would be able to see her at least one more time, is enough to have even the slightest bit of hope. The time from when Julie and Maddie were first separated to when they saw each other at last was over six months, and I know that (from personal experience) it is the hardest thing to be separated from your best friend for that long. In that time, there was not a page or confession that went by that either Julie or Maddie mentioned the worry they had about the other person. Therefore, the most prominent theme in the book *Code Name Verity* is that friendship is the most important thing in life.

## Mood and Tone

The mood of *Code Name Verity* is suspense and fear, because you almost never know what will happen next. The book is set in a prison for enemy spies during World War II. Therefore, without even having to think about it much or even read the book, there will always be a mood of suspense because anything can happen in the camp. Sometimes during the book, especially when Julie was being interrogated by the leader of that prison, SS-Hauptsturmführer von Linden (von Linden for short), I was scared. Because von Linden held the most power in that establishment and he was the most highly authorized staff member in the prison, it was always scary when he entered the interrogation room, or even Julie's private quarters. I think the author was also trying to convey this mood

*(Continued)*

(Continued)

through her tone. She made the book suspenseful so that you wouldn't expect what was about to happen, or you were fearful about certain things in the book, such as what punishment the Nazis will decide on after Julie has not been cooperating. Also, in the beginning of the book especially, there is an overwhelming fear that Julie will not be able to confess everything she knows in the two weeks she is given, similar to how a student may feel when only given a few days for a seemingly large project. This tone and mood is only exuded during the parts where Julie is writing about her experiences in the prison. Julie also writes stories about her and Maddie in their youth and their experiences outside of their involvement in the war. These stories of before the war have a mood and tone that is a lot more happy and relaxed. I conveyed these themes in my book trailer. The music I chose for the background started out quiet and gradually got louder and more suspenseful, especially when I got into more detail about the book. For example, in the beginning when I was only talking about Maddie and Julie's friendship and the setting, the music was (relatively) calm. However, when I began getting into the details of the two girls flying into France and how their plane got shot down, the music got louder and more powerful so that I could exaggerate the mood and tone of the book and the confessions within.

## Quotes

In the trailer I produced, I included three quotes. The first quote, which I shortened a little to fit the trailer and the phrase I was going for, was "We make a *sensational* team" (p. 68). I used this quote to represent the theme of the book, which is that friendship is the most important thing in life and can even blossom in the midst of crisis. This quote was used a few times in the book, and it shows how even though there is a war to be fought around them and they almost get hit by an airborne airplane, they are still so passionate about taking a break from their jobs as pilots and radio operators to be friends. The next quote I used, from page 68, was "It's like being in love, discovering your best friend." This quote also represents the theme of the book. This is because it was the beginning of the best friendship that Maddie and Julie would ever know, and it shows, even from the way beginning, they knew they were going to be friends for a long time. The last quote is from page 237, "Incredible what slender threads you begin to hang your hopes on." This quote also somewhat represents the theme because a theme—going along with the overall message—is that the thought and illusion of something good is enough to be hopeful. In this case, during Maddie's part of the book, Maddie was saying how horrible it was not knowing what is going on in Julie's life, and whether or not she is being continuously tortured. However, just the thought and slim chance that Julie could still be alive and well was enough for Maddie to have hope. I used these quotes in my trailer not only because that is how I wanted to convey the theme of the book, but also because I wanted the watchers of the trailer to understand the connection that Julie and Maddie shared. I wanted the people watching to understand how close and meaningful their relationship was.

## Directorial Decisions

I made many beneficial choices as the director of this trailer to optimize the trailer itself. First, the music I chose was meant to be suspenseful and dark at certain points. In fact, to find the music I used, I went on YouTube and searched "suspenseful music" and scavenged through the results in order to find the perfect audio. I made sure that the music had the right effect for each part during my trailer. For example, in the beginning, when mentioning the setting and characters, the music was subtle. Then, as soon as I mentioned that they flew into Nazi-occupied France, the music picked up in speed and suspense. Next, when I started describing how Maddie and Julie's plane crashed and that Julie was arrested by the Gestapo, the music became very intense. This created power and suspense in my trailer. Another decision I made was to use only pictures and video that were actually from the time period around World War II. The air force combat videos I included were actually from World War II, as well as (most of) the images. The app I used to create my trailer was iMovie, and within iMovie there are options that allow you to edit the picture or video you used. One of the filters is called "Aged Film," which is the effect I used on most of the videos and pictures. Sometimes, however, I used a filter called "Film Grain," which has a similar effect to Aged Film. In these ways, I gave the trailer authenticity to the time period and setting of the book. My main goal in any of my directorial decisions was to make it accurate to the book, whether that is the suspense, theme, or setting, and I think I did a good job doing that.

## Works Cited

Elizabeth L. Gardner of Rockford, Illinois, WASP (Women's Airforce Service Pilot) pilot, takes a look around before sending her plane streaking down the runway at the air base. Digital image. *National Archives Catalog*. N.p., n.d. Web. 16 Apr. 2016. <https://research.archives.gov/id/542191>.

*(Continued)*

(Continued)

*Epic Suspenseful Action Music "ENEMY" Original Film Movie Soundtracks, Dramatic*. FesliyanStudios, 25 Jan. 2014. Web. 16 Apr. 2016. <https://www.youtube.com/watch?v=4izl7DgWNmc>.

*German Invasion of Russia (distressing Footage)*. War Archives, 10 Aug. 2012. Web. 16 Apr. 2016. <https://www.youtube.com/watch?v=pSCqpqNJ7uY>.

Greene, Anne. Image of Radio Operators during World War 2. Digital image. *Heroes, Heroines, & Historu*. Blogger, 14 Feb. 2015. Web. 16 Apr. 2016. <http://www.hhhistory.com/2015/02/wacs-serve-in-world-war-ii.html>.

Image of Interrogation of Female. Digital image. *Beautypendence*. N.p., 21 Oct. 2011. Web. 16 Apr. 2016. <http://www.beautypendence.com/tag/interrogation/>.

Image of two female pilots beside a plane. Digital image. *Hellphie's Fiendish Fiction*. N.p., 28 Apr. 2014. Web. 16 Apr. 2016. <https://hellphiesfiendishfiction.wordpress.com/tag/verity/>.

Klein, Kate. Women Airforce Service Pilots (WASPs) in front of a Boeing B-17 Flying Fortress at Fort Myers, Florida, in 1944. Digital image. *Ezra Magazine*. Cornell University, 2009. Web. <http://ezramagazine.cornell.edu/Update/Nov14/EU.Dawn.Seymour.html>.

Lee, Matthew. *Code Name Verity* Book Cover Image. Digital image. *Twitch Film*. N.p., 9 Oct. 2012. Web. 16 Apr. 2016. <http://twitchfilm.com/2012/10/books-to-be-scene-elizabeth-weins-code-name-verity.html>.

*Pen to Paper*. Digital image. *Gabriellasalmon.com*. N.p., 17 Aug. 2014. Web. <http://www.gabriellasalmon.com/pen-to-paper-magic-spells/>.

*Portrait of Two New Women's Air Force Pilots During WWII*. Digital image. *Gettyimages.com*. Getty Images, n.d. Web. 16 Apr. 2016. <http://www.gettyimages.com/pictures/man-sized-jobs-are-ahead-for-these-girls-who-were-among-23-news-photo-515554388>.

*Research Reveals Secrets of Gestapo*. Digital image. Liverpool John Moores University, 8 Oct. 2015. Web. 16 Apr. 2016. <https://www.ljmu.ac.uk/about-us/news/research-reveals-secrets-of-gestapo>.

Sherman, Stephen. Douglas A-20 Havoc, tail #2-86657(?), 1943 roundel, in flight. Digital image. *Ace Pilots*. N.p., n.d. Web. 16 Apr. 2016. <http://acepilots.com/archives/Photos/light-bombers.html>.

Truth blurred i---mage. Digital image. *Diggerfortruth.com*. Wordpress.com, n.d. Web. 16 Apr. 2016. <https://diggerfortruth.wordpress.com/2015/01/26/the-truth-is/>.

Wein, Elizabeth. *Code Name Verity*. New York: Hyperion, 2012. Print.

*World War II Air Combat Color Footage*. Military World, 29 June 2014. Web. 16 Apr. 2016. <https://www.youtube.com/watch?v=tQYuP84bsSg>.

WW2 Aircraft Crashes in the Cavendish area. Digital image. The Foxearth and District Local History Society, n.d. Web. 16 Apr. 2016. <http://www.foxearth.org.uk/ww2Crashes.html>.

## AUTHOR STUDIES

Author studies are independent projects in which students delve deeply into one author's works. Students choose an author whose work they love, and they analyze that author's craft, style, themes, and more by reading as much as they can and writing about their findings.

We can encourage students to find authors they love because that is what readers do: readers go through binges of reading everything they can find by an author, and they become experts on that writer. Studying the craft similarities and differences across several works by an author not only falls right into the expectations of the standards, but also allows our students to become experts on a writer they love. Whether it's John Green, Jacqueline Woodson, or Gene Luen Yang, let students go deep and see what makes that author special, and then allow students to share their expertise with others.

## How to Stay Sane When Grading

### RUBRICS

Rubrics are not a fuddy-duddy formula—they are a godsend in being clear about what we expect and inviting students in on how to be successful in our class. Avoid the trap I fell into when I started teaching, coming up with how I'd grade at the end of a unit, and instead let students know right away what you'll assess and how. The amount of high-ranking work shoots up, not because we lowered our standards but because we made those standards transparent. Rubrics allow us to zero in on just what we want to assess, which makes grading simplified and faster. Whatever isn't on the rubric, let it go.

### LIMITED COMMENTS

How often do we stay up late, writing copious comments on students' work, only to find their essays shoved into notebooks after checking out the grade or, worse, on the floor or in the trash? All those precious kernels of advice and wisdom ignored, and rarely applied to the next work they do... Save your time, and keep comments focused to just a few key issues that you taught and most value. Resist the urge to fix it all. Students won't absorb lots of advice anyway, and too many suggestions set them up for frustration. Writing comments all over drafts might make us feel virtuous, but it does little for our students, crushes their motivation, and keeps us from living a life.

## SELF-ASSESSMENT

Anything we grade can be graded by our students first. Again, we don't need to be the be-all end-all determiners of what is good and what isn't. Students should be part of this process, and by thinking through how well their work meets expectations, we are sharing that important evaluator role. These two (or three, if you're including a peer assessment) perspectives can be combined and averaged in whatever way you see best.

## "OFFICE HOURS"

We don't have to have an office for our students to find us. We can be accessible in person instead of filling their work with our written feedback and comments. Advocating for themselves, reaching out and initiating communication, and seeking out rather than passively receiving feedback are all essential skills for young adults. Students can initiate these conversations and feedback through a class website, a once-a-week lunch period, or a routine time in class. These talks can be powerful opportunities to create a partnership in their learning.

## POWER OF PRAISE

Find what is working. In fact, try this with the next round of work that you collect. Dare yourself to comment only on what is working. The fact that this will feel so challenging and new is a sign that we are not trained, sadly, to look for what *is* there. We grew up getting feedback, typically, on what was lacking, and now we pass on this habit as assessors of student work. This isn't a sign that we're jerks. In fact, it's often a mark of our extreme compassion and desire to help our students. We see what they sorely need and point it out to help them catch up. But the result is that multiple suggestions for improvement tend to discourage, overwhelm, and reinforce most of our students' already fragile sense that they are not up to par.

What we can do to shift this is identify the positives. And they *are* there. As we practice looking for what a student is doing, we start seeing little nuggets of brilliance over and over again (Bomer, 2010). By pointing these out, we invigorate our students to do more and more of that. Praise begets more good work.

Just remember that this can be hard to do at first, and that middle and high school students are experts at sniffing out false praise. Make it genuine and from the heart. When they hear that and start to believe it—watch out. You will witness them investing in their work about reading like never before.

## CHAPTER EIGHT

# BUILDING TEACHER–STUDENT RELATIONSHIPS THROUGH THE BLENDED MODEL

Years ago, I had a staff developer in my classroom ask me which students I avoided. "Me?" I asked, aghast. "No one—I treat all my students the same!"

She pushed: "Come on. Who do you kind of wish would get mono and be out for six weeks?" I protested, as if I would ever. Then, I pointed to the group of boys in the back. They were intimidatingly cool, sometimes outwardly hostile, and just enough on task to ignore.

"Them," I said. "A really long, drawn-out case of it."

"Go to them," she told me. I nodded, starting toward the group of sweet girls in the front. I'd get there eventually. "Go there first," she added. Sheepishly, I headed to the back.

I squatted next to one particularly annoying kid and started a conversation about his work. It went against my instincts and felt more than a bit uncomfortable, and our talk wasn't particularly enlightening. Not that first time anyway. But it did melt something in us both. The act of listening, of asking questions, of giving my undivided attention, again and again over the next few weeks, so each of these boys started to trust me, changed everything.

This group was notorious around school; the students served as constant fodder in the staff room and were easily written off as lackluster, lazy, annoying, not so bright, or outright unlikable. Then they became individuals. They were people with names who I discovered liked skateboarding, cracked jokes, liked poetry and graphic novels, hated poetry and loved sports biographies, struggled to read, got confused, questioned texts, and thrived on praise and attention. Indeed, they all had a lot to say that was worth hearing.

I realized there were whole swaths of students I had been avoiding, and that avoiding them wasn't doing any of us a lick of good. These students consumed a lot of energy to manage, or even to ignore. And I had been failing them—failing to do my job and discover who they were and what they needed.

And doing right by them wasn't hard. It meant getting past my discomfort, opening up a dialogue, and forging a relationship. The rest was teaching them what I knew already: how to read and write well. Through the simple act of talking to my students, we became a community of learners. And every one of us was a member.

## Why the Blended Model Opens Up Space for Powerful One-on-One Teaching

When we spend most of our class time learning about one book, it's hard to pay attention to more than the grade grubbers (bless their hearts, again) and those who are actively off task because they will demand most of our attention. Even those students, however, we don't necessarily get to know that well. Teaching this way requires us to be "on" a lot, and there just isn't time to get to know every student, especially by middle and high school, when we may teach over a hundred students.

Forging a relationship can take until the end of the year, and likely, it happens more through interactions outside of class. We get to know our students by coaching their team after school or working with them on the literary magazine or newspaper.

By devoting a large amount of time in class to what we value most, reading, we also open up space to show our students whom we value most: them. It's tempting, of course, to use the time that they read to read our own books, too. But that would be a wasted opportunity—here we have this gorgeous stretch of time to teach them in personalized meaningful ways: by talking to them one-on-one.

## WE BUILD RELATIONSHIPS WITH
## STUDENTS AROUND BOOKS

By talking to them about their reading, we effortlessly get to know their interests, passions, challenges, questions, struggles, and habits. Books become a vehicle to understand who they are, and vice versa. It might be helpful at first to think of these talks as if you're with your favorite book club group, just without the wine. You're simply talking to other readers, sharing your opinions and ideas, and using your reading to share about yourself.

Officially, in the world of education, these conversations are usually referred to as reading conferences. Hosts of excellent books by educators such as Carl Anderson (2000), Jennifer Serravallo (2013, 2015), and others can guide you in moving readers through thoughtful and structured reading conferences.

I'm resisting the term *conferences*, however, in favor of *conversations*. This whole change from a class novel to choice reading may be a brave leap into uncharted territory, and I want to make the trip as smooth as possible. By simply talking and listening to your readers, you will witness growth and open up your teaching practice. Reading conferences are, at their essence, a conversation. Start there.

Just go, as my staff developer said. Just go and talk to your students.

## CONVERSATION ALLOWS FOR
## SEAMLESS DIFFERENTIATION

*Differentiation* is a buzzword for good reason. Our middle and high school students are in no way uniform, and teaching them the same thing in the same way guarantees we will meet only some, and perhaps only a few, of their needs. Teaching the whole class the same way is like a doctor going to every one of her hundred patients and telling them each to take penicillin and put an ace bandage on their ankle. Our students are individuals with unique challenges, needs, and strengths that we can teach to. Talking to them one-on-one is a natural painless way to do so.

Having conversations with our readers can engage 100 percent of our students, because they all get what they need. The English language learner who needs help with fluency, the high flyer who is ready to compare books across a genre, the reluctant reader who needs the right book, the insecure reader who needs specific praise for a job well done, the confused reader who needs a reminder to reread—through talking to them, we deliver the treatment they need to improve.

## CONVERSATION CEMENTS
## STUDENTS' IDENTITIES AS READERS

By talking to them about their reading, we cement our students' identity as bona fide readers. They carry on in-depth conversations with us about books, and contrary to reading the class novel, each is the lone expert on his or her book. Who doesn't respond to feeling like an expert, especially teens? Listening to them validates their expertise in an authentic way and helps them get better and better as readers.

It is a sad misconception that teens need less attention than younger students. Think of a toddler begging repeatedly, "Watch me! Look at me!" Teens are just better at masking a craving for your attention because it's not exactly cool. But the desire for your approval and focus is there. Satisfying that craving is easy to do and produces wild results. This is our opportunity to look at our students, listen to them, and help carve their paths on a journey to being readers.

## STUDENTS NEED ONE-ON-ONE
## TIME WITH CARING ADULTS

Middle and high school students shift the bulk of their time to being with peers. That's natural and age-appropriate, but they still need the caring perspective of smart adults in their lives. One-on-one time with adults outside of their family, however, is preciously rare if not wholly nonexistent. Unless they take piano lessons, they are almost always lumped with other groups of teens when they're with grown-ups.

Talking to students about their reading isn't therapy; it's time to help them be better readers. There are all kinds of fringe benefits, such as the way teens thrive on our undivided attention. For instance, students get to hear all kinds of bigger life advice even when we say it about reading. Encouraging them to read every night, even if they don't fulfill their page requirement, is a reminder that it's always better in life to do something than nothing. Asking where they saw that character change is advice to support opinions with evidence. Listening to them is a reminder that they matter—that they have something worth saying.

## STUDENTS DON'T NEED
## ANOTHER DISAPPROVING PERSPECTIVE

When you tell people that you teach teens, how many times do they respond, "Oh, I could never do that. Teens are the worst!" as if anyone over twelve is an alien species, as if we were never that age? Most likely, however, we teach middle and high school because we actually *like* teens. Getting to know them through books is a way to show them we champion teenagers; we're not just surviving the day with their adolescent hormonal selves. Well, usually.

How many of us hold visceral memories of not being understood as a teen? Maybe our boredom was seen as rudeness, challenging the status quo was a seen as a threat, or our confusion was seen as lazy or dumb. We easily see over a hundred students a day, and without the opportunity to listen to them on their own, it is all too easy to lump them into a stereotype or negative label. When they feel seen and understood by us, teens respond in all kinds of beautiful ways.

## How to Talk to Students About Their Reading

I've seen many smart passionate teachers embrace this model, then balk when it's time to talk to readers. I get it. This is out of our comfort zone. We may not have had a teacher talk one-on-one with us about our reading, unless we were in trouble, so there's no model to rely on. Then, there's this whole matter of not having read our students' books. What are we supposed to say? There's no way to prepare for the conversation, and like good teachers everywhere, we feel immense pressure to come up with something smart to say, right on the spot. It's enough to drag out Dickens and do a read-aloud—at least we know how to do that!

But this fear, while totally normal, is unwarranted. In reality, we not only don't need something brilliant to say on the spot; we don't have to say much at all!

Teens are grateful to have an adult who listens. And they're shocked when an adult doesn't come with all the answers or a lecture on what to do.

Take off the hair shirt, or at least the pressure to say amazing things when you talk to them.

Think about the way you talk to a friend or your sister or the salesperson at the bookstore about a book. What do you say? Start there. Ask open-ended questions that make your students feel like this is not an oral pop quiz, but a natural conversation. Think about questions like

> Teens are grateful to have an adult who listens. And they're shocked when an adult doesn't come with all the answers or a lecture on what to do.

*"What are you working on?"*

*"How's it going?"*

*"Talk to me."*

*"What are you thinking about?"*

Go for casual, not intimidating (Anderson, 2000).

Teens might feel awkward, too. They're not used to being an expert, carrying on a conversation about a book, or getting your undivided attention. That discomfort might initially result in sabotaging the conversation in ways that only teens can master: One-word answers. Grunts. Silence. A few of those, and you might long to analyze symbolism in *The Scarlet Letter*.

Don't give up, however. Show your students you value them as readers by talking to and teaching each of them how to do it well.

## HOW TO HELP STUDENTS TALK TO YOU ABOUT READING

These talks may feel like an awkward first date at the beginning, but they don't have to stay that way for long. They can quickly transition to short powerful discussions that move every reader. You can do a lot to help students get ready to make that happen.

Model the good and the bad. Ask students or colleagues to talk to you about their reading, and purposefully show them everything you *want* to happen:

- Students do most of the talking.

- They're ready to talk when you sit down next to them.

- They talk about what they're trying as a reader, rather than giving a long summary of their books.

- They talk about
    - What they're proud of
    - What's hard
    - Important ideas in their notes
    - Honest assessments of their reading
    - Evidence to back up their opinions
    - And more

Then, because it's fun and useful, model what you *don't* want to happen:

- Students give a coma-inducing play-by-play of their book.

- They give one-word answers.

- They fake answers.

- They don't look at you.

Chart each of the things students should do and not do in a conversation about reading, and let them practice. Suggest ideas and topics they can get ready to talk about, which will include

- All the strategies you've taught so far about reading well

- Something they loved and why

- What confused them

- What they're trying to do to get better at reading

- Sharing their goals, asking questions, and more

Post a list of conversation "pointers" and let them practice those, too.

Let students know when you're coming to speak individually to them. They will have so much more to say, and more smart things to say, when they've had time to prepare mentally.

Here are a couple of ways I've seen teachers give students the heads-up that they'll be talking soon so students can feel ready to talk. One teacher posts a rotating list on the SMART Board during each reading time, outlining what every reader is doing that day, like this:

| Getting Lost in Books, Thinking About Reading, and Taking Notes | Getting Ready to Talk to Mr. Suarez by Jotting Down Questions and Looking Over Notes | Talking to Mr. Suarez Individually or in Groups as Noted |
|---|---|---|
| Shuyler, Rahul, Lexi, Xavier, Ben, Alexis C. | Vinny, Breanna, Ryan, Zack, Alexis P., Matthew | Danielle, Santi, Jennifer |

Other examples of posted schedules are shown here.

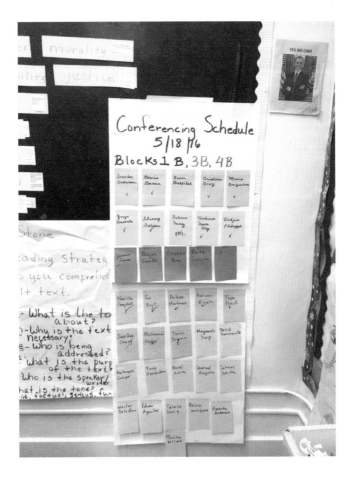

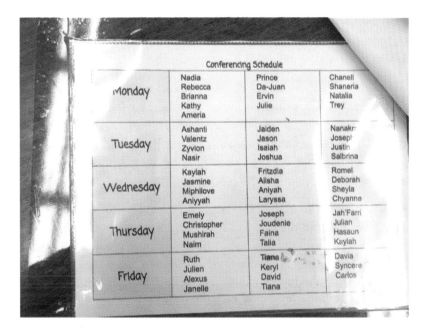

You can also show students what a good conversation might look like. Invite them to use conversation starters to help them prepare so they don't feel like they're in the spotlight sitting across from you. You might share a list like the following:

| Things You Can Talk About in Your Book With Ms. Gordon |
| --- |
| Why you chose this book |
| What makes it a favorite or not-so-favorite |
| What you're planning on reading next and why |
| Your reading goals and how you're doing with them |
| A theory you have about a character |
| How you're applying the thinking we're doing in the class novel to your own book |
| A favorite notebook entry |
| A question or struggle you're having |
| What you're noticing about this author's writing style |
| Questions about my reading, though I mostly want to hear from you ☺ |

Two theatric middle school teachers I work with, playing the part of teacher and student, created short videos modeling what to do and what not to do in a

Teacher modeling what not to do in a conference

Teacher modeling what to do in a conference

conversation about reading. One shows "the student" prepared with a book and something to talk about. The other shows "the student" forgetting a book, supplying one-word answers, and avoiding eye contact. Not only did the students love watching their teachers be a bit silly, but their conversations improved!

You can, as time goes on, consider assessing students or having them self-assess on how well they're using this one-on-one time with you. However, I caution against doing this right away and recommend you build up to it slowly. Attaching a grade to how your students talk to you runs the risk of shutting down, not nurturing, conversations.

I work with a group of teachers who wanted to create a low-stakes rubric showing students what to do when talking about reading, and they did so after months of informal conversations and developing relationships with readers. Starting off expecting students to master this right away would be asking a lot. But, it's something to work toward so conversations have more and more impact.

## Independent Reading: Expectations for When You Talk to Your Teacher

|  | Not yet | Starting to | Yes |
|---|---|---|---|
| I started off with an explanation of what I'm working on as a reader, what I'm struggling with, and/or what's going well |  |  |  |
| I pointed out specific parts of the text to back up my thinking |  |  |  |
| I gave my own thoughts and insights about the text |  |  |  |
| I didn't spend a long time summarizing the book |  |  |  |
| I wrote down what my teacher told me in my notes |  |  |  |
| Total out of 25 points (× 4): |  |  |  |

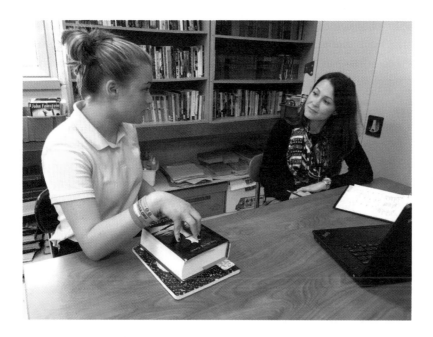

Notice the text is written in the first person so students can use it as a self-assessment tool, helping them to get better at using this time and talking in more sophisticated ways. You could use something similar to help your students get better at these reading conversations, even if what they're saying at first isn't the most scintillating or insightful. To begin, a simple checklist could show that you want them to have their book on hand and be ready to share one or two thoughts about it. Reassure them you'll help them go from there. It's okay to build up to great conversations.

## WHY IT'S OKAY THAT YOU HAVEN'T READ THEIR BOOK

Trust me—it's even better that we don't know students' choice books inside and out. It relieves us from feeling as if we need to teach those books to the students, and it encourages them to do that hard work on their own. Not knowing their book forces us to ask more questions, listen harder, and talk less. There's no risk of exhaustion on our part, and more focused learning on theirs.

Also, as strong readers ourselves, we know more than we realize about their books just by looking at the cover jacket and hearing them talk for a few minutes. Once we start immersing ourselves in the kinds of books our students like to read, even if not the *exact* books, we tend to get a good sense of how those books "go."

And even if we are completely clueless about a book, that cluelessness is a gift of sorts. Not being the expert on a student's book forces us to make the conversation less about getting something "right." We can't say things like "Yes, you got the relationship between those characters right!" or "Yes, you arrived at my conclusion for what the dying rose symbolizes!" Instead, we listen for and talk about the habits, moves, and strategies that good readers use whenever they read.

We can talk about whether students are backing up theories with evidence, tracking character change, or questioning whose voice is represented and whose is left out. These guiding questions are easy to listen for whether we read the book or not, and the questions empower our readers to do something smart in any book they read, not just the one in their hands.

## TIPS SO CONVERSATIONS HELP READERS

The most important thing is to just go talk to your readers. As my staff developer once told me, "Go!" You will learn so much through trial and error, and your teens will forgive a lot because they'll see you earnestly trying to get to know them as readers. That said, you can do some things to make your conversations with readers go well right away.

### Management

Listening and talking in a one-on-one conversation will demand that management is solid. You can't pay attention to one student if you're worried that, behind you, all the other students are getting out phones or starting to talk. If that's the case, return to Chapter 3 and revisit the lessons that help establish habits of focused reading, and hold students accountable for quietly reading during the designated time. Make a quiet room of readers a nonnegotiable before you dive into talking.

### Notes

Keep track of whom you talk to. Remember, we all unconsciously avoid certain students! By checking off those we talk to each day, we know.

In addition to tracking whom you talk to, find a way to jot down notes. You are telling your students to try important reading moves, and those are worth documenting. Teachers can keep track of what they talk about with readers in a million ways, and you'll likely need to try a few before settling on the one

that fits you. I like a clipboard with a sheet for each reader, and I jot down notes on that one page every time I talk to a student. That way, I see patterns across our talks.

Remember, middle and high school students are old enough to write down notes from our conversations, too. They can also take responsibility for seeing what patterns emerge, and they can use these notes as something to talk about (e.g., "Well, last time you suggested a book/reminded me to pay attention to minor characters/questioned the author's bias, and guess what . . .").

## Length and Frequency of Conversations

Aim to see each of your students at least once every two weeks. Of course, more is ideal, but if you have thirty students in a class, it's unrealistic that you'll get to talk to them all in a meaningful way every week.

I can usually talk to about five readers while the class is quietly reading for about thirty minutes. It's a red flag if I find myself talking to many more than that: then I'm just checking in with them and not getting to anything of substance. Any more than eight minutes with a reader, unless it's a very reluctant reader or reticent talker, and I'm teetering toward a therapy session, talking too much, or letting them barrage me with a plot summary. None are very effective in helping readers, while having them read is always helpful. So, when in doubt, give students time to read rather than time to talk.

If you're scheduling a certain number of readers to talk to each day, don't schedule more than three. Remember you'll need time to jot down notes, perhaps manage the class a bit, circulate, and more. You can always add in more impromptu conversations with readers who want to talk or have questions.

### Praise

Tell them what they're doing right.

Praise is so effective. In fact, if we don't know what to tell our students, we can never go wrong by pointing out something specific to keep doing and build on. It's not fluffy kumbaya, either. Typically I witness the student I praised doing much more work, not less!

> *Tell them what they're doing right. Typically I witness the student I praised doing much more work, not less!*

I always start a conversation with something the reader is doing well. This is a fairly standard procedure for reading conferences for a reason. It boosts students up, tells them what to keep doing, and helps them listen to what you say next.

### Independence

The goal of these conversations should always be students leading the way. The more they talk, the more they set the agenda, and the more they tell us what's working and what isn't, the more we're empowering them to manage their reading lives independently. It's our job to guide them, and it's their job to lead the way.

## What We Can Expect as a Result of Talking to Students About Reading

There's a reason my daughter's piano teacher charges well more than a dollar a minute. It's one-on-one expertise, guided to just what my kid needs. It's feedback that is personalized and nearly magical in nurturing growth. Similarly, you're giving each of your students priceless feedback, and it will produce results.

Developing the habit of reading is a milestone in middle and high school English classrooms. Nurturing students' thinking as readers happens most organically and productively when we can talk to them one-on-one.

Fisher, Frey, and Hattie's (2016) research shows that the most effective teaching practices are encompassed in a structure of talking to students. The top practices that have the most effect include providing formative evaluation, interventions, teacher clarity, and feedback, all of which are embedded in these conversations. Teacher–student relationships, in fact, are ten times more effective than class sizes! Many experts refer to conferring as the "heart" of a reading workshop because of the transcendent power of talking to students in thoughtful structured ways. Carl Anderson (2000) refers to these kinds of conferring conversations as the most essential component of teaching. They are not the icing on the cake, but the cake itself. Talk doesn't just feel good; it is good.

Remember the unease you felt when you went over your interpretation of a class novel and wondered how many of your students "got it"? Talking to them removes any doubt of what they know or don't know. The proof is right there. They're telling you how they're making the transfer from the class novel to their own books. And you're part of that conversation.

> "I have had so many successful moments in my reading conferences, and I can't believe what it has done for my relationships with some of the students in just one week. It's insane!"
>
> —Vanessa Astore, middle school teacher

Profound connections, and likely a renewed joy in your job, will be established with your students.

Talk fosters meaningful relationships, and those relationships foster meaningful work. Teens need to feel connected to us to want to learn. One-on-one time with a knowledgeable adult who cares is rare in their lives, and precious. This is how we use it for good: we open up their lives as readers.

We share ourselves as readers, and so do they. By talking about characters, plots, interests, questions, and what confuses, surprises, and wows us in our books, we grow and connect in profound ways.

All of these moves toward sharing yourself as a reader, building up your students as readers, and pushing it all forward through conversations will feel natural: it is how we all read, think, and learn.

> One-on-one time with a knowledgeable adult who cares is rare in their lives, and precious. This is how we use it for good: we open up their lives as readers.

Finally, creating a community of readers through conversation starts to form links among all your students. You are modeling the kinds of connections they can make with one another, based on the authentic connections and emotions that arise when we read.

We'll end with some examples of students' jottings when asked how lines in their books represented "truisms" from their own lives. Their universal stories link them to characters in their chosen books, and also to one another. Helping our teens feel connected to others is a triumph, and doing so through books is even more so.

# "HOW Are Our Stories Really Everyone's Stories?"

"He's mad at me... For not being like him." (Eleanor and Park)

Truth: In life, some people are angry and offended by us because we are not like them.

"I thought I'd died and gone to heaven... no one could tell that I was fat, that I had acne... no one could even touch me. In here, I was safe." (Ready Player One)

Truth: People feel safer when they aren't seen

"Online, I didn't have a problem talking to people or making friends. But in the real world, interacting with other people — especially kids my own age — made me a nervous wreck." (Ready Player One 30)

Truth: Children & teens are spending so much time in games & inside it may be harming their social skills.

"Like I'm trying to be something that I'm not. [...] It was the trying part that was so disgusting."

Truth: You should not try to be something you are not. You should work on being yourself.

"There are plenty of Reardan kids who get ignored by their parents." (The Absolutely True Diary of a Part-Time Indian)

"On the Rez... We KNOW each other. Everybody knows everybody." (Part-Time Indian)

Truth: The Indian and white community are very different in connectivity.

"A thick film of neglect still covered everything in sight. The streets, the buildings, the people." — Ready Player One

Truth: The world will be a terrible place if we don't take care of it and ignorance will make it worse.

"He stopped trying to bring her back. She only came back when she felt like it, in dreams, and lies and broken-down déjà vu." (Eleanor and Park)

truth: It's harder to hold on than to let go

"She never felt like she belonged anywhere, except when she was lying on her bed, pretending to be someone else." (Eleanor and Park)

Truth: Sometimes we feel like we're not good enough to belong somewhere.

"And that, Colin found himself thinking, must mean that we are friends. Almost by accident, and in just two days. Colin had made his second friend ever."

— An Abundance of Katherines

Truth: Someone trusting you with something can sometimes be the turning point in any relationship and friendship.

"It's okay; I miss my sisrr, too, I love her" (216)

Part-time indian

Truth: Everybody is suffering and we are not aware.

"But the risk of being able to win over anyone, he found himself thinking, was that you might pick the wrong people"

— An Abundance of Katherines

Truth: Sometimes even having alot of friends doesn't always guarantee life-long friendships or having people that will always be there for you.

"He stopped trying to bring her back. She only came back when she felt like it, in dreams. and lies and broken-down déjà vu"
(Eleanor and Park)

truth: It's harder to hold on than to let go

"She never felt like she belonged anywhere, except when she was lying on her bed, pretending to be someone else." (Eleanor and Park)

## Time to Embrace Change

Apple just got rid of the headphone jack, and there's a fair bit of outrage on social media. Probably by the time you read this book, the notion of a cord tying us to our device will feel sweetly antiquated, but at the moment, we're resisting the change.

The time to pull the plug on the class novel is now, and kudos to you for overcoming resistance to change and embracing lifelong reading habits for your students. Just because we were taught a certain way doesn't mean it's still relevant, or that it was useful then. We (maybe) succeeded in the model of a novel every six to eight weeks, but plenty of kids around us came to hate English and reading. My own favorite reading memories as a teen have nothing to do with class novels, but lots to do with stolen moments with favorite books, and books that teachers suggested just for me.

Now is the time to merge our favorite literature with our students', many yet unfound, favorite books. It is thrilling to think of how quickly education might be shifting along with our global world, but in many ways, our shifts are not fast enough. Your students will be one step closer to moving into a relevant, updated model of being sophisticated and able readers. Keep pushing for that change in ways all your own. Take this blend and mix it up even further. Add new ingredients and ditch outdated ones. Abandon what doesn't click and fold in what does. Then let me and other teachers know about it! beritgordon47@gmail.com

# RESOURCES

All resources in this section are available for
download on the companion website at
resources.corwin.com/nofakereading.

# Our Book Reviews: Sample Assignment for Sharing Choice Books

For this marking period, we will still be sharing our books with our classmates; however, we will be sharing them in a much more interactive and creative way! We will be designing book spines for our books and creating a unique QR code to share our reviews. We will then have the opportunity to scan our classmates' codes to hear their reviews and generate titles to add to our own "To Read" lists. Please see below for detailed step-by-step directions on how to complete this assignment.

Note: Four spines are due this marking period; books over 350 pages count as two books (and two spines).

1. Once you have finished your book, please be sure to update your reading log and genre list.

2. Gather the materials needed to create your book spine and let your creativity soar! You must include the title and author of your novel, along with a visual depiction.

3. Complete a "Book Review Template." You'll be reading this sheet for your recording, so write neatly so you can decipher your own handwriting.

Name: _____     Date: _____

                                    Period: 1  2  4  5  8

**Book Review Template: Teaser or Paragraph Reading**

If you choose "Teaser":

**Directions:** Complete this script completely and accurately to use while recording your QR code. When recording, be sure to speak slowly and clearly so your listener can hear you, and have fun! Please attach additional paper, if necessary.

**Title:**

**Author** (your name):

**Teaser** (e.g., Do you like [a type of genre]? What are some similar stories that your reader might be familiar with? Why else should your reader immerse him- or herself in your story?): _____

_____

_____

_____

_____

_____

_____

_____

If you choose "Paragraph":

**Directions:** Complete this script completely and accurately to use while recording your QR code. When recording, be sure to speak slowly and clearly so your listener can hear you, and have fun! Please attach additional paper, if necessary.

**Title:**

**Author** (your name):

**Background** (i.e., What's going on in your story that we need to know in order to understand the particular paragraph that you're going to be sharing?):

_____

_____

_____

_____

_____

*(Continued)*

(Continued)

_____

_____

_____

**Why did you choose this paragraph to share?**

_____

_____

_____

_____

_____

_____

_____

**Read your actual paragraph.**

Creating the QR code:

4. Just like we did with our short stories, visit Vocaroo.com to record your review.

5. On Google Classroom, you have been provided with a "Google Sheet" to use for creating your unique code. Log in to this sheet and copy your recording into Cell C. This will produce your code.

6. Submit your sheet to me, and we will print your code, which you will attach to your spine.

7. All done! Submit your spine and immerse yourself in a new read! Scan your classmates' reviews for some ideas!

# Technology Integration Ideas to Support Choice Reading

*Note: This is a working document that will develop throughout the year. Please feel free to add your own technology integration ideas, or add a comment indicating questions or where further support is needed.*

| Technology Tool | Language Arts Alignment | Tips |
|---|---|---|
| "We are readers" Padlet wall | Model *ourselves* as readers | • Continue to post recommendations<br><br>• Share our wall with colleagues outside of the department to post |
| Padlet | Create an online space for *students* to share what they are reading | • Follow this guide when using Padlet with students and eliminate anonymous posting |
| Google Classroom | | • Post a question using the Google Classroom support resource where students can respond |
| Google Drawings | | • Create a digital, collaborative bulletin board for students to upload photos of books and link to recorded or typed recommendations |
| Verso | | • Assign an activity in which students comment on what they are reading<br><br>   o Keep posts anonymous to students, but viewable for the teacher |

*(Continued)*

(Continued)

| Technology Tool | Language Arts Alignment | Tips |
|---|---|---|
| Google Forms | Confer with students | • Streamline the record-keeping process<br>  o Include class period, date, a dropdown list of students, and a notes field for quick input |
| Recap | Create opportunities for students to reflect on learning and self-assess progress | • Have students record a short reflection video (the teacher can designate a time constraint) or answer reflection questions |
| Screencastify | Record student book buzzes | • Record video from a tab or webcam and save it to Google Drive<br>  o Invite camera-shy students to record an image of the book and do a voiceover |
| Camera | | • Ask students to use the camera on their own device to record a quick video (videos can then be submitted through Google Classroom) |
| Tweet from class | Tweet book buzzes | • Have your students post book buzzes to a class Twitter account for an authentic audience |
| Google Forms | | • Create a text question that limits the number of characters a student can submit |
| Google Drawings (or, for students using their own devices, any photo-editing app) | Have students visually share and reflect on what they are currently reading, then mark up | • Have students submit their work through Google Classroom or the "upload file" feature in Google Forms |

| Technology Tool | Language Arts Alignment | Tips |
| --- | --- | --- |
| | a photo of a specific quote from a page of their book to identify key takeaways, reactions, and so on | • Search #BookSnaps on social media<br>• Learn more from Tara M. Martin, originator of the #BookSnaps idea, at www.tarammartin.com/booksnaps-snapping-for-learning/ |
| Timer | Create consistent time in class to read | • Use a timer (available from a Google search) to help students stay focused and build stamina while reading<br>• Encourage students to use their own devices to set a timer when reading at home |
| Goodreads | Have students create a "what to read next" list and a timeline of books read | • Have students create "bookshelves" of books read, books currently reading, and books they want to read |
| Google Calendar | | • Have students create a reader calendar where they track the books they are reading and how long it takes to finish a book<br>  o Invite them to use the "task" feature to keep a list of books to read next |
| Google Keep | | • Have students keep "notes" that include books they want to read |

# My Reading Goals: Student Sample

**Volume:** I was able to finish about a book a week by reading in class and a little bit outside of class some days on the bus to games or if I didn't have a lot of homework. But now I'm reading <u>Unbroken</u>, and it's going a lot slower. It's hard because there's a lot of information about World War II that I don't know about. In order to finish this book in less than two weeks, I need to find more time outside of school. I'm going to try reading on the weekends before I start my other homework.

**Habits:** I really don't like doing a lot of writing about reading, but it's making the writing assignments hard to do because I don't have a lot of notes. In order to write about <u>Unbroken</u>, I need to keep notes from my research and from my reading. I'm going to start keeping sticky notes with me when I read.

**Genre:** I'm surprised that I like this nonfiction book. Carlos suggested it, and it's really good. I usually read fiction. I'm going to try another book by Laura Hillenbrand after this. My teacher wants me to try some poetry, too. I'm not sure about that yet. I tried a poetry book, and it was kind of boring. But I will try a biography before the end of the marking period.

**RESOURCE 4**

## Bookmark Calendar Template

| Name: | | |
|---|---|---|
| Title: | | |
| Author: | | |

| Date | Pages | Y/N |
|---|---|---|
| | | |
| | | |
| | | |
| | | |
| | | |
| | | |
| | | |
| | | |
| | | |
| Date Completed: | | |

online resources

# Sample Grade 10 Unit Plan: *The Scarlet Letter*

**Fiction**

**Mentor Text/Class Novel:** *The Scarlet Letter* by Nathaniel Hawthorne (Penguin Books, 2003)

**Standards Addressed:** RL.9–10.1, RL.9–10.2, RL.9–10.3, RL.9–10.4, RL.9–10.5, RI.9–10.9

| | Teaching Point | Possible Text Excerpts | What Students Will Try |
|---|---|---|---|
| 1 | *Readers take careful note of all the important information conveyed in the beginning of a book; knowing the way the author structures the beginning is important.* | pp. 7–8 The introduction's first two pages<br>p. 28 "But the past was not dead . . ."<br>p. 29 "But one idle and rainy day . . ."<br>p. 31 "The object that most drew my attention . . ."<br>p. 36 ". . . he need never try to write romances."<br>The teacher thinks aloud about what he or she notices while reading the introduction, rereading key parts such as those noted above. Think-aloud topics might include how the intro frames the narrative, the narrator and his role in retelling a story, and the category of "romance" of the narrator's fictional account of the history of the scarlet *A*. The teacher can also think aloud about the structure of this long essay and how it sets the atmosphere, provides essential information, establishes the conflict, provides the basis for the story, and defines the work's genre (romance). | Students take a few minutes to read or reread the beginning of their book, jot down what they notice, then share with a partner about what they notice about how the book begins and how that information is conveyed. They all work to answer: what purpose does the structure of the beginning serve? |

| Teaching Point | Possible Text Excerpts | What Students Will Try |
|---|---|---|
| | Presented here, too, is an opportunity to acknowledge what many students consider confusing—Old English—and how the teacher, as a strong reader, makes sense of it. | |
| 2 *Readers analyze the author's choice of narrator, considering the purpose and impact of that perspective.* | p. 13 "Doubtless . . ." <br><br> p. 18 "It would be sad injustice . . ." <br><br> p. 32 "In the absorbing contemplation . . ." <br><br> p. 40 "In short, unpleasant as was my predicament . . ." <br><br> Students read in pairs, or with the teacher, and briefly consider implications of the surveyor's perspective. For instance, what is the impact of Hawthorne telling the story twice removed through Jonathan Pue, what are the similarities to Hawthorne's views, are such parallels relevant, and how is the narrator's perspective as an outsider similar to Hester Prynne's? | Readers consider the implications of the narrator's perspective in their books. They consider and take note of the following: <br><br> • What role does the narrator serve, other than simply conveying the events? <br><br> • What information is the narrator privy to, and what is he or she unaware of? <br><br> Students should write about a half page about why their author may have chosen that narrator, and how that perspective is relevant. |

*(Continued)*

| Teaching Point | Possible Text Excerpts | What Students Will Try |
|---|---|---|
| 3 | *Readers can do additional "sleuthing" to understand the cultural context in which a text was written, and thereby have a more nuanced understanding of the book.* | The teacher jots down questions generated from the reading so far, such as the following:<br><br>• What was life like in these colonies?<br>• What was the relationship between law and religion?<br>• What is a custom house?<br>• Why is the condemnation of Hester so public?<br>• Why is there this obsession over sin?<br>• What was the Puritans' notion of what was sinful?<br><br>Then, the teacher shares researched information that answers those questions. Research includes the main tenets of Puritanism and its views on sin. Modeled notes will also include what that information does for students' understanding of key scenes so far, such as Hester's public condemnation and why she was punished for adultery in such a way. | Students write down questions from their reading so far. Then, they go about getting answers to those questions online and chart how that information affects their understanding of the text. |

| Questions | Information | New Understandings |
|---|---|---|
|  |  |  |

| Questions | Information | New Understandings |
|---|---|---|
|  |  |  |

| | Teaching Point | Possible Text Excerpts | What Students Will Try |
|---|---|---|---|
| 4 | *Readers pay attention to significant and repeated images and consider what those images might symbolize in the larger context of the novel.* | p. 45 Descriptions of the prison door, such as "heavily timbered with oak, and studded with iron spikes," "marked with weather-stains and other indications of age," and "beetle-browed and gloomy front." Descriptions of the rosebush with "delicate gems," and a "fragile beauty." Students briefly consider in pairs the possible significance of these images, and the teacher may add on his or her thinking as well—for instance, how the unrelenting, imposing, dark door versus the beauty of the rosebush shows the contradiction between the harshness of the Puritan society and the out-of-place natural beauty of the "sweet moral blossom" or how the rose (romance) is trying to survive among the gloomy surroundings. Another image to explore: p. 50 Descriptions of the scarlet letter, such as "On the breast of her gown, in fine red cloth surrounded | Students take notes as they read, considering the following questions: <br><br> • What images, objects, colors, and settings are described in detail; seem to come up again and again; or simply seem potentially relevant and put there for a reason by the author? <br><br> • What is their significance, based on how they are described? <br><br> • What ideas do they reinforce in your book? <br><br> • How do they deepen or change your understanding of the big ideas in your book? |

online resources ↖ Full unit plan available for download from resources.corwin.com/nofakereading

# Unit Planning Template

**Grade ___ Unit Plan**
**Fiction**
**Mentor Text/Class Novel:**
**Standards Addressed:**

| Lesson 1 | Lesson 2 | Lesson 3 | Lesson 4 | Lesson 5 |
|---|---|---|---|---|
| What readers pay attention to, question, and think about . . . | What readers pay attention to, question, and think about . . . | What readers pay attention to, question, and think about . . . | What readers pay attention to, question, and think about . . . | What readers pay attention to, question, and think about . . . |
| Text excerpt: | Text excerpt: | Text excerpt: | Text excerpt: | Text excerpt: |

 Full unit planning template available for download from resources.corwin.com/nofakereading

## Sample Grade 8 Unit Plan: *The Outsiders*

Fiction

Mentor Text/Class Novel: *The Outsiders* by S. E. Hinton (Penguin Books, 2012)

Standards Addressed: RL.8.1, RL.8.2, RL.8.3, RL.8.4, RL.8.6

| Lesson 1 | Lesson 2 | Lesson 3 | Lesson 4 | Lesson 5 |
|---|---|---|---|---|
| *Readers slow down and pay attention to the beginning of a novel where there is essential information about setting and character relationships.* <br><br> Text excerpt: pp. 1–3 "That's just the way things are . . ." <br><br> The teacher models, "What I've learned so far about . . ." | *Readers think about the setting in ways that go further than basic facts of time and place. They can take a nuanced look at the values, rules, and social norms for race, class, gender, age, sexuality, and more for that time and place.* <br><br> Text excerpt: p. 12, "tough and tuff are two different words . . ." | *Readers start imagining each distinct character beyond just his or her physical characteristics.* <br><br> Text excerpt: pp. 1–3 citing what we know about Ponyboy, even though we don't know his name yet <br><br> The teacher might say, "I'm not thinking of Ponyboy as a generic guy, but I'm using every detail I can glean to get a crisp picture of who he is and more. | *Readers can take note of multiple conflicts in a novel. We're used to looking for one obvious plot-driving conflict, but there are often underlying conflicts that we can track, too.* <br><br> Text excerpt: pp. 31–33 <br><br> There is a major conflict: two social groups don't get along. | *Readers can identify antagonists and think about their role in moving the plot forward. It helps if we take time to understand what the antagonists want, and what is their backstory. This also gets us to a more sophisticated, perhaps empathetic understanding of the antagonist beyond "the bad guy."* |

 **Full unit plan available for download from resources.corwin.com/nofakereading**

## Sample Grade 11 Unit Plan: *Narrative of the Life of Frederick Douglass, an American Slave*

### Nonfiction

**Text:** *Narrative of the Life of Frederick Douglass, an American Slave* by Frederick Douglass (Simon & Brown, 2012)

**Standards Addressed:** RI.1, RI.2, RI.3, RI.4, RI.6

| Lesson 1 | Lesson 2 | Lesson 3 | Lesson 4 | Lesson 5 |
|---|---|---|---|---|
| *Readers use all the information available before diving into Chapter 1.* | *Readers of nonfiction pay close attention to the context in which it was written.* | *Readers of nonfiction pay attention to character (or subjects) just as they do in fiction. What are the traits of the characters or subjects we can notice in our autobiographies?* | *Readers of autobiographies, biographies, and memoirs infer all they can about relationships between the subject and other key players, using explicit and nuanced evidence to support their theories.* | *Readers of nonfiction try to read as much as they can about that one subject, choosing easier books on a challenging topic first to better acquaint themselves with more background knowledge.* |
| There is a rich amount of valuable information to pay attention to outside of the "beginning" of many biographies and other nonfiction texts—the front- and back-cover blurbs, of course, but also the table of contents in addition to (in this case) a short bio, timeline, preface, introduction, and letter. | Readers might ask themselves questions: Who is speaking? What perspective do they represent? Whose voice was not represented? What were the conflicts at the time? Who had power? Who did not?

Text excerpt: p. 1 of preface, including | Text excerpt: p. 18 "I never saw my mother . . ."

This paragraph conveys a great deal about Douglass's mother, such as her capacity for silent suffering and her dedication to her child, | Text excerpt: p. 17 "White children could tell their ages. I could not tell why I ought to be deprived of the same privilege."

pp. 18–19 ". . . such slaves . . ." when footnote at the bottom explaining who William Garrison was and what group he represented. | The teacher models questions that arise while reading *Narrative*, such as the laws regarding children born from rape, the prohibition of education, and the differences |

 Full unit plan available for download from resources.corwin.com/nofakereading

# Reading Notebook Prompts:
## Transfer of Skills to Choice Books

| Focus | Fiction Notebook Prompts: Transfer of Skills to Choice Books |
|---|---|
| Plot and Structure | • What event or conflict gets the story started right away? Why would the author start there?<br>• What was the most important event in the story so far? Why? What prompted the main character to act as he or she did?<br>• What was the climax of the story? How do you know it was the climax?<br>• What hardships did the main character have to deal with?<br>• What are two or three of the turning points in the story?<br>• What scenes got left out? How do you know they happened even though they weren't explicitly written?<br>• What parts of the book move slowly, and what parts move quickly?<br>• How much time passes throughout the entire book? Where does time move the fastest? Slowest? Why did the author write it that way?<br>• What is the flow of chapters? Why did the author tell the story in that order?<br>• How does tension build throughout the text? How does the author make you want to keep reading, or when does the author lose you? Why? |
| Character | • How does the author paint a picture of this character?<br>• What are the multiple, even conflicting, characteristics of the main character? How do you know these are characteristics and not just one-time emotions?<br>• What conflicts does the character face? How does he or she resolve them?<br>• Who is the antagonist in your book, and how does this character shape the decisions of the main character? |

*(Continued)*

| Focus | Fiction Notebook Prompts: Transfer of Skills to Choice Books |
|-------|--------------------------------------------------------------|
|  | • How does the main character grow or change across the book?<br><br>• What is the single most important decision the main character makes in the story? Why?<br><br>• Write an obituary for one of the characters.<br><br>• Tell about one of your favorite characters in the book. What makes you like him or her?<br><br>• Refer to one section of dialogue and discuss what is said and what is not said. What does that teach you about the characters?<br><br>• What factors, relationships, and events shaped the main characters the most?<br><br>• Try answering any of the above questions for minor characters in your book.<br><br>• Do any minor characters become more like main characters or key players by the end? How does their role shift?<br><br>• Who is a minor character that the book could not exist without? Why? |
| Setting | • How does the author introduce details of setting? How do you learn about where this story takes place?<br><br>• What is significant about this story's setting other than time and place? For instance, what are the cultural values, social hierarchies, and unspoken rules?<br><br>• How does the author make this setting believable? How does the author make an unfamiliar place feel familiar, like you can picture it in your head?<br><br>• Show how a character is affected or changed by the setting. How does he or she act differently based on different environments?<br><br>• Why might the author have chosen this setting? How does the setting play a crucial part in how the story unfolds? What aspects of the story could not exist in a different setting?<br><br>• Describe how the setting impacts multiple characters in different ways. |

| Focus | Fiction Notebook Prompts: Transfer of Skills to Choice Books |
|---|---|
| Symbols | • What special value do any of the symbols carry for one character, and how is that value different for another character? Show your thinking in a table, or graph if you prefer.<br><br>• How does the symbol help advance the plot or show character change throughout the book? Give specific evidence to back up your thinking from more than one place in the book.<br><br>• You found a repeating image. What is the larger theme or idea that the author is getting to by bringing up that image again and again? |
| Foreshadowing and Flashbacks | • Were there clues that led you to believe something would happen?<br><br>• Share a short excerpt or refer to a passage that includes foreshadowing. Describe how the author plants a seed for something to come.<br><br>• Looking back at foreshadowing "clues," how might you notice these on a first read in a future book? What patterns of foreshadowing make you think it's a hint of what's to come, not just a random description or detail?<br><br>• Does the author use shifts in time? Cite a place in the book and explain why the author might have used time shifts there. What new information does the flashback or flashforward provide? |
| Title | • How does the title fit the book? Does your understanding of the title change throughout the book?<br><br>• Is the title of the book a good fit? Why or why not?<br><br>• If chapters are titled, how do they help you predict what might happen? Is there a pattern to the chapter titles? How do they fit with the book's title? |
| Narrator | • Who is the narrator in the story, and why do you think the author chose this narrator?<br><br>• Is the book written in first or third person? Share an example from the text to show how you know. |

*(Continued)*

| Focus | Fiction Notebook Prompts: Transfer of Skills to Choice Books |
|---|---|
| | • If the author changed between narrators, who are they? Why do you think the author told the story from multiple perspectives?<br><br>  o How do the perspectives rotate, and why do you hear from some voices when you do? |
| Theme | • What does the main character learn, what realization does he or she have, or how does he or she grow across this text? Explain how that can serve as a theme to this book.<br><br>• Identify a theme in this book in a complete sentence, not simply a word. What does the author seem to be saying about that theme?<br><br>• Identify another theme in this book. What does the author want the reader to consider about that big idea?<br><br>• After you've looked at more than one theme, which is the most important? Why?<br><br>• What was the author showing about life through this story?<br><br>• What can be learned from this novel?<br><br>• Revisit one of your initial theme statements. Does it still hold true? How has your thinking changed about the theme now that you have read more of the book? Revise your theme statement.<br><br>• What caused the plot to end as it did—luck, hard work, coincidence, skill, ideas, or others' influences? Or some combination thereof? How does the cause of that ending contribute to the overall theme?<br><br>• Do you see a theme in this book that you have also seen in another book? How might that theme extend to your life? What would your life's "theme" be in relation to the book's?<br><br>• Is the theme a cliché, or is it realistic? Why? |
| Language and Word Choice | • Does this author use a formal or informal kind of language? What impact does that have on the book? Does it change throughout? Why?<br><br>• Jot down words that intrigue you as you read today, then look them up on your phone. |

| Focus | Fiction Notebook Prompts: Transfer of Skills to Choice Books |
|---|---|
| | • If your book has a lot of words that you don't understand, write about how that's affecting your reading. What do you do to help? What parts do you choose to reread or not? Would you choose another book that is this difficult again or not? Why?<br><br>• Jot down words as you read today that are essential to understanding this text. Explain why those words are particularly significant.<br><br>• Choose a descriptive passage and jot down the language that makes that passage come to life in your mind. Which nouns, verbs, and adjectives stand out? Why did the author choose those words over others? |
| Connections | • What other books have you read by this author? How are they similar, and how are they different?<br><br>• Finish one of these prompts:<br>  o This book reminds me of . . . (my life, family, experiences, places I've been)<br>  o I understand how the character feels because . . .<br>  o I can connect with . . . because . . .<br>  o This book is similar to/different from . . . (genre, text structure, theme, plot, character, use of language)<br>  o This book is similar to/different from . . . (something I've seen on TV, a current event, a newspaper article, a topic in another class, real-world happenings, a conversation)<br><br>• If the theme of one text carries over into others, how does each author revise that idea in his or her text?<br><br>• If you see characters that are similar to other characters, do they fall under archetype patterns? Why or why not?<br><br>• If this book references other texts, stop and jot those references down. Then go back to them and look them up if you need to. Why does the author include those? What do they mean in relation to the larger text? |

# Examples of Realistic Fiction
# Book Club Annotations and Analysis

*Use your annotations to extend your thoughts for discussion now, and so you'll have developed body paragraphs for your literary analysis paper later.*

*Remember, you want to analyze HOW the author uses that element of realistic fiction to create realistic writing and WHY that element/way it is written is effective in creating writing that seems real. This is NOT a summary, but an ANALYSIS.*

## HOW TO STRUCTURE YOUR
## EXTENDED THOUGHT PARAGRAPH

*(Each body paragraph should include transition, example, and explanation.)*

1. The author uses _____ in order to _____.

2. For example, _____.

*(Provide specific examples of how the author makes the writing seem real WITH PAGE NUMBER.)*

3. This makes the writing seem real because _____.

or

This is effective because _____.

*(Explain how the evidence you provide for the part you chose seems real.)*

You want to make sure you explain **HOW the author uses** that specific element

and

**WHY the way it is written is effective** in making the writing seem real.

**Effects of the structure (*How* does the way the book is written create realistic characters, plot, setting, etc.?)**

**Here is an example of what I'm looking for, using *Tears of a Tiger*:**

p. 3, paragraphs 1–3 (*Tears of a Tiger*): Written like a conversation and not like normal dialogue—makes it seem like I'm overhearing a real conversation

One example of how the author uses realistic dialogue to make the plot seem real is how the author writes in "conversation." Even though there is technically dialogue since two people are talking, the author creates a sense that there is a real conversation you are overhearing. She doesn't use traditional dialogue grammar, such as quotation marks or dialogue tags. For example, this is seen on page 3, when Rob is speaking with Andy. The book states,

— Hey, Rob! Live game, man . . .

— Yo, Andy, my main man! I see you . . .

As you can see, there are no quotation marks used, and there is no narrator who is stating, "He said . . . She said . . ." There is also no mention of who is speaking other than when the person uses names in speech (such as in the first quote the reader knows that someone is talking to Rob, and then we find out that Rob is talking to Andy, so the reader can now follow who is speaking from that point forward). This makes it seem more real because in life, there is no narrator, and if you overhear a conversation, you don't get background information regarding what is being said. You are put right into the moment with the characters and you have to follow the conversation to see who is speaking. By writing as if we are overhearing the conversation, it makes the plot and overall context of the book seem like real life.

— Hey, Rob! Live game, man. You be flyin' with the hoops, man! Swoosh! Ain't nobody better, 'cept maybe me.

— Yo, Andy, my main man! I see you been eatin' bull crap for dinner again! You only wish you was as good as me! I, Robert Orlando Washington, will be makin' *billions* of dollars playin' for the N.B.A.! Want me to save you a ticket to one of my games?

*(Continued)*

(Continued)

— Man, you be trippin'! You better be lookin' out for *me*—here's my card—Andy Jackson—superstar shooter and lover to the ladies—'cause I'm gonna be the high-point man on the opposin' team—the team that wipes the floor with you and your billion dollars!

**Includes realistic language (*How* does the use of dialogue and dialect add to the realistic effect? *How* does the narration or way the characters speak create realistic effects?)**
**Again, here is an example of appropriate analysis with references to the text:**

p. 3, paragraphs 1–3 (*Tears of a Tiger*): Informal speech/improper grammar—sounds like my friends and people I overhear talking

Another way that the author uses realistic dialogue to make the characters seem real is through the use of informal speech. The author uses a specific informal language that is not proper English. This is reminiscent of language I hear on a regular basis, which makes me relate more to the characters and makes them seem like real people. For example, on page 3, the author uses the words *ain't*, *'cept*, and *'cause* in the dialogue. The author also has the boys speak without the use of *g* when saying *–ing*. This makes it seem like the boys are comfortable with each other. Since they're ragging on each other but also not using proper English, it's clear they're probably close friends. This makes it seem real because there is a difference between how you talk with your friends and how you talk with a stranger, a teacher, or your parents. Since they are using words like *ain't* and *'cause* and not using *g* at the end of sentences, it seems very informal and casual. This is how friends in real life actually speak. In fact, this is how I speak with my friends. When reading the dialogue between characters, because of the use of language, I felt like I could be listening in on a conversation between my friends and me. This makes the characters seem more real.

# Choice Read or Class Novel Check-In: How Do You Know They're Really Reading?

Name:

Book title:

Current page:

Date:

Author:

Expects to finish by:

| Explanation of randomly pulled page/quote: | **1** **2** **3** |
|---|---|
| 1 point | • Offers few details<br><br>• Says little, makes vague comments, or makes comments that could have come from the book jacket<br><br>• Is confused or unclear about basic plot lines |
| 2 points | • Names characters and plot lines but may struggle to place the passage<br><br>• Speaks at some length about the book even if the excerpt is not contextualized |
| 3 points | • Contextualizes what happened before and afterward<br><br>• References who is talking or who is in the scene<br><br>• Knows the character's objective<br><br>• Explains how the passage relates to the whole |

Reschedule date (optional): _____

# Reading Notebook Rubric Sample 1

| JOURNALS<br>Expectation | Needs Much Work | Developing | Satisfactory | Excellent |
|---|---|---|---|---|
| Writing is thoughtful in both content and form. Journal entries cover the entirety of the novel (amount, length, mechanics, grammar, spelling, etc.). | 3 points | 4–5 points | 7–8 points | 9–10 points |
| Reader has made appropriately challenging choices and has made a conscious effort to achieve some variety in reading and writing. | 3 points | 4–5 points | 7–8 points | 9–10 points |
| Reader presents original creative ideas, insights, and interpretations and **uses evidence from the text to back them up.** | 5 points | 8–10 points | 11–15 points | 18–20 points |

| JOURNALS Expectation | Needs Much Work | Developing | Satisfactory | Excellent |
|---|---|---|---|---|
| Reader shows basic comprehension of text, but thinks critically and thinks beyond the text as well. Reader connects/ analyzes/evaluates text, ideas, themes, and author's craft. | 5 points | 8–10 points | 11–15 points | 18–20 points |
| Vocabulary is chosen throughout the entirety of the novel. It is kept in a neat separate section of the journal, and all assigned parts are complete. | 3 points | 4–5 points | 7–8 points | 9–10 points |
| Journal is handed in on time. | 1 point | 3 points | 4 points | 5 points |

**TOTAL:** _____/75 points

# Reading Notebook Rubric Sample 2

**Name:** _____

## Reader's Notebook Rubric

### MARKING PERIOD 1

| 4 points | 6 points | 8 points | 10 points |
|---|---|---|---|
| Notebook entries are brief (often less than three sentences). Ideas and opinions are not supported with evidence. Questions or original thoughts about books read are not attempted. There is no evidence of interest or growth in the reader. The notebook is lacking notes as a whole and is largely disorganized. | Notebook entries include opinions and summaries with little evidence from the book. Little to no questions are raised about the books being read. There is little to no interest in reading or evidence of growth in the reader. Entries are missing from the table of contents and actual body of the notebook. | Notebook entries reflect a solid understanding of the book, as well as theories and ideas regarding character and theme that are supported with ample evidence from the book. Questions may be raised and/or answered by the reader. Entries may also show evidence of interest in reading and/or growth by the reader. All entries are completed and organized according to the table of contents. | Notebook entries indicate an excellent understanding of the books. All ideas and writings about character and theme are supported with evidence from the test, as well as follow-up thinking and explanations. Entries reflect a strong interest in reading as well as evidenced growth across the marking periods. All entries are completed and organized according to the table of contents. |

# Reading Notebook Rubric Sample 3

## Reader's Notebook Check

|  | Student | Teacher |
|---|---|---|
| **Updated Reading List and Genre Graph** | ___/2 | ___/2 |

- *Reading list is complete with*

  o *Title*

  o *Author*

  o *Date started and completed*

  o *Pages read*

  o *Rating*

- *Genre graph correctly reflects the number of books read*

| **Things Good Readers Do List** | ___/1 | ___/1 |
|---|---|---|

*Objectives for each lesson written down*

| **Learning From the Blurb** | ___/2 | ___/2 |
|---|---|---|

*Notes from the blurb of your book*

*(Continued)*

(Continued)

|  | Student | Teacher |
|---|---|---|
| **Reading Strategies Evidence** | ___/4 | ___/4 |

- *Notes on each strategy written down in notebook*

- *Book title and author*

- *Strategy applied at length in notebook entry*

- *Text evidence or specific reference to text*

- *Page number(s) included*

- *Total of four strategy responses*

| **Appearance** | ___/1 | ___/1 |
|---|---|---|

*Notebook is neat and easy to read. Notes/jots are organized with pages in numerical order. It is obvious that the reader takes pride in his/her work. Handwriting is legible to anyone.*

**Total: ___/10**

online resources

# Sample Essay Assignment, Outline, and Rubric Using Choice Book

## Your Choice—Essay Outline

### INTRODUCTION

1. Construct a compelling introductory statement that includes the title and author of the story.

   _____

   _____

   _____

2. Provide a BRIEF summary of the story. Only include enough background information to prepare the reader for the rest of the essay. *(What is the general plot of the story?)*

   _____

   _____

   _____

   _____

3. THESIS STATEMENT *(What is the author's main point/theme?)* Remember that the thesis statement controls the ENTIRE ESSAY and should represent the main idea.

   _____

   _____

   _____

*(Continued)*

## BODY PARAGRAPHS

*Provide *evidence* to *support the thesis.*

*Only address one piece of evidence per paragraph.

*Don't stray off topic or summarize the plot.

**Topic Sentence** *(Describe one example.)*

_____

_____

_____

**Examples/Explanation** *(Explain and provide specific details from the novel. Include a QUOTE to support your explanation.)*

_____

_____

_____

_____

_____

_____

_____

_____

**Concluding Statement**  *(Link your ideas back to the thesis statement.)*

_____

_____

_____

**Topic Sentence** *(Transition to your second example.)*

_____

_____

_____

_____

**Examples/Explanation** *(Explain and provide specific details from the novel. Include a QUOTE to support your explanation.)*

_____

_____

_____

_____

_____

_____

_____

_____

_____

**Concluding Statement** *(Link your ideas back to the thesis statement.)*

_____

_____

_____

_____

_____

*(Continued)*

**Topic Sentence** *(Transition to your final example.)* \*\*\*THIS PARAGRAPH IS OPTIONAL\*\*\*

_____

_____

_____

_____

**Examples/Explanation** *(Explain and provide specific details from the novel. Include a QUOTE to support your explanation.)*

_____

_____

_____

_____

_____

_____

_____

_____

_____

**Concluding Statement** *(Link your ideas back to the thesis statement.)*

_____

_____

_____

_____

## CONCLUSION

*Bring together the ideas and reinforce the thesis statement.
*What theme is prominent throughout this novel?*

_____

_____

_____

_____

*Reiterate how the theme is shown through the literature.*

_____

_____

_____

_____

_____

_____

_____

CLINCHER STATEMENT  (**Rephrase your thesis statement.**)

*What message does the author want you to take away from this piece?*

_____

_____

_____

_____

*(Continued)*

(Continued)

## FOCUS CORRECTION AREAS

**Reading Comprehension and Analysis**          /20

**Goal:** A well-developed analysis supported by effective text evidence

**Structure and Organization**          /20

**Goal:** A four- to five-paragraph essay that demonstrates coherence and unity

**Writing Skills**          /10

**Goal: To** utilize active- and present-tense verbs while avoiding fragments and run-ons

# Sample Literary Analysis
# Essay Assignment for Choice Book

**LA 1**

**Final Essay**

**Independent Choice Book**

**50 points**

For your final literary essay, you may respond to one of the following prompts. Both explore themes that we have discussed at length in connection with *Great Expectations*. You will now apply these ideas to your choice book. Be sure to consider the Focus Correction Areas and to use your best reading and writing skills. Your essay will go through the writing process of drafting, revising, editing, and conferencing.

**SCHEDULE**

**Rough Draft:** Thursday, January 19 (bring colored pencils to class)

**Final Draft:** Monday, January 23

**Choice 1:** Analyze the role of social class in your novel. How are characters treated, and what sort of power do they hold because of wealth and class? Additionally, how are those of a lower socioeconomic class regarded, and what role does ambition and the desire for self-advancement play in the novel?

**Choice 2:** Analyze the treatment of children and its long-term effect on them as they reach adulthood. Were any of your characters victims of mistreatment and/or abuse, and how did this shape them later on in their lives? Were there expectations put in place for them, and how did this affect them as young adults?

*(Continued)*

(Continued)

## FOCUS CORRECTION AREAS

**Reading Comprehension and Analysis** /20

**Goal:** A well-developed analysis supported by effective text evidence

**Structure and Organization** /20

**Goal:** A four- to five-paragraph essay that demonstrates coherence and unity

**Writing Skills** /10

**Goal: To** utilize active- and present-tense verbs while avoiding fragments and run-ons

# References

Alliance for Excellent Education. (2006, July 11). *Reading next: A vision for action and research in middle and high school literacy*. Retrieved from http://all4ed.org/reports-factsheets/reading-next-a-vision-for-action-and-research-in-middle-and-high-school-literacy/

Allington, R. (2002, June). What I've learned about effective reading instruction from a decade of studying exemplary classroom teachers. *Phi Delta Kappan, 83*(10), 740–747. Retrieved from http://www.jstor.org/stable/20440246?origin=JSTOR-pdf&seq=1#page_scan_tab_contents

Allington, R. (2013). What really matters when working with struggling readers. *The Reading Teacher, 66*(7), 520–530. Retrieved from https://cr4yrnvsd44.files.wordpress.com/2014/12/allington-what-really-works-for-struggling-readers.pdf

Anderson, C. (2000). *How's it going? A practical guide to conferring with student writers*. Portsmouth, NH: Heinemann.

Atwell, N. (2007). *The reading zone*. New York, NY: Scholastic.

Beers, K. (2003). *When kids can't read*. Portsmouth, NH: Heinemann.

Beers, K., & Probst, R. (2016). *Reading nonfiction: Stances, signposts, and strategies*. Portsmouth, NH: Heinemann.

Belluck, P. (2014, October 3). For better social skills, scientists recommend a little Chekov. *New York Times*.

Bidwell, A. (2014, November 13). Average student loan debt reaches $30,000. *U.S. News & World Report*. Retrieved from http://www.usnews.com/news/articles/2014/11/13/average-student-loan-debt-hits-30-000

Bomer, K. (2010). *Hidden gems: Naming and teaching from the brilliance in every student's writing*. Portsmouth, NH: Heinemann.

Calkins, L. (2000). *The art of teaching reading*. Upper Saddle River, NJ: Pearson.

Center for Teaching and Learning. (2017). *High school readers*. Retrieved from http://c-t-l.org/high-school-readers/

Daniels, H., & Daniels, E. (2013). The best-kept teaching secret: How written conversations engage kids, activate learning, and grow fluent writers, K–12. Thousand Oaks, CA: Corwin.

Daniels, H., & Steinke, N. (2011). *Texts and lessons for content-area reading*. Portsmouth, NH: Heinemann.

Delpit, L. (2012). "Multiplication is for White people": Raising expectations for other people's children. New York, NY: New Press.

Denby, D. (2016). *Lit up: One reporter, three schools, twenty-four books that can change lives*. New York, NY: Holt.

Douglass, F. (2003). *Narrative of the Life of Frederick Douglass, an American Slave*. New York, NY: Barnes & Noble Books. (Original work published 1845)

Fisher, A. (2013, July 10). Giving a speech? Conquer the five-minute attention span. *Fortune*. Retrieved from http://fortune.com/2013/07/10/giving-a-speech-conquer-the-five-minute-attention-span/

Fisher, D. (2008). Effective use of the gradual release of responsibility model. *Author Monographs*. Retrieved from https://www.mheonline.com/_treasures/pdf/douglas_fisher.pdf

Fisher, D., Frey, N., & Anderson, H. L. (2015). *Text-dependent questions, grades 6–12: Pathways to close and critical reading*. Thousand Oaks, CA: Corwin.

Fisher, D., Frey, N., & Hattie, J. (2016). *Visible learning for literacy*. Thousand Oaks, CA: Corwin.

Gallagher, K. (2009). *Readicide: How schools are killing reading and what you can do about it*. Portland, ME: Stenhouse.

Gladwell, M. (2012). *Outliers: The story of success*. Retrieved from http://www.lequydonhanoi.edu.vn/upload_images/S%C3%A1ch%20ngo%E1%BA%A1i%20ng%E1%BB%AF/Outliers-%20The%20Story%20of%20Success.pdf

Godsey, M. (2016, March 17). The value of using podcasts in class. *Atlantic*. Retrieved from http://www.theatlantic.com/education/archive/2016/03/the-benefits-of-podcasts-in-class/473925/

Goldman, C. (2012, September 7). This is your brain on Jane Austen, and Stanford researchers are taking notes. *Stanford News*. Retrieved from http://news.stanford.edu/news/2012/september/austen-reading-fmri-090712.html

Goodreads. (2017). *Popular teen books*. Retrieved from https://www.goodreads.com/shelf/show/teen

Harry Ransom Center. (2010). Teaching materials from the David Foster Wallace archive. *University of Texas at Austin*. Retrieved from http://www.hrc.utexas.edu/press/releases/2010/dfw/teaching/

Hawthorne, N. (2003). *The scarlet letter*. New York, NY: Penguin Books. (Original work published 1850)

Hinton, S. E. (2012). *The outsiders*. New York, NY: Penguin Books. (Original work published 1967)

Ivey, G., & Johnston, P. H. (2015). Engaged reading as a collaborative transformative process. *Journal of Literacy Research, 47*(3), 297–327. Retrieved from https://www.uwlax.edu/uploadedFiles/Academics/conted/Reading_Research_Symposium/2016-RRS-handout-Ivey-Reading-Collaborative.pdf

Johnston, P. (2012, July 23). Blogstitute Week 5: Reducing instruction, increasing engagement. *The Stenhouse Blog*. Retrieved from http://blog.stenhouse.com/archives/2012/07/23/blogstitute-week-5-reducing-instruction-increasing-engagement/

Kidd, D., & Castano, E. (2013, October 18). Reading literary fiction improves theory of mind. *Science*. Retrieved from http://science.sciencemag.org/content/342/6156/377

Kittle, P. (2013). *Book love*. Portsmouth, NH: Heinemann.

Kittle, P. (2014). *Custom booklist*. Retrieved from http://pennykittle.net/uploads/images/PDFs/Reading_Lists/Book_Love_2014_HS_book_list.pdf

Krashen, S. (2004a). *The power of reading: Insights from the research.* Portsmouth, NH: Heinemann.

Krashen, S. (2004b, June 24). *Free voluntary reading: New research, applications, and controversies.* Presented at PAC5, Vladivostok, Russia. Retrieved from http://www.sdkrashen.com/content/articles/pac5.pdf

McSpadden, K. (2015, May 13). You now have a shorter attention span than a goldfish. *Time.* Retrieved from http://time.com/3858309/attention-spans-goldfish/

Mikaelsen, B. (2001). *Touching spirit bear.* New York, NY: HarperCollins.

Miller, D. (2014). *Reading in the wild: The Book Whisperer's keys to cultivating lifelong reading habits.* New York, NY: Scholastic.

National Center for Education Statistics. (2002, April). *Adult literacy in America: A first look at the findings of the National Adult Literacy Survey* (3rd ed.). Retrieved from https://nces.ed.gov/pubs93/93275.pdf

National Center for Education Statistics. (2010). *Digest of Education Statistics: Table 241.* Retrieved from https://nces.ed.gov/pubs93/93275.pdf

*Nerdy Book Club.* (2015). Nerdy book awards. Retrieved from https://nerdybookclub.wordpress.com/nerdy-book-awards/2015-nerdy-book-awards/

*Nerdy Book Club.* (2017). Top ten lists. Retrieved from https://nerdybookclub.wordpress.com/category/top-ten-lists/

O'Donnell-Allen, C. (2006). The book club companion: Fostering strategic readers in the secondary classroom. Portsmouth, NH: Heinemann.

Oswald, T. (2012, September 14). Reading the classics: It's more than just for fun. *MSU Today.* Retrieved from http://msutoday.msu.edu/news/2012/reading-the-classics-its-more-than-just-for-fun/

Schaub, M. (2015, October 28). Obama: "The most important stuff I've learned I think I've learned from novels." *Los Angeles Times.* Retrieved from http://www.latimes.com/books/jacketcopy/la-et-jc-obama-learned-from-novels-20151028-story.html

Selingo, J. J. (2017, January 30). Wanted: Factory workers, degree required. *New York Times.* Retrieved from https://www.nytimes.com/2017/01/30/education/edlife/factory-workers-college-degree-apprenticeships.html?_r=0

Serravallo, J. (2013). *The literacy teacher's playbook, grades 3–6.* Portsmouth, NH: Heinemann.

Serravallo, J. (2015). *The reading strategies book.* Portsmouth, NH: Heinemann.

Siegler, M. G. (2010, August 4). Eric Schmidt: Every 2 days we create as much information as we did up to 2003. *TechCrunch.* Retrieved from https://techcrunch.com/2010/08/04/schmidt-data/

Steinbeck, J. (1993). *Of mice and men.* New York, NY: Penguin Books. (Original work published 1937)

Tatum, A. (2005). *Teaching reading to Black adolescent males.* Portland, ME: Stenhouse.

Tomlinson, C. A. (2014). *The differentiated classroom: Responding to the needs of all learners.* Alexandria, VA: ASCD.

*VCloudNews.* (2015, April 5). Every day big data statistics—2.5 quintillion bytes of data created daily. Retrieved from http://www.vcloudnews.com/every-day-big-data-statistics-2-5-quintillion-bytes-of-data-created-daily/

Wesson, K. (2012, March 1). Learning and memory: How do we remember and why do we often forget? *BrainWorld*. Retrieved from http://brainworldmagazine.com/learning-memory-how-do-we-remember-and-why-do-we-often-forget/

Wheeler, L. K. (2017). *Classical literature*. Retrieved from https://web.cn.edu/kwheeler/resource_lit.classics.html

Wilhelm, J. D. (2001). *Improving comprehension with think-aloud strategies*. New York, NY: Scholastic Professional.

Wilhelm, J., & Smith, M. (2017). *Diving deep into nonfiction, grades 6–12*. Thousand Oaks, CA: Corwin.

# Index

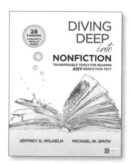

### Patty McGee

Helps you transform student writers by showing you what to do to build tone, trust, motivation, and choice into your daily lessons, conferences, and revision suggestions.

### Laura Robb

Discover classroom structures that create the time and space for students to have productive talk and written discourse about texts.

### Gravity Goldberg, Renee Houser

Take the guesswork out of planning with a protocol that shows you how to mine readers' writing and book discussions for next steps.

### Leslie Blauman

Use these lesson structures to each your students how to support their thinking whether writing a paragraph, an essay, or a test response.

### Jim Burke

Learn what the standards really say, really mean, and how to put them into action, Grades 6–8 and 9–12.

### Jim Burke

This new version of *The Common Core Companion* provides an index for states implementing state-specific ELA standards, allowing you to tap into the potency of standards-based teaching ideas.

CL CORWIN LITERACY

CORWIN
A SAGE Publishing Company

N17679

A SAGE Publishing Company

**CORWIN HAS ONE MISSION:** to enhance education through intentional professional learning.

We build long-term relationships with our authors, educators, clients, and associations who partner with us to develop and continuously improve the best evidence-based practices that establish and support lifelong learning.